Leigh Bowery

Performative Costuming and Live Art

Sofia Vranou

Bristol, UK / Chicago, USA

First published in the UK in 2025 by
Intellect, The Mill, Parnall Road, Fishponds, Bristol, BS16 3JG, UK

First published in the USA in 2025 by
Intellect, The University of Chicago Press, 1427 E. 60th Street, Chicago, IL 60637, USA

A catalogue record for this book is available from the British Library.

Copy editor: MPS Limited
Cover designer: Tanya Montefusco
Cover image: Werner Pawlok, Leigh Bowery, 1988. © Werner Pawlok.
Production editor: Sophia Munyengeterwa
Typesetting: MPS Limited

Hardback ISBN 978-1-83595-113-2
Paperback ISBN 978-1-83595-123-1
ePDF ISBN 978-1-83595-115-6
ePUB ISBN 978-1-83595-114-9

To find out about all our publications, please visit our website.
There you can subscribe to our e-newsletter, browse or download our current catalogue, and buy any titles that are in print.

www.intellectbooks.com

This is a peer-reviewed publication.

Printed and bound by Short Run

Contents

Figures

Foreword

Boy George

I know Leigh Bowery would love the idea of exhibitions and books and the continued celebration of his colourful legacy. Those who knew him just wish he was still here and wonder how he would operate in this new politically correct universe. What would Leigh's pronouns be and would he be cancelled for spraying the contents of his bowels over the dance floor? Most importantly, I wonder what he would be wearing and where he would have taken it visually. It is clear, when you look at *RuPaul's Drag Race* and fashion, how much Leigh has influenced everything weird and wondrous, but no one does it quite like Leigh. He was the freakiest freak on the freaking planet.

Leigh was an agitator, provocateur and a sight for sore eyes. His favourite snack was pesto on toast and he was ahead of the game with sun-dried tomatoes. He was sarcastic with a twisted sense of humour and hated to explain himself. I always loved seeing him arrive at a club or fashion show because just when you thought he could take it no further he would appear in some genius creation that defied gravity and logic. Leigh Bowery always tried to defy gravity and logic and he did it with undeniable panache.

We must never underestimate the influence of Leigh's widow Nicola Bateman Bowery Binnie Rainbird who was absolutely instrumental in helping Leigh create his groundbreaking looks. Skilfully sewing a million sequins onto voluminous skirts for days or weeks on end. Her own looks were equally astounding and she is as interesting now as she ever was. So much so, I have dedicated a new song to her and her sister Christine, called simply 'The Bateman Sisters'.

Acknowledgements

This is the first scholarly monograph dedicated to Leigh Bowery's vibrant and multifaceted practice, much of which was developed under the supervision of Dominic Johnson at Queen Mary, University of London. I am sincerely thankful for his guidance, unwavering support, and kindness throughout my academic journey and beyond.

Several individuals generously devoted their time and energy for this research project. I am indebted to Nicola Bateman and Matthew Glamorre for granting me access to archival material and engaging in insightful conversations with me. Rob van de Ven at *Zapp Magazine* and Dick Jewell wholeheartedly shared their video recordings. Charlotte Hellicar, Allen Pelling and David Wood at Torture Garden provided valuable information. Ernie Glam was wonderfully kind to recount his memories of Bowery in New York and compile a publicly accessible archive of *Project X*. I extend my thanks to Sue Tilley, Michael Costiff, and Boy George for their positive responses and encouragement. I'm also grateful to Martin Gayford and Anne Marsh for trusting me with their scripts; Gary Needham and Anna Hickey for their valuable comments and insights; and Donatella Barbieri and Stephen Farrier for their support and kind words. I thank Vincent Trasov, Mary Duffy, James Pretlove and John Mozzer for their interest and enthusiasm.

I feel particularly fortunate for the funding and academic opportunities provided by the Drama Department at Queen Mary, which significantly facilitated the development of my research. My interactions with fellow researchers and staff members were instrumental in deepening my understanding of performance and cultural politics. Special thanks to Shane Boyle, Jen Harvie and Martin O'Brien. Additionally, my appreciation goes out to the staff at the Library Services at Queen Mary for their assistance and expertise. Several institutions contributed to the materialization of this project. I express my gratitude to the staff at: Live Art Development Agency, Bishopsgate Institute, Tate Archives, National Art Library, National Portrait Gallery, British Library, Lux Moving Image, Michael Hoppen

Gallery, Central Saint Martins Special Collections, University of the Arts, London; The Robert Mapplethorpe Foundation, Luhring Augustine, New York; Bancroft Library, University of California, Berkeley; ONE Archives, University of Southern California, Los Angeles; and Morris and Helen Belkin Art Gallery, University of British Columbia, Vancouver.

I am greatly indebted to the photographers who documented and preserved Bowery's work and who generously supported this book: Fergus Greer, Gordon Rainsford, Johnny Rozsa, Tim Bauer, Josef Astor, David Gwinnutt, Leo Erken, René Habermacher, Don Pollard, Robert Rosen, Fiona Freund, Tom Pilston, Nils Jorgensen, Sheila Rock and Werner Pawlok. Special thanks to Del LaGrace Volcano, Sheree Rose, Austin Young, Dona Ann McAdams and James Caswell for their outstanding work and generosity.

An excerpt from Chapter 1 benefited from questions and suggestions following my presentation at *Fashion, Costume and Visual Cultures* international conference at the University of Zagreb, which was kindly supported by the Glynne Wickham Scholarship fund. An earlier version of part of Chapter 1 is published as: '"Pakis from Outer Space": Oriental Postmodernity in Leigh Bowery's Performative Costuming', *Studies in Costume and Performance*, 5.1 (2020), 73–84. An earlier version of part of Chapter 2 is published as: 'Performing the Subcultural Freak: Leigh Bowery's Peculiar Narcissism and the Disruption of Normativity', *Contemporary Theatre Review*, 30.3 (2020), 326–39. A revised excerpt of Chapter 3 is published online as: 'Leigh Bowery: Glitter, Shit, and the Performance of Decadence', *Staging Decadence*, 5 February 2024, <https://www.stagingdecadence.com/blog/leigh-bowery>. I thank Adam Alston for the invitation. An introductory text about Bowery's practice is published as 'Leigh Bowery', in *Fifty Key Performance Artists*, ed. by T. Nikki Cesare Schotzko and Adriana Disman (New York: Routledge, forthcoming).

My collaboration with Arts Feminism Queer (commonly known as Cuntemporary) opened new horizons and got me deeper into club performance. I thank Giulia Cassalini, Diana Georgiou, Natalia Damigou-Papoti and all the creatures of the night for their friendship and fabulousness. Finally, I would like to extend my heartfelt thanks to the production team at Intellect for their invaluable support and professionalism. Their commitment to publishing high-quality academic work has been essential in bringing this project to fruition.

Introduction: Larger than Life

In the finale of an early episode of *The Clothes Show*, a popular British television programme about fashion, a self-proclaimed avant-garde designer by the name of Leigh Bowery welcomes the camera into the dressing room of his flamboyant flat for a quick showcase of some of his latest outfits. Covered with clownish make-up, wearing a pair of painted glasses featuring two big dots for eyes, and adorned with a strange spiky headpiece that resembles a sea urchin, the emerging designer peeks playfully behind his colourful door and invites the viewers in. For the next few minutes he is shown modelling a series of outlandish costumes and bizarre accessories that he describes in what would commonly be perceived as an exaggerated posh British accent: 'I think things should be larger than life', he says and resumes posing and acting in a well-calculated theatrical manner. His presence is buzzing camp as he gestures and spins gracefully, wrapped up in layered frills inside his gloriously garish dimly lit flat. Most of the costumes Bowery wears have been designed for the stage, but he does not hesitaté to wear them in public, especially in nightclubs, which, as he states immersed in a red tulle ball ensemble, play 'a very important part' in his life.[1]

More than three decades later, Bowery is commonly remembered as an eccentric costume maker of the 1980s who came to inspire some of the most ingenious contemporary fashion designers; a nightclub persona and free-spirited performance artist; an unlikely muse for painter Lucian Freud; but above all, a visual provocateur with a highly distinctive and unprecedented practice of creative self-fashioning (Figure I.1). Bowery started making extravagant costumes that he mainly showed off in London's nightclubs as an ambitious and aspiring fashion designer, soon turning into a subcultural icon who constantly blurred the boundaries between fashion, art and life. Being at odds

Figure I.1: Tim Bauer, *Leigh Bowery*, 1986. © Tim Bauer.

with mainstream trends and normative ideals of beauty, he soon abandoned his initial plans for a career in the fashion industry and focused on constructing unusual and often monstrous looks that became over time an inseparable part of his subjectivity, signalling a deep investment in the intersection of self-costuming and performance. Tall with a corpulent physique, Bowery manipulated his appearance drastically with sculptural garments, strange headpieces, layers of make-up and huge platform shoes that made him a towering figure more than seven feet high. Apart from his costumes and the wide range of creative projects he was involved in during his deciduous but multifarious artistic journey, Bowery left behind a peculiar body of work in live art that has for a long time remained puzzling.

The mastery of the fine balance between fashion and art that Bowery attained is rare – if not unique – among artists of his generation. He has been variously described as 'outrageous', 'beautiful', 'genius', 'terrifying' and 'sick', but it is the words of fellow club freak and collaborator Boy George, for whom Bowery designed some of his early career outfits, that seem to most vividly capture his unsettling presence when the latter famously described him as 'modern art on legs'. As compelling and accurate as this might sound in underlining the fact that Bowery's perpetual costuming is foremost a form of performative art that extends beyond the confines of the gallery, it also hints at a possible explanation as to why he has remained a marginal and slippery figure when it comes to the absorption of his work into dominant art narratives.

The ephemerality, complexity and mobility of Bowery's practice, which embraced pop sensibilities and was for the most part exercised in subcultural or unconventional settings like nightclubs, constitute the main factors of its difficulty in being accepted and treated as an important art form. This is the case with many so-called 'underground' artists – from Genesis P-Orridge and Kembra Pfahler to Johanna Went and David Hoyle – whose distinctive practices developed outside institutional art spaces and the disciplinary grid, encompassing a wide range of cultural influences and expressions that for the most part remained inaccessible to the restrained sphere of 'high' art. Bowery's costumes, nevertheless, many of which have been extensively documented by photographer Fergus Greer, were swiftly appreciated in fashion discourse for their strong impact, bold shapes, innovative vision and craftsmanship, despite the fact that they were never conceived as fashion – at least in the typical sense – but as strictly personal performative devices. Bowery is perhaps the only performance artist who is widely labelled as such, but he is particularly celebrated as a designer and relatively very little has been critically explored about his performances. It almost feels like his costumes, the surviving relics of his idiosyncratic practice, have turned into autonomous artefacts whose powerful brilliance has overshadowed their performative purpose.

It was an image of Bowery in one of his arresting costumes that first caught my attention as I was browsing through *The Artist's Body* (2000), an illustrated art book. As usual, he was mentioned briefly and in relation to his series of performances at the Anthony d'Offay Gallery, his only solo show in a commercial gallery and the one that is most often referenced in art publications. My enthusiasm to find out more about this 'icon in underground culture' who turned into walking art 'to examine prevailing judgements of what is perverse and what is normal' was cut short as very limited and scattered information was available or accessible to me at the time.[2] A biography written shortly after his death by his close friend Sue Tilley had been out of print for years, becoming a rare and treasured cult find. When I managed to lay my hands on it and lose myself in Bowery's fascinating life through amusing anecdotes and glimpses of his complex body of work, I felt that his fairly unexplored practice would make for a promising research project, given its significance to live art studies and visual culture as well as its potential to penetrate various discourses beyond art.

Bowery's short life was saturated with excessive experimentation with self-display and the ceaseless pursuit of creative possibilities driven by his fame-hungry ambition. Born in 1961 in Sunshine, a small working-class suburb in Melbourne, he shared a happy childhood with his younger sister in a conventional family that valued good manners and discipline, with both parents actively involved in the Salvation Army. He was an introverted child who excelled at school and the piano and had shown an interest in crochet and lace tatting from an early age. By the time he enrolled at the Royal Melbourne Institute of Technology to study fashion his creativity and flamboyant side had started to show, but he soon grew dissatisfied with the curriculum and abandoned the course, which he found conservative and boring. Approximately a year later, in late

1980, Bowery was on his way to London with few savings and his portable sewing machine, hoping to pursue a career in fashion and mix with the trendy club crowd he had only seen in magazines. Even though his path to subcultural notoriety was thorny and involved financial hardship and many shifts at Burger King to support himself at the beginning, he steadily built a strong network of like-minded creative friends, most of whom he met at clubs like Cha Cha, Club for Heroes and Asylum.

When Bowery started to get noticed as an emerging fashion designer by making clothes for his scenester friends and having achieved significant connections and exposure with shows in the United Kingdom and internationally, he realized that he disliked the idea of having his designs available on the market. What Bowery craved instead was all spotlights on himself as he paraded his unique and extravagant looks in London's most fashionable nightclubs. His big breakthrough came in 1985 when he became the public face of legendary club night Taboo: 'the apotheosis of a flamboyant life plan which [...] aimed to formulate an alternative to the philistine ruthlessness of neoliberalism, whose visual metaphor could be found in the rigid hairstyle of Margaret Thatcher', Thomas Mießgang characteristically writes.[3]

Taboo expanded Bowery's reputation as an eccentric club persona and motivated his increasingly excessive outfits, which subsequently started to turn into highly crafted avant-garde looks with the valuable help of his assistants Nicola Bateman and Lee Benjamin. From that point on, Bowery embarked on a mission to constantly push the boundaries with his often-provocative performative costuming and engaged in a variety of creative projects and collaborations. Never abandoning the honorary title of nightclub freak, he developed such an ambiguous identity and diverse body of work that essentially rendered him unclassifiable. During a near-decade of intense productivity, approximately from 1985 until his death in 1994 from an AIDS-related illness, Bowery had been known as a fashion and costume designer, club promoter, television persona, painter's model, performance artist, theatre actor and aspiring pop star.

A Peculiar Body of Work

Bowery's creative adventure started shortly after his relocation to London by designing clothes on commission for friends, showcasing his work in nightclubs and setting up a stall at Kensington Market where he sold his early New Romantic-inspired garments. Influenced at the time by Vivienne Westwood's collection *Buffalo Girls/Nostalgia of Mud* (Autumn/Winter 1982), he made baggy clothes, such as long woolly skirts and cotton dresses, playing with different materials, patterns and patchwork techniques.

Bowery started to create a name for himself in fashion after 1983 when he met club and fashion impresario Susanne Bartsch who included his work in *New London in New York* (1983 and 1984), two massive runway shows of twenty emerging designers from the United Kingdom that she produced at The Roxy and The Limelight. It was around that time when Bowery discovered he was not interested in a career as a mainstream fashion designer and started exploring more experimental ideas of dressing. His collection *Mincing Queens* (1984) was presented at *Performing Clothes* (1984), a two-week fashion and dance event at the Institute of Contemporary Arts in London, with the show being repeated at The Haçienda club in Manchester and The Caley Picture House in Edinburgh.

Evidently more daring than his previous work, the collection featured frilly knickers and shoes, garments with unusual cuttings and uneven parts in baby pink, brown and white, big floppy hats and painted faces. Bowery, who also modelled his outfits on the catwalk leaving his ass bare, did not rehearse his show but instead enticed the models with alcohol and other psychotropic substances, encouraging an improvised spectacle of disaster that involved bumping into each other and tumbling. Later that year, Bartsch took Bowery's collection and other UK-based designers to Tokyo for *London Goes to Tokyo*, a collective fashion show that was sponsored by the Hanae Mori Foundation (Figure I.2). Information and material regarding these shows and Bowery's early steps in fashion are limited, but Bartsch, whose later successful career as a New York-based club organizer was very much inspired by Bowery's party ethic, undoubtedly gave him the opportunity to expand his creative network and subcultural stardom outside London.

Another success story from Bowery's brief but impactful fashion career was his contribution to a Levi's jacket project that *BLITZ* magazine initiated in 1986. The iconic style magazine commissioned 22 of the most forward-thinking designers,

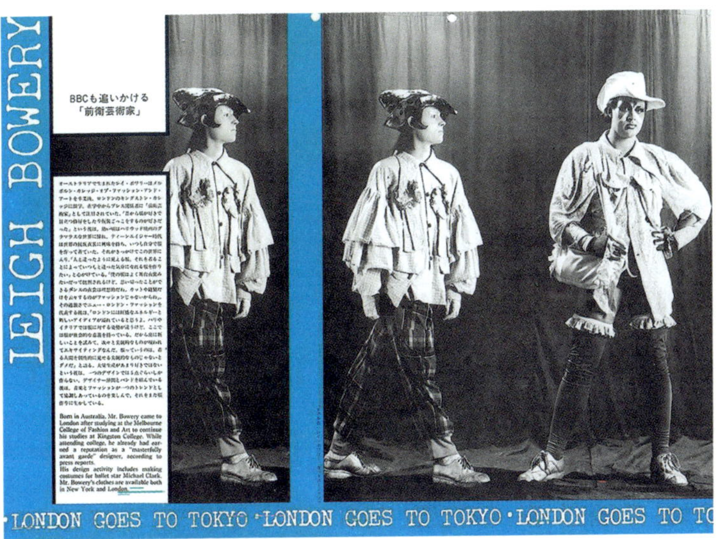

Figure I.2: Page from the Japanese catalogue of *London Goes to Tokyo* featuring Trojan and Leigh Bowery, 1984. Photographer unknown. Courtesy of Michael Costiff.

including John Galliano, Vivienne Westwood, Stevie Stewart and David Holah of BodyMap, Rifat Ozbek, duo Bernstock Speirs, and Judy Blame, to customize Levi's classic denim jacket. Bowery's piece – now acquired by the Victoria and Albert Museum in London – was completely covered with blond shiny hair grips and was lined on the inside with applied silver plastic discs. The works were presented in a heavily publicized fundraising gala for The Prince's Trust at the Albery Theatre in London's West End where a number of celebrities took the stage with professional models in individual choreographed routines, showcasing the jackets. Not only was Bowery the only designer who modelled his own jacket, but he did so in clownish make-up, performing a spoof fall before leaving the stage.

A milestone in Bowery's artistic development is undeniably his long-term collaboration with the choreographer Michael Clark and his dance company. The two met at a nightclub in the early 1980s and Clark was immediately drawn to Bowery's charisma and extravagant style; he likely identified its potential in dynamically complementing his unconventional post-punk ballet choreographies and productions, most of which toured nationally and abroad. Bowery was initially only making costumes for Clark – for which he and fashion label BodyMap won a Bessie award in 1986 – but eventually became a prominent performer in many of the company's shows, including *Because We Must* (1987), *Pure Pre-Scenes* (1987) and *Mmm* ... (1992). Sustained by a strong friendship and a shared appetite for provocation, their lasting collaboration proved a fruitful exchange that benefitted Clark's longing for visual edge and modernization of ballet (often attributed by critics to Bowery's 'bad' influence) and opened new horizons for Bowery in meeting and working with various creatives and becoming more comfortable – and more ambitious probably – with performance beyond the nightclub.

Bowery's most unexpected collaboration, nevertheless, is with painter Lucian Freud when the latter famously immortalized his unadorned body in numerous paintings and etchings. Their unlikely association and friendship started after 1988 when they first met through the artist Cerith Wyn Evans. Bowery posed in the nude regularly for the painter until his death, with Freud producing during this time some of his greatest late works. They have been variously exhibited in many renowned museums worldwide, planting Bowery's imposing figure in the very centre of the art elite and prompting Freud's unsympathetic critics to denounce the works as, in Martin Gayford's words, 'a sort of freak show in oil paint'.[4]

Film director and video artist Charles Atlas, a pioneer in developing screen dance with an impressive list of collaborations, filmed Bowery for numerous projects. They first worked together in *Hail the New Puritan* (1986), a fictionalized poetic documentary about Clark that constitutes an important document of Bowery's early costumes in dance: tall hats, bodysuits that exposed the buttocks, uncomfortably high platform shoes, frilly aprons with bare backs, wigs, childish ensembles with big polka dots and oversized cardigans with huge shoulders decorate the dancers' bodies as they flow spasmodically to post-punk music by The Fall. Bowery also appears briefly in the film, most notably in a scene shot in his actual living room, plastered with tacky Star Trek wallpaper, where he experiments with various looks in front of the mirror before a night out with friends Trojan, Rachel Auburn and Clark. In *Because We Must* (1989), a poetic film based on Clark's original stage production, a provocative mix of choreography and fantasy in classical and post-punk music features a variety of Bowery's impressive costumes worn by the dancers as well as himself. Dressed as an androgynous creature, a teapot, a shiny star or with lightbulbs on the sides of his head, Bowery is a prominent member of the cast shown playing the piano, delivering lines and dancing. He is also featured in two subsequent video portraits by Atlas discussed later: *Teach* (1992), which shows Bowery trying to lip-sync with plastic lips attached through the piercings on his facial cheeks, and *Mrs. Peanut Visits New York* (1992), a video that involves Bowery parading the streets of downtown New York in one of his most recognized costumes.

Bowery's arresting looks worked like a magnet for experimental video artists who wanted to include in their works even a few shots of him, such as Wyn Evans and John Maybury.[5] Photographers were equally drawn to Bowery, who frequently posed for many over the years, most notably Greer, whose comprehensive collection of Bowery's most iconic looks serves as an important archive. Not only did photography function as a strong aesthetic platform for documenting and preserving Bowery's looks, but, as Katharina Sykora observes, it 'induced and made possible this very particular adventure of the ego' that typifies his practice.[6] Craving the spotlight, Bowery appeared in various television programmes and talk shows many times, at first to showcase his collections and later as a captivating designer, artist and subcultural star utilizing strange costuming. His talents shone through a variety of roles he undertook throughout the years, sustaining his dedication to bringing performance, fashion and music together: as a chat show host in *Take the Blame* for European MTV; an iconic figure in commercials (for Pepe Jeans) and music videos (for The Fall, Jesus Loves You and Lana Pellay); or a background dancing freak on the stage of *Top of the Pops* for 'Don't You Want Me' (1992) by Felix.

Less-known ventures in Bowery's rich experience include his work for the Italian brand Calugi e Giannelli, his tutoring in a creative foundation course at the Architectural Association in London, and his collaboration with Marina Abramović in her performance *Delusional* (1994). Furthermore, having achieved significant recognition in New York's party scene, Bowery was one of the MCs at Love Ball I and II (1989 and 1991), two significant AIDS fundraising events organized by Bartsch that celebrated ballroom culture and raised millions of US dollars.

Whether showcasing his collections, sharing the stage with Clark's dancers, posing for Freud and photographers or appearing in music clips and experimental videos, Bowery's endeavours – if not his theatrical self-fashioning alone – emit a strong sense of performance. In 1986, he experimented for the first time with acting when he starred in *Hey! Luciani: The Life and Codex of John Paul I*, an intricate play bristling with absurd conspiracy theories written by Mark E. Smith, frontman of The Fall. It was staged only for a couple of weeks at the Riverside Studios in London, and the main cast comprised Smith, Bowery, Trevor Stewart, and Lucy Burge, with The Fall providing music interventions, and Clark and Pellay also appearing briefly. Smith's ambitious attempt at playwriting and his atypical crew were received with tepid bewilderment by critics. Bowery's final acting experience came in 1993 when he embodied Madame Garbo in *The Homosexual: or, the Difficulty of Sexpressing Oneself*, which toured nationally. In an essay discussing the work, Peta Tait was not surprised to see Bowery in one of the leading roles, considering the play's unconventional narrative that is determined by '"unnatural" physical bodies and their bodily functions'.[7]

Having been adequately familiar with the precepts of dance and theatrical performance in dignified institutional spaces, Bowery identified as an artist whose main outlet remained the nightclub for its anarchic and spontaneous mix of bodies, music and fashion, and its relatively greater freedom in expression. In parallel with his busy and diverse work schedule and especially after the success of Taboo, he continued performing throughout the years in the most remarkable nightclubs of the period in Europe and New York: Heaven, Camden Palace, Empire Ballroom, The Limelight, RoXY, Café de Paris and Jackie 60 are just a few. Bowery was also a contestant twice in Andrew Logan's recurring event Alternative Miss World, which fused queerness, art and fashion. In 1985 he entered as 'Miss Leigh Bowerie' and in 1986 he competed alongside a friend as 'Miss Fuck It', leaving a memorable mark in the history of the competition (Figure I.3).

Figure I.3: Fat Gill and Leigh Bowery performing as 'Miss Fuck It' at Andrew Logan's Alternative Miss World event at the Brixton Academy, London, 1986. Photograph by Robert Rosen. © Robert Rosen.

Bowery's outrageous presence was usually enough to turn any situation into an event, but his first advertised performance took place as early as 1984 at The Crypt near Warren Street in London. The event was organized by the Neo Naturists, an avant-garde live art group initiated in 1981 by Christine and Jennifer Binnie, and Wilma Johnson. Bowery performed with his close friend Trojan in one of their most distinctive looks that became known – problematically – as 'Pakis from Outer Space'. Tilley briefly describes their performance, which involved both of them stripping naked, with Bowery's freshly pierced nipple bleeding after it was accidentally snagged.[8] He next put on a white lab coat and pretended to push syringes into Trojan's body who proceeded to spill some lighter fuel on the floor and light it. To finish, Bowery urinated into a glass; Trojan managed to drink half of it before putting out the flames with the rest.

Many club performances followed, most of them unfortunately remaining difficult to recover, inadequately documented or forgotten. Perhaps his most notorious club performance was for an AIDS benefit at The Fridge in 1990 that ended with Bowery spraying the audience with an enema. This and his few major performances that are described below succinctly are unpacked in detail in the chapters of the book.

Bowery's most meticulously organized performance, after which he gravitated more consciously towards the genre, was arguably his series at the Anthony d'Offay Gallery in 1988 for which he installed himself in one of the gallery rooms as an art object. Later that year he repeated the performance, slightly modified, in the shop window of Parco department store in Tokyo. An exhibition titled *Ruined Clothes*, which involved a collection of photographs depicting some of Bowery's garments strategically scattered on the ground outside the council estate he was living in, ran simultaneously in a gallery upstairs. The following year he performed a dress-up transformation at the opening of *Success Is a Job in New York: The Early Art and Business of Andy Warhol* (1989) at the Serpentine Gallery. Assisted by Mr. Pearl and Bateman, Bowery slipped into a tight shape-shifting bodysuit, elevating the act into a shared ritual of queer becoming. Yet, his most celebrated queer performance is a birth re-enactment that was carried out numerous times in clubs and festivals, most famously at Wigstock in 1993, a popular outdoor drag festival in downtown New York. Bowery's final performance idea was presented at *The Laugh of No. 12* (1994), a multimedia exhibition at Fort Asperen in the Netherlands for which he came up with a piece with the same title, inspired by tarot mysticism and BDSM aesthetics.

Particularly excited by the prospect of a career in pop music – albeit with a distorted twist of performance that could hardly lead to commercial success – Bowery formed in 1992 the short-lived group Quality Street Wrappers with Sheila Tequila and Stella Stein, devising short club performances that involved singing out of tune, outrageous costumes and nudity. They soon changed their name to Raw Sewage and continued doing shows in various clubs in the United Kingdom and abroad, which by then had evolved more into intoxicated abject improvisations. A sense of their avant-garde drag is captured in a deliberately tacky music video they produced at Star Trax, a karaoke booth located at the London Trocadero shopping centre that was accessible for a few pounds to (typically) teenagers wanting to have some fun by making their own pop video. Sporting ridiculous costumes and – probably questionable – painted-black faces, in the video they follow a sloppy dance routine during which they end up naked with tucked genitals, delivering a terrible singing performance of 'Walk This Way' (1986) by Run-DMC featuring Aerosmith while various visual effects of urban landscapes run in the background via lo-fi greenscreen technology. When their collaboration ended in drama due to their differing levels of engagement, Bowery, along with Richard Torry, went on to form the alternative art band Minty in 1993, with Bateman and Matthew Glamorre joining as core members soon after. This was a much more concentrated effort to break into the music business and reach a wider indie audience that, apart from their highly theatrical performances in clubs, included plans for an album release and promotional activities. Their energetic performances involved elaborate costumes, explicit lyrics and abject acts, such as simulated drinking of urine, vomiting and Bowery 'giving birth' to Bateman on stage, which became their trademark act.

In 1994, Minty performed alongside Gavin Turk and Wyn Evans at The Fete Worse than Death, a memorable art gala with public interventions and stalls by young artists at once run-down Hoxton Square in London, organized by progressive curator Joshua Compston.[9] Their final performance with Bowery took place at the Freedom Café in London, shortly before his hospitalization and death.[10] What Bowery considered his most intimate performance had occurred just a few months earlier at the Bow Registry Office where he secretly married his trusted assistant Bateman, with Wyn Evans as the best man and Bateman's sister Christine as the bridesmaid. An openly gay man, Bowery never gave a frank explanation for this decision, which was possibly driven by his HIV-positive status and the fear of an inevitable death that could lead to legal complexities over the council flat he shared with Bateman or disputes over his archive and creative legacy.

Bowery's work has been hosted posthumously in numerous group exhibitions worldwide, exploring themes like unconventional fashion and design, masquerade, postmodernism, club culture, post-punk, and queer identity politics. As his work started to increasingly attract institutional attention at the dawn of the new millennium, he still remained an enigmatic figure that troubled the curatorial tendency for categorization, destabilizing and upsetting the modes that represented him. Plenty of labels are used to describe him in exhibition catalogues in an attempt to communicate the complex nature of his work production. Yet, he enjoyed and desired this ambivalence: 'If you label me you negate me', Bowery famously stated, declaring his contempt and defiance for any kind of categorization.[11]

Considering the challenges posed by Bowery's diverse and anti-disciplinary work, this book seeks to critically engage with his performative costuming and non-theatrical performances through live art narratives and the broader context of visual culture. Emphasis is therefore placed both on the practice of constructing a dissonant subjectivity as an aesthetic and performative venture and on his known club, street and art performances that are either overlooked or obscured by their cult marginality. His choreographed performances in Clark's magnificent productions and a deep engagement with his brief experience with theatre and acting as well as his music-oriented projects are beyond the scope of the book, not least because some of them have been adequately accounted for by other scholars or writers and, as more conventional modes of performance, they fall outside my research interests and, possibly, expertise.

Performative Costuming and Live Art

Critic and independent curator Bob Nickas wrote in a brief article in *Artforum* in 2004: 'The Bowery moment we're going through now is testament to an unfolding fascination for an artist who continues to be rediscovered.'[12] Almost a decade after Bowery's death his life and work started to gain wider visibility first through an award-winning documentary, *The Legend of Leigh Bowery* (2002), directed by Atlas, followed by a stage musical about London's nightlife in the 1980s, titled *Taboo* (2002), and the massive retrospective *Take a Bowery: The Art and (Larger than) Life of Leigh Bowery* (2003) at the Museum of Contemporary Art in Sydney. Simply put, no scholarly writings were published on Bowery's practice during his lifetime. The only publications from prior to 1994 include brief articles, magazine editorials and interviews in commercial-style magazines (most prominently *The Face* and *i-D*), mainly focusing on his outrageous presence in nightclubs and referring occasionally to his creative projects, and an insightful article by cultural commentator Michael Bracewell, first published in *Frieze* shortly before Bowery's death. Bracewell positions Bowery within the trajectory of transgression in fashion and pop culture that erupted during the 1970s with David Bowie, but he struggles to find a comparison to his performative costuming 'in fine art terms': 'the nearest [...] would be [Andy] Warhol's superstars, but Bowery has exchanged the traditions of simple drag for a personal surrealism', he writes.[13]

Scholarly writings on Bowery's practice started to appear timidly in the mid-2000s and increased significantly during the last few years. These are structured around a repertoire of themes and discourses, predictably focusing mostly on his profound experimentation with embodiment and attempting to make sense of it through fashion studies and its impact on visual culture, the liberating tenets of the carnival and the socially disruptive power of the grotesque or identity politics with a reasonable emphasis on his significance to queer studies and drag refashioning. They have certainly informed many of the core ideas explored in this book and provided useful (and often surprising) contexts for thinking about such a distinct body of work. However, although the concept of the body as an art object is prevalent and recurring in these discussions, a deep engagement with Bowery primarily as a performance artist – an identification he felt at ease with the most – through performance art narratives and art discourses is deafeningly absent.

This book is deeply motivated by this absence and seeks to counterbalance the disproportionate attention to fashion Bowery's legacy relished throughout the years by prioritizing the performative quality of his practice. Its objective is twofold: first, to theorize Bowery's outlandish costumes as fundamentally performative, emphasizing that they were not just well-designed corporeal objects but instrumental mediums for performance; and second, to critically reframe his costumed body within live art narratives as both significantly disruptive and capable of addressing pressing social issues, rather than serving merely as a superficial fashion spectacle. While Bowery abstained from referring to the outfits he created as costumes – possibly due to the association of 'costume' with theatricality and fancy dress – the term is productive in conveying notions of performativity, intentionality and temporality. For this reason, it is widely adopted by scholars discussing his work and is also used here. Additionally, terms such as 'self-fashioning', 'costuming' and 'dressing' are used interchangeably in the text, despite their potential theoretical distinctions for fashion experts.

Pamela Karantonis previously described Bowery's costumes as 'performative' for '[t]hey altered the spectator's perspective on the object or source he was imitating and always destabilized the genre it inhabited'.[14] Furthermore, I maintain that just being in them in public was enough to transform the simplest act into a spectacular performance and they were also often designed and adapted to facilitate specific performance ideas. Bowery's costumes appear to be inextricably linked to him – his energetic dancing in nightclubs, his live art and his wild public behaviour – that when viewed on mannequins in recent exhibitions they look lifeless and deflated, creepy sad reminders of loss unable to convey the vivacity and threat of Bowery's live presence.

Framing Bowery's costuming as performative and approaching it critically is imperative in examining his status in contemporary art and culture; not least because costume, when employed as an 'interventional practice' that is distinct from conventional modes of dress and fashion, 'represents a potential strategy for subverting the ongoing repetitions of body politics', Rachel Hann writes.[15] Costuming can radically complicate and threaten normative ideas of appearance usually imposed by fashion, which operates as an ideological system traditionally upholding identity construction, and dress, which often functions as a repetitive standardizing practice that reinforces fashion conventions. It is perhaps this tension between the exciting prospects offered by performative costuming and the disciplined imagination of commercial fashion that gradually but permanently distanced Bowery from a career in the fashion industry. His extreme practice is exemplary of the type of costuming and subversive qualities that Hann articulates and demands a critical approach, for it does not only destabilize the politics of appearance, but, as I demonstrate in the following chapters, it shatters deeper understandings of identity tied to gender, sexuality and personhood.

Eluding accepted histories and conventions of artistic production and reception, Bowery's ambiguously anti-disciplinary performative costuming troubles the way canons are traditionally constructed for art and performance and requires a new or revised practice of historiography. It is for this reason that I find 'live art' a more useful critical term than 'performance art' in describing and framing his peculiar body of work. Although it is frequently used interchangeably with the latter since both terms appeared in art discourse in the late 1970s broadly designating the same thing – that is the experience of liveness in art-making – live art has increasingly grown into an independent cultural sector in the United Kingdom (which, however, remains sidelined) that appears to be at odds with the formalities of international performance art. Live art operates as a more inclusive territory, embracing a variety of artists adopting not only traditional aspects of performance art but also more experimental practices that favour miscellaneous disciplines and deviate from or refuse the legacies pertaining to international performance art. Remaining equally resistant to specific definition, live art is described by Lois Keidan, co-founder and former director of the Live Art Development Agency in London, as 'a framing device for a catalogue of approaches to the possibilities of liveness by artists who choose to work across, in between, and at the edges of more traditional artistic forms'.[16] Bowery's unorthodox practice, which stands awkwardly on the periphery of art discourse and became largely outshined by his impressive costumes, seems to fit well within the fluid boundaries of what is now understood as live art.

Noise and Absence

This first monographic study of Bowery's live art and performative costuming strongly engages with a broad spectrum of visual culture and an array of cultural practices and histories of performance. It contributes to a relatively recent scholarly context in the historiography of marginal or heterogeneous art practices in which scholars in art history and performance studies have sought to recover artists whose complexity and often anti-institutional demeanour have hindered the acknowledgement of their cultural significance in dominant narratives after 1960.

In a bid to reckon with Bowery's gravity in contemporary visual culture and performance studies, I move beyond the limitations of traditional forms of criticism and undertake a critical visual analysis, often informed by intertextuality, favouring a distinctive interdisciplinary methodology that spans from performance studies and art history to subcultural theory, with a strong emphasis on disability discourse, gender, and trans studies. Feminism, fashion and the critique of orientalism are also key to the development of my arguments at various points in the chapters. This diverse approach is partly informed by Jennifer Doyle's analysis in *Hold It against Me: Difficulty and Emotion in Contemporary Art* (2013), an exploration of politically confrontational (and often overlooked) works whose controversial status, in subject matter or form, poses a challenge to institutional politeness and exposes the limits of traditional art criticism that tends to dismiss anti-disciplinary or overly political works for disengaging from aesthetic criteria.

Citing the relationship of noise and music as a productive analogy, Doyle describes such multifaceted works as 'noisy' for their ability to interfere with and disrupt the supposedly harmonious order of art discourse with their problematic attachment to specific genres and disciplines: 'They appear to be at odds with Art, or they contain within them elements that seem to come from the "outside"', she writes.[17] Grounded in her first-hand viewing experiences of and emotional responses to her case studies, Doyle's close readings draw on a variety of fields, such as cultural studies, film criticism and feminist and queer critical theory. Delving into other disciplines for insight appears to be an essential strategy in opening up to the social turn of such 'noisy' works and practices that otherwise cause awkwardness to those art critics who avoid popular culture and the methodologies pertaining to its analysis. What Doyle suggests and this book attempts to put to the test is 'a different kind of conversation'.[18] That said, my analysis tends to be rather removed from Doyle's deeply personal emotive readings. While she experienced many of the performances she discusses first hand, which facilitates her affect-driven analysis, my approach to reading Bowery's live art is inevitably limited to studying documentation and oral histories, allowing (but not necessarily following from) a comprehensive evaluation resulting from historical and physical distance. This, indeed, appears at odds with the ontology of performance that Peggy Phelan so assertively defends for its presentist and nonreproductive quality, but it, nevertheless, constitutes a productive strategy in accessing and examining work.[19]

In this respect, my methodology mirrors that of Amelia Jones who in critically unveiling histories of performance art – most notably the body art practices that defined the 1970s – resorts to photographic, textual, film and oral documentation often. She argues that knowledge developed through documentation is of equal significance to that generated by witnessing a performance live or getting to know the artist's intentions for 'there is no possibility of an unmediated relationship to any kind of cultural product' and 'the documentary exchange [...] is equally intersubjective' to that of the live experience.[20] Referring to Carolee Schneemann's famous performance *Interior Scroll* (1975), Jones characteristically writes: 'Having direct physical contact with an artist who pulls a scroll from her vaginal canal does not ensure "knowledge" of her subjectivity or intentionality any more than does looking at a film or picture of this activity.'[21] Furthermore, historical distance in evaluating performance art (through its documentation) is almost essential for coming to grips with the contexts and narratives that surrounded the work at the time. Certain works become indeed more meaningful when re-visited later as 'it is hard to identify the patterns of history while one is embedded in them', Jones also observes.[22] This resonates profoundly with the work of artists like Bowery who in hindsight are often loosely celebrated as 'ahead of their times', but they have, for various reasons, managed to escape critical attention in their time. Although documentation can be emotionally detaching, it has served as the main source for analysis in this study. The historical distance from Bowery's work, however, has proven to be a privilege as it revealed his ongoing relevance by allowing his work to converse and resonate with a variety of contemporary concerns revolving around performativity and identity politics.

Researching such a disparate and almost uncharted territory, as is the case with Bowery's less renowned performances – if not his work at large – inevitably comes with certain difficult challenges, the most common being sparse documentation and scattered or insufficient information and material. In addition, Bowery's personal archives that I consulted in person – just like his practice – remain chaotic and uncatalogued in storage boxes in a private residence, while his marginalized status until recently translated to limited scholarly attention. I also often identified and sought to correct inaccuracies and inconsistencies in chronologies and events, on one memorable occasion coming from Bowery himself. It is widely known among his friends how he enjoyed constantly confusing people by spreading outrageous lies or twisting the facts. Tilley must have fallen into this trap when she believed and later reproduced in his biography that Anthony d'Offay personally invited Bowery to perform at his gallery after being mesmerized by a series of seasonal cards featuring Bowery displayed on a shop window; Bowery did make these images and cards with photographer Johnny Rozsa and he appears in some of them disguised as a cake, or a Christmas tree (Figure I.4). However, gallerist Lorcan O'Neill's account of the events (who was working closely with d'Offay at the time) presents elsewhere a less sensational – and rather more plausible – story.[23] It was Clark who was at first approached for a performance at the gallery but, due to his busy schedule, Bowery took on the offer. As intricate as it might have been, researching Bowery at times turned unexpectedly entertaining.

Figure I.4: Johnny Rozsa, *Leigh Bowery as a Christmas Tree*, 1986. © Johnny Rozsa.

He left behind a colourful body of work that sustained my enthusiasm and dedication throughout the research process and drafting of this book despite the awkwardness caused sometimes by his politically provocative costumes or my concerns about his ambivalent politics in a number of instances. I consider the creative weaknesses that I detect in Bowery's work an interesting and important part of his artistic identity and my subsequent frustration a fascinating aspect of what constitutes an exciting and challenging research project.

Structure and Chapter Summaries

Leigh Bowery: Performative Costuming and Live Art attempts to read Bowery as a multifaceted performance artist whose costumed body – his main expressive medium – allows him to penetrate multiple theoretical discourses and contexts of visual culture. By carving out a space for Bowery in relation to dominant art narratives, the first chapter establishes a vital understanding of his performative costuming as art and provides the foundation for further interdisciplinary analysis. In subsequent chapters, I carry out a close and extended study of Bowery's key looks and performances through a number of research contexts and analysis of relevant visual culture material to argue that his influential performative costuming and live art, which often appear politically precarious, constitute critical postmodernist interventions that not only trouble conventional historiography but also effectively challenge notions of normative embodiment, defy stereotypical representations of illness and bolster queer visibility. After I theorize Bowery's extravagant performative costuming as art in the first chapter, my attention shifts to its critical manifestation of subcultural freakishness, Bowery's extreme practices and body modification, and eventually his phenomenal queer embodiments. Throughout this narrative I engage with Bowery's live art substantially, with every chapter – save for the first – being thematically structured around at least one major performance that is discussed in detail.

Starting from the premise that Bowery's highly artificial self-fashioning constitutes an enigmatic and contradicting welding of avant-garde experimentation and postmodernist aesthetics, Chapter 1 negotiates Bowery's place in art history through some of the most authoritative voices in art theory and performance studies, namely Peter Bürger, Allan Kaprow and Fredric Jameson. I engage the narrative from modernism and the historical avant-garde to the emergence of postmodernism to argue that Bowery's performative costuming effectively merges art and life while often presenting questionable shock tactics to stir controversy. To critically situate Bowery's practice within the wider domain of postmodern art and to call attention to the marginalization of performative costuming in the broader context of art history, I look at his public intervention *Mrs. Peanut Visits New York* (1992), captured on film by Atlas, as well as the Dada embodiments of Baroness Elsa von Freytag-Loringhoven, an artist whose unruly practice in the early twentieth century remains enchanting. Three of Bowery's most controversial and potentially offensive looks that are exemplary of his postmodernist ethos – known as 'A Cunt', 'Nazi Dominatrix' and the 'Pakis from Outer Space' – are also discussed in depth and in relation to their problematic attachment to political matters pertaining to feminism, appropriation and subcultural aesthetics, and orientalist representation, respectively.

Chapter 2 expands on the sociocultural dimensions of Bowery's performative costuming through a critical investigation of the figure of the freak and examines his series of performances at the Anthony d'Offay Gallery (1988) as a distinctive manifestation of what Robin Blyn calls 'freak-garde'. Deviating from the flamboyant ethos of the New Romantics, which motivated his early sartorial experimentations, I demonstrate how Bowery evolved into the epitome of subcultural freakishness in London's club scene via his club night Taboo and the various niche media that supported it, most importantly *The Face* and *i-D* magazines whose contribution I historicize throughout in line with Sarah Thornton's seminal work on club cultures and subcultural capital. Bowery's solo performances of notorious self-made freakishness at d'Offay's gallery – a series of *tableaux vivants* that turned his costumed body into an art installation – can be viewed, I argue, as a postmodernist interpretation of the historical institution of the freak show, in which 'human oddities' were exhibited for entertainment and profit. In contrast to Bowery's passive objectification, artists Mat Fraser in *Sealboy: Freak* (2001) and Mary Duffy in *Stories of a Body* (1990) deal much more explicitly with 'freak' as a stigmatizing marker of disability and seek to address through agency the intrusive stare their unusually formed bodies elicit. The different ways the interrogating stare is negotiated in the performances under study enable me to propose an original dialogue around notions of normativity and otherness, narcissism and agency, and disability and queerness. Drawing on the writings of disability studies scholars, such as Rosemarie Garland Thomson and Petra Kuppers as well as Jones's work on narcissism and body art, I conclude that Bowery's narcissistic desire, flamboyant demeanour and dedication to transforming the body beyond accepted norms constitute an effective strategy of asserting difference and questioning the idea of the normative body.

Following the theorization of Bowery's freakishness as a performative mode, Chapter 3 elaborates on his fixation on bodily extremity, most evidently expressed through abject performances (namely, a performance at Industria in 1993, *The Laugh of No. 12* at Fort Asperen in 1994 and an enema performance at The Fridge in 1990), BDSM aesthetics (widely understood as the sexual practice of Bondage, Discipline, Sadism and Masochism) and the profound manipulation of the body as art material. I approach his restrictive shape-shifting costumes and experimentation with body modification – evident in various looks as well as in Atlas's film *Teach* (1992) – as painful means of a performance of endurance that aligns him with histories of extreme body-focused practices as they have been theorized by scholars like Kathy O'Dell and Dominic Johnson. Yet, I argue that pain in Bowery's practice arises as an inevitable consequence of the desire for the impeccable, exaggerated look and requires a new theory. His performance *The Laugh of No. 12*, which explicitly communicates this fascination with BDSM style and tactics, evokes the similarly intense body works of Bob Flanagan and Ron Athey, whose investment in extremity is openly informed by personal experiences of illness and disability and serves as a form of tacit activism. I specifically examine Flanagan's touring exhibition *Visiting Hours* (1992–95) and Athey's *Torture Trilogy* (1992–95), both dealing with illness and loss by employing ritualistic BDSM and body modification as empowering strategies. Even though I find Bowery's particular performance to be unconvincing in relation to a critical engagement with extremity, by shifting my focus to his enema performance at The Fridge for an AIDS benefit I argue that at times Bowery reveals a more politically promising aspect of his practice through perverted humour and the glorious staging of a sick queer body that refuses to crumble.

Bowery's unmissable queerness – the most frequently occurring motif in analyses of his practice – is meticulously addressed and developed in Chapter 4, which examines his important contribution to gender expression, sexuality and the representation of non-normative procreation. To effectively intervene and build on the existing relevant scholarship of his practice, I discuss several case studies from Bowery's diverse body of work and the expanded field of visual culture. His performance at the Serpentine Gallery (1989), a camp appropriation of an iconic billboard advertisement that became known as 'Hello Boys' (1994) and his 'Birth' performance at Wigstock drag festival (1993) are some examples I examine in detail. Bowery's camp and hybrid visual language, which, I argue, transcends conservative drag practices and effectively challenges the presumed gender binary, is re-worked towards a more robust framing of his work as an act of disidentification with heteronormative mass culture and as fundamentally reflective of – what writer Sandy Stone calls – a 'posttranssexual' ethos, which troubles not only understandings of gender but the limits of the human as well. Judith Butler's influential work on gender, José Esteban Muñoz's concept of disidentification and Donna Haraway's feminist reframing of the cyborg are some of the theories I engage with throughout the chapter. Employing the work of photographer Del LaGrace Volcano to guide the analysis allows me to initiate a discussion about non-normative procreation and the ways it poetically crops up in Bowery's work, whether through his performative costuming or, more explicitly, the infamous 'Birth' performance that constitutes the climax of his creative journey.

In the Epilogue I assess Bowery's legacy in the present moment – 30-plus years after his death – by tracing his enduring impact on club culture histories and alternative drag practices. I specifically discuss Minty's video *Like a Dream* (2019) as an intimate posthumous gesture and an emotionally charged creative tribute by close friends to honour Bowery's memory. I also argue for his broader significance and relevance as a queer icon with a far-reaching influence on various scenes and movements, such as New York's so-called 'Club Kids' of the late 1980s and 1990s, the emergence of Tranimal drag in Los Angeles at the end of 2000s and Bowerytopia, an annual queer event in Brisbane that grew from a series of Bowery-inspired parties happening since 2016. Bowery's lasting legacy attests to a powerful practice of performative costuming that is still urgent and present in various contemporary club cultures and queer drag scenes, disseminating a politically compelling queer ethos that reaches beyond fashion or art.

Notes

1. Leigh Bowery in *The Clothes Show*, BBC One, 17 November 1986. Author's transcription.
2. Amelia Jones, *The Artist's Body*, ed. by Tracey Warr (London: Phaidon, 2000), p. 187.
3. Thomas Mießgang, 'Die Kunst des Ausgehens: Wie Leigh Bowery im Rausch des Londoner Nachtlebens seinen Körper lesbar machte und als Regisseur eines Theaters der Künstlichkeit in Erscheinung trat', in *Leigh Bowery: Verwandlungskünstler*, ed. by Angela Stief (Vienna: Piet Meyer Verlag, 2015), pp. 53–71 (p. 57). Author's translation.
4. Martin Gayford, 'Ein riesiger unbekümmerter Narrenprinz: Lucian Freuds Bilder von Leigh Bowery', in *Leigh Bowery: Verwandlungskünstler*, ed. by Angela Stief (Vienna: Piet Meyer Verlag, 2015), pp. 261–81 (p. 261). A script in English was provided by the author.
5. Bowery appears in Wyn Evans's *Epiphany* (1984) and *Degrees of Blindness* (1988) as well as Maybury's *Read Only Memory* (1998) and *The Union Jacking Up* (1985). He is also featured in Dick Jewell's *Headcases* (1989), a three-part documentary showcasing London-based creatives discussing their views and physical attributes. A rare find is *Unstitched* (1990) by Baillie Walsh, which portrays Bowery having his cheeks pierced.
6. Katharina Sykora, 'Ego-Abenteuer zwischen Aktion und Bild', in *Leigh Bowery: Verwandlungskünstler*, ed. by Angela Stief (Vienna: Piet Meyer Verlag, 2015), pp. 209–32 (p. 210). Author's translation.
7. Peta Tait, 'Performing Shamelessness: Leigh Bowery, Copi and Queer Body Physicality', in *What a Man's Gotta Do?: Masculinities in Performance*, ed. by Adrian Kiernander, Jonathan Bollen and Bruce Parr (Armidale: CALLTS, 2006), pp. 208–21 (p. 213).
8. See Sue Tilley, *Leigh Bowery: The Life and Times of an Icon* (London: Hodder & Stoughton, 1997).
9. Bowery was also involved in the previous year's fete where he painted the faces and privates of then-emerging artists Damien Hirst and Angus Fairhurst. During the street celebration, the duo, dressed as

clowns, created spin paintings for 50p and invited the curious to peek at Bowery's hidden artwork for the same price.

10. Minty only managed to record one single with Bowery, titled 'Useless Man' (1994), which became a chart success in the Netherlands and turned into a cult anthem with numerous re-mixed versions. After his death, three more singles were released: 'Plastic Bag' (1995), 'That's Nice' (1996) and 'Nothing' (1997); and an album titled *Open Wide* (1997).
11. 'What Is Your Idea of Perfect Happiness?' in *Leigh Bowery*, ed. by Robert Violette (London: Violette Editions, 1998), pp. 8–9 (p. 9).
12. Bob Nickas, 'Talk of the Gown: Bob Nickas on Leigh Bowery', *Artforum*, February 2004, p. 52.
13. Michael Bracewell, 'Leigh Bowery's Immaculate Conception', in *The Space Between: Selected Writings on Art*, ed. by Doro Globus (London: Ridinghouse, 2012), pp. 126–33 (p. 129).
14. Pamela Karantonis, '"Punk's Dead, Michael": Artifice, Independence and Authenticity in Leigh Bowery's Self-Fashioned Post-Punk Performative', *Punk and Post-Punk*, 4.2–3 (2015), 205–22 (p. 210).
15. Rachel Hann, 'Debating Critical Costume: Negotiating Ideologies of Appearance, Performance and Disciplinarity', *Studies in Theatre and Performance*, 39.1 (2019), 21–37 (p. 25).
16. Quoted in Dominic Johnson, 'Marginalia: Towards a Historiography of Live Art', in *Critical Live Art: Contemporary Histories of Performance in the UK*, ed. by Dominic Johnson (Oxford: Routledge, 2013), pp. 13–30 (p. 22).
17. Jennifer Doyle, *Hold It against Me: Difficulty and Emotion in Contemporary Art* (Durham, NC: Duke University Press, 2013), p. 22.
18. Doyle, p. 21.
19. See Peggy Phelan, *Unmarked: The Politics of Performance* (Oxford: Routledge, 1993).
20. Amelia Jones, '"Presence in Absentia": Experiencing Performance as Documentation', *Art Journal*, 56.4 (1997), 11–18 (p. 12).
21. Jones, '"Presence in Absentia"', p. 13.
22. Jones, '"Presence in Absentia"', p. 12.
23. See 'Lorcan O'Neil', in *Michael Clark*, ed. by Suzanne Cotter and Robert Violette (London: Violette Editions, 2011), pp. 115–16 (p. 115).

Chapter 1 Performative Costuming: Merging Fashion, Art and Life

Performative costuming is at the core of Leigh Bowery's versatile body of work. A simple image search for Bowery online results in a colourful mosaic of assorted looks, most of them carefully staged and framed as glossy fashion shots. Yet, deeper research into his life and work reveals that his costumed personas were not just isolated creative instances for the camera but have in fact been inseparable from his ordinary public presentation of self. Bowery's performative costuming reflects in a prolific manner his hybrid aesthetic and ability to fuse a wide range of visual elements stemming from haute couture elegance, fine art, pop culture and underground practices that together render his extravagant presence highly enigmatic. An initial interest in fashion has, in Bowery's case, progressively culminated in a full-blown malleable performance of subjectivity.

Since Bowery started running club night Taboo in 1985, his looks became increasingly inventive and eccentric. This was around the time he decided to shave all of his hair off and use his head as a canvas by placing splashes of coloured PVA glue on (the pigment of which varied according to the outfit) and letting them drip evenly to the sides of his heavily made-up face. Fergus Greer photographed Bowery modelling the 'Drip' look against a dark background that contrasts with his vibrant make-up and lime green outfit (Figure 1.1). Bowery appears elegant and smooth as

Figure 1.1: Fergus Greer, *Leigh Bowery: Session I, Look 2*, 1988. © Fergus Greer. Courtesy of the artist and the Michael Hoppen Gallery, London.

he softly stares into the camera. His face and the flesh of his chest, squeezed in a way that creates the illusion of a bust, are lightly tinted white while blue pigment descends from the top of his hairless head. He has thick dark eyebrows painted on that frame his pink smokey eye make-up, blending seamlessly with the orange on his cheeks. The lips are overdrawn and distorted, with the bottom lip painted bright red and the upper darker. Yet, his outfit looks luxurious: satin long-sleeves and an exaggerated U-neckline emphasize his curvaceous bust and expand into a feathery balloon-shaped skirt that finishes just above the knees, creating the illusion of a round waist-less silhouette. Fully embroidered leggings with green and red sequins cover his legs and Victorian-style green ankle boots with golden laces and plain white gloves complete the look. High-fashion demeanour and clownish quirkiness merge harmoniously in Bowery's look, constructing a bizarre nightclub creature of sorts.

Even though during his early years in London Bowery had achieved some recognition as a new and promising fashion designer, he soon grew dissatisfied with the idea of mass-producing his garments and potentially having to compromise his extravagant vision to satisfy the commercial demands of the fashion industry. The prevailing general rule in fashion of regularly setting and catering to popular trends appeared at odds with Bowery's desire to explore the body's ability to transform and the idea of costuming as a means of forming and performing a unique subjectivity. Denying the accessibility and commercialization of his designs, Bowery divests them of their functionality as fashion to warrant them the status of strictly personal wearable art in the form of performative costuming that came to define his life and fluid practice across media: from impromptu interventions in nightclubs or the street and more structured performances in art spaces to posing and performing for the camera.

In an episode of the offbeat documentary series *South of Watford*, dedicated to Bowery as London's unconventional design phenomenon and club icon, the camera follows him through the narrow streets of the East End. Fully costumed in a flashy assemble and with a painted face one can hardly miss, he is shown walking hastily through the busy crowd and scouring textile shops for materials. 'I can't really tell the difference between the stage and the street', he states attired in his 'Drip' look.[1] With his extraordinary presence, Bowery negotiates the complex relationship between performance, everyday life and public space.

Examined within the wider context of canonical art history, it is tempting to look at Bowery as nothing other than a postmodern descendant of similar manifestations of performance encountered in the historical avant-garde of the early twentieth century, both in terms of his desire to be distant from the highly capitalist fashion industry in favour of experimentation and in terms of practice or form. This connection has been acknowledged by previous commentators on his work. Pamela Karantonis reads his ostentatious self-fashioning of pure artifice as a post-punk parody of the dehumanizing effect of late-capitalist culture, appearing, therefore, to be in line with the radical anti-establishment values espoused by the historical avant-garde.[2] In terms of aesthetics and expressive means, Anne Marsh similarly links Bowery's practice to the experimentation found in Dada cabaret or the antics of the Russian Futurists who paraded the streets in outlandish costumes and painted faces against *comme il faut* bourgeois taste, the Surrealists' fixation on physical transgression and Oskar Schlemmer's unorthodox costumes for the Triadic Ballet that spread the constructivist ethos of the Bauhaus. Yet, as Marsh admits, Bowery occupies a precarious space in theoretical discourse for his intricate practice upsets the linear progression of canonical art history:

> Bowery's art bridges high and popular-subculture in dynamic ways. His 'looks' developed from street culture to become hybrid high art, *haute couture*, and avant-garde performances. [...] [He] can be seen as a modernist in terms of his design but he was also a postmodern, post-punk, new romantic, performatively transgendered, artist who operated on the extremes of the fashion industry and the art world.[3]

Marsh attests to the diversity and acute fluidity of Bowery's practice that seems to trouble the attempt for a straightforward art-historical approach. The heterogeneity that defines his work, which is typical of a postmodernist ethos that dominated visual arts after the late 1950s, merges with the now fairly deflated spirit of avant-garde experimentation and innovation, which presumably failed to live up to its expectation for anti-institutional art integrated with life. Bowery's paradigm makes justice a practice that remained theoretically and critically neglected in art-historical accounts of modernism. Operating on the extremes or margins of fashion and art and resisting categorization, his performative costuming has brought him closer to avant-garde ideals than those more authoritative figures in art history and offers opportunities for critical analysis and reflection on his dubious shock tactics as a postmodernist provocation.

Towards a Practice of Lifelike Art

Bowery's performative costuming, exercised for the most part in non-institutional contexts, can be viewed as a form of 'lifelike art', a herald of the expanded field of performance art in which performativity displaced the traditional object-based art production, collapsing the boundaries between art and life, an ambition the historical avant-garde unsuccessfully strived for. An unruly and disruptive practice, performative costuming routinely existed on the periphery of established art developments and discourse since modernism and arguably gained momentum relatively recently through the increased visibility of Bowery's work; an artist who seems to curiously personify a theoretically compromised postmodern return to the principles of the historical avant-garde.

The historical avant-garde is firmly attached to the modernist era, which commenced in Europe during the late nineteenth century as an artistic backlash to the crisis of modernity and as an endeavour into non-representational styles in fine arts that best reflected the prevailing spirit of relinquishing tradition. The plethora of movements and styles that dominated the rather busy terrain of modernism overcame pure imitation and realism – something that art historian Ernst Gombrich attributes merely to the invention of photography becoming more accessible – to produce art that critically and authentically expressed the excitement or concerns of a dramatically changed world and required a potentially more philosophical approach.[4] The obsessive emphasis on new visual languages by artists fostered a growing fascination with expressive mediums and the ways they can be worked to create an aesthetic dialogue between form and colour. At the same time, a developing art market and an increasing number of intellectuals and critics started valuing originality and innovation in art techniques. While modernist art was targeted at a cultivated audience, its supposed antithesis was what art critic Clement Greenberg calls 'kitsch', namely the various products of the industrial revolution in the form of 'popular, commercial art and literature with their chromeotypes, magazine covers, illustrations, ads, slick and pulp fiction, comics, Tin Pan Alley music, tap dancing, Hollywood movies, etc., etc.', which along with representational 'lower quality' art were consumed, he claims, by the ignorant masses who were unable to appreciate 'high' art.[5]

Parallel to modernism but distinct in emphasis, the historical avant-garde of the early twentieth century encompassed 'the idea of radical art merging with revolutionary politics', Günter Berghaus clarifies in a study of its significance in shaping contemporary theatre practice.[6] Thoroughly critical of art evolving into an autonomous institution separated from the practice of real life, the heterogeneous avant-garde that operated in small close-knit groups attacked dominant ideologies and aesthetic conventions of bourgeois society and opposed the capitalist idea of art as a marketable commodity. In its quest for radical uncompromising art capable of provoking social change, the avant-garde resorted to transgression and shock tactics, refusing to cooperate with the bourgeois institutions of art. The ephemerality and immediacy of non-theatrical performance (often the chosen medium among avant-garde artists) were promising qualities for directly addressing their concerns, reaching a wider audience and effectively steering clear of the capitalist exploitation of art at the time. Nonetheless, the historical avant-garde was ultimately accepted, imitated and excitedly welcomed by the establishment.

The failure of the historical avant-garde to live up to its expectations is most assertively argued by Peter Bürger who specifically traces the emergence of Dada, early Surrealism and Russian experimental art after the October Revolution as an attack on the autonomous status that art had acquired with the rise of bourgeois culture.[7] Bürger illustrates the historical avant-garde as an attempt at introducing art into the practice of life, mounting at the same time a critique towards art as an institution and not necessarily towards past artistic styles as art movements had been traditionally expected to. The infamous *Fountain* that Marcel Duchamp submitted for the inaugural exhibition of the Society of

Independent Artists in New York in 1917 (only to be rejected by the committee) became an emblem of object-based avant-garde and one of the most influential pieces in the history of modern art. It is famously an industrially produced porcelain urinal rotated from its usual axis and signed 'R. Mutt', which Bürger reads as a conceptual gesture against the excessive focus on individual creation and the artist as the central figure of the creative process, both highly valued in art production since the Renaissance and especially in then-emergent modernism. The exhibition of a mass-produced object as art, a 'readymade' as such exhibits became widely known, negates notions of authenticity and individual production, with the pseudonymous signature inscribed on it serving as acute criticism of the art market where the signature overshadows the quality of the work.

For Bürger, the readymades, which became synonymous with Duchamp and Dada, are not works of art per se but 'manifestations' that sought to dismantle the modernist idea of the work of art and invalidate by extension the bourgeois institution of the museum that maintained its autonomous status.[8] However, these provocative 'manifestations' were quickly accepted as revolutionary art objects that deserved a place in museums or, making things worse, in commercial galleries for purchase by prosperous art collectors. The original *Fountain*, lost shortly after it had been submitted for exhibition, was later recreated in sixteen replicas by Duchamp and his art dealer Arturo Schwartz that are now scattered across some of the best-known institutions and private collections worldwide. Ultimately, Duchamp did not prove so immune to the prospect of fame, possible financial gain and a prestigious place in art history as a 'genius' artist. The historical avant-garde may have not succeeded in dismantling the institution of art and reintegrating art and life by these means, but it managed to modify the idea of art significantly.

Subsequent movements in the 1960s that have been credited as neo-avant-garde, namely Pop Art and Minimalism, retained some of the discursive edge of their predecessors, albeit fully adapted to the art market and often viewed by critics as occurrences of an inauthentic protest of a long-faded provocation. In defence of the neo-avant-garde, art critic Hal Foster maintains that it perpetuates past strategies in a fresh critical context without replicating the historical avant-garde but appropriating it to devise new hybrid practices that would pave the way for postmodernism: 'If minimalism and pop do mark a historical crux [...] they will suggest not only a perspective on modernist art but also a genealogy of postmodernist art.'[9]

Since the institution of art proved resistant to the attack of the historical avant-garde, the integration of art with the practice of life ought to be realized solely outside the institutional framework of the museum, art gallery and the market, either through site-specificity or the dematerialization of the work of art. For Bürger, all object art after the historical avant-garde is doomed, it 'can either resign itself to its autonomous status or "organize happenings" to break through that status' without, however, hoping for an equivalent 'protest value' or shock effect like that of the Dada manifestations, he claims.[10]

Developed by performance art pioneer Allan Kaprow during the 1950s in New York, 'happenings' can loosely be described as multidisciplinary art events incorporating chance, performativity and various objects in attempting to shift the inflexible experience of object-based art production towards collective occasions of everyday life. Similar radical art activities in search of new outlets that moved away from the conservative then modernist formalism appeared elsewhere as well, with most prominent those of the Gutai group in Osaka. Paradoxically, it was the action painting of Abstract Expressionism 'hero' Jackson Pollock, lauded by Greenberg who saw on his canvases the apotheosis of pure late-modernist formalism, that opened up new creative horizons for Kaprow's conception of happenings. In his seminal text 'The Legacy of Jackson Pollock' (1958), Kaprow extols Pollock for destroying the tenets of traditional painting by placing his large canvases on the floor and letting colour drip on the surface in fluid almost dance-like movement, adding a performative ritualistic dimension to the process of painting.[11] Taking Pollock's action painting further, Kaprow almost prophetically urges the artists of his time to utilize all their senses and 'become preoccupied with and even dazzled by the space and objects of [their] everyday life, either [their] bodies, clothes, rooms, or, if need be, the vastness of Forty-second Street'.[12] As a walking art piece, Bowery seems to represent the culmination of many of the trajectories of happenings, which defined this ideological and creative shift towards the development of performance art.

In a later reflection, Kaprow articulates a clear distinction between two avant-garde histories: one of a conventional 'artlike art' evident in Dada's manifestations that preserves its seriousness and medium purity, relishing institutional acceptance; and a contrasting, liberating 'lifelike art' that is foremost connected to the experience of life and avoids tradition.[13] Lifelike art is overall not concerned with new art genres and adopts a more flexible and inclusive approach to art. It moves away from familiar institutional contexts to engage with unexpected environments. It favours various performative modes and real processes, blurring the boundaries between art and life. It renders art experts and critics obsolete for what matters is the random (or not so random) participants and interactions in the real world. It unfolds with life and can be therapeutic. Bowery's practice, which certainly refused categorization, fits well into Kaprow's schema of lifelike art, sharing many of its principles. Not quite fashion and not exactly art in the conventional sense, his elusive performative costuming comfortably occupies a highly creative grey area and operates mainly within the rubric of the everyday, transforming, via extreme looks, mundane experiences into small instances of performance whether by walking down the street, dancing in a nightclub or just being in public space. Remaining anarchic and versatile, his practice appears alien to the conservatism of art institutions and critics. Away from elitist art specialists, Bowery generously offers unsuspecting audiences spontaneous encounters with art just by living out his experiments with embodied subjectivity and alternative modes of being openly and as cathartic acts. Most importantly, his obsession with refashioning the body speaks to wider social anxieties surrounding notions of normativity, tolerance and repressed desire, with potentially powerful liberating effects that reach beyond art discourse.

This lifelike art represents only a strand of what loosely became known as postmodernist art, understood by critics such as Rosalind Krauss and Douglas Crimp as a radical break with the dominant culture and modernist aesthetics witnessed in the late 1950s and early 1960s.[14] Contemplating Jean-François Lyotard's seminal definition of the postmodern as 'incredulity towards metanarratives', namely the discourses of grand universal truths and ideologies governing societies since the Enlightenment, postmodernist art as a whole can be viewed as a repudiation of the metanarrative of modernism via its unprecedented diversity of hybrid styles and voices.[15] What, however, should not be ignored is the fact that such practices involving performativity existed in the margins of art history and the historical avant-garde long before the explosion of postmodernism.

The Performance of Subjectivity and the Historical Avant-Garde

Bowery developed his performative costuming within the subcultural milieu of London's nightclubs in the 1980s and persisted in viewing such alternative spaces – certainly marginal to the conservative gaze – as the main outlet for his artistic practice. This does not mean that he rejected the commercial gallery and theatre sectors per se; his experience includes performances in institutional venues such as the Anthony d'Offay and the Serpentine galleries, while during his collaboration with the Michael Clark Company he had the opportunity to perform in prestigious theatres in the United Kingdom, such as the Royal Opera House, Sadler's Wells, and the Riverside Studios in London, and overseas. However, he found conventional spaces somewhat limiting in comparison to the freedom and spontaneity of the nightclub that allowed him to combine all the things he was passionate about, namely performance, music and fashion.

Besides the fact that art is almost always under negotiation in institutional venues, Bowery realized the dynamic effect and interactive quality of his performative costuming in everyday situations that involved an incidental crowd: 'Art has such hoity-toity connotations and appeals to really boring middle-class people. [...] I think when I'm dressed up I reach more people than a painting in a gallery', he stated.[16] His more conventional daytime looks that involved a variety of scroungy wigs and subtle transformative techniques, such as tightly sellotaping the skin on one side to create the illusion of a misshapen face or wearing high heels inside his trainers to look taller, were equally performative, making his presence more disturbing than his highly theatricalized embodiments.

A short video by Charles Atlas titled *Mrs. Peanut Visits New York* (1992) shows Bowery in one of his most iconic costumes catwalking the streets of downtown New York, causing bewilderment and excitement to unsuspected spectators

(Figure 1.2). The ‘Mrs. Peanut’ look consists of a full body and face Lycra construction in beige colour with a disanalogous bulgy leg enveloped in a floral long dress and a matching tilted top hat. The head is completely covered and has only two half-circular blue shapes for eyes and a perfectly round red hole, giving the impression of a pout. Inspired by a picture of Audrey Hepburn in haute couture by Yves Saint Laurent, the gown was made of cheap fabric from Shepherd’s Bush Market. It is a one-shoulder dress with a thigh slit that was heavily corseted with cast-iron bones intended for orthopaedic patients. Walking in it must have been a challenging task, not least on account of the corseted torso but also because of restricted sight and breathing.

In the video he roams the streets gracefully early one morning and mixes with the commuters, exaggerating the fashion walk and posing vigorously in front of the least glamorous urban sights imagined: first a bus stop, then a pile of rubbish and a decayed wall with graffiti. A blend of retro peanut-related pop songs, jazz,

Figure 1.2: Charles Atlas, *Mrs. Peanut Visits New York*, 1992. Video stills. © Charles Atlas. Courtesy of the artist and Luhring Augustine, New York.

experimental sounds, rock 'n' roll and Queen's hit 'Killer Queen' (1974), written about a high-class call girl with a lavish taste for luxury, complements the lo-fi footage, which creates a similar effect to John Waters's improvised scenes of his muse Divine cheerfully walking the busy streets of Baltimore. In a volume cataloguing his various art projects, Atlas recalls his experience with filming Bowery on this occasion:

> We walked around the Meatpacking District and found an area with garbage and graffiti where we thought he looked good. This was before the area was fancy; back then it was still the real meat market. I was used to going out with Leigh, but people on the street were surprised. He was an especially strange sight during the daytime, and a passerby called out, 'Mrs. Peanut!' We loved the idea that Leigh was Mr. Peanut's wife, and that's how this look got its name.[17]

Atlas points at the powerful impact Bowery's intervention had and the productive exchange between the performer and an incidental spectator that resulted in the work taking its name from a funny comment, regardless of whether conservative-looking Mr. Peanut would deserve so sassy a wife.

The mascot of American snack-food company Planters, Mr. Peanut, was at the time one of the most recognizable icons in advertising history. He is depicted as an anthropomorphic peanut in its shell dressed in the formal clothing of an old-fashioned gentleman: a top hat, monocle, white gloves, spats and a cane. Bowery's round-constructed beige head with the hat could indeed with a little imagination allude to that of Mr. Peanut. Notably, Mr. Peanut made his way into performance art history when he became the alter-ego of Canadian artist Vincent Trasov who in exploring anthropomorphism, identity and contemporary mythology created in 1969 a papier-mâché costume identical to the mascot's, which he would wear while strolling through the city or playing his violin and tap dancing in the street with his fellow 'Peanettes'. Trasov's grandest performance as Mr. Peanut, however, was undoubtedly when he ran for Mayor of Vancouver in the civic elections of 1974 with the slogan 'Mr. Peanut ... Not just another nut in politics'. Following a hectic campaign schedule (ideated by fellow artist and campaign manager John Mitchell) that involved dancing and singing interventions in public spaces and televised political debates and being formally endorsed by William Burroughs, he received a respectable percentage of the vote, adding a bit of amusing absurdity to the otherwise dull civic bureaucracy and explicitly exemplifying the avant-garde ideal of lifelike art (Figure 1.3).[18]

Live gestures like Bowery's and Trasov's have consistently been employed as avant-garde expressions to challenge the conventions of institutional art as early as the 1910s, but they have been largely ignored or inadequately addressed in the discourse of modernist art that seemed firmly fixed on the art object. It was much later, during the 1970s, that performance art more broadly became accepted as an artistic genre worthy of critical attention. In the first history of performance art, RoseLee Goldberg acknowledges the importance of Futurism, Russian Constructivism, Dada, Surrealism and the Bauhaus in sowing the seeds for the gradual development and visibility of performance art after the mid-century.[19] Some of the strategies employed by the neglected segments of the historical avant-garde involve the dialogue between performative costuming and public space that artists like Bowery and Trasov resurrected decades later. The Russian Futurists, for instance, (such as Vladimir Mayakovsky and David Burlyuk) were regularly seen in public in outrageous costumes and painted faces, manifesting their rejection of aesthetic uniformity and restrictive conventions that disconnected art from life. Their meeting point, the Stray Dog café in St Petersburg, functioned in a similar manner to Taboo, one might say, that is as a creative locale for experimenting with dissonant subjectivities. The same might be said of Cabaret Voltaire in Zurich, a Dada nightclub where Hugo Ball performed as Magical Bishop in a hand-crafted costume, while in the tragic aftermath of the First World War, George Grosz walked the Kurfürstendamm in Berlin dressed as Death.

Especially in its most improvisational form, lifelike art appeared to be marginal and stigmatizing for its rebellious and often anarchic connotations as an anti-materialist, anti-commercial and devotedly presentist mode that evaded institutional assimilation. It also constituted an enticing, rarefied and evasive expressive medium that troubled its incorporation into dominant histories of art, leading to Duchamp's readymades being widely perceived in dominant narratives of the historical avant-garde as definite key origins of

Figure 1.3: Vincent Trasov performing as Mr. Peanut at the steps of the Vancouver Court House, Vancouver, 1974. Photograph by Bob Strazicich. Courtesy of the artist and the Morris and Helen Belkin Art Gallery, University of British Columbia, Vancouver.

institutional critique and dialectical precursors of progressive postmodernist art. This widely accepted model skilfully praises male artists by excluding women and queers, neutralizing, as Amelia Jones puts it, 'irrational aspects of subjectivity and practice'.[20] In her critical interpretation of New York Dada through the bohemian life and works of Baroness Elsa von Freytag-Loringhoven, Jones argues for an alternative outlook on the historical avant-garde that rehabilitates the obscured foundations of radical performance practice.

New York became a focal point in artistic development when, under the threat of First World War, many European artists like Duchamp relocated to the city. Baroness Elsa was well known in avant-garde circles as a multi-talented persona – Jones describes her as a 'self-performative cultural provocateur' – who arrived in the city from Germany in 1913 after having lived a turbulent nonconformist life.[21] During the ten years of her stay, she socialized with the cutting-edge art scene, turning into a symbol of Greenwich Village bohemia mainly due to her highly unusual sense of dress that resulted in her appearing frequently in stories in the daily press and even being arrested by the police. In a cultural biography of Baroness Elsa, Irene Gammel recounts how with her 'outrageous costumes' she became 'a New York landmark at subway stations, in public offices, in museums, at exhibitions, in department stores, and on the major thoroughfares':

> Her head: shaved and occasionally shellacked in striking colors like vermilion red. Her makeup: yellow face powder, black lipstick, and an American stamp on her cheek. Her jewels: utilitarian, mass-produced objects like teaspoons as earrings or large buttons as finger rings. Her accessories: tomato cans and celluloid rings adorning her body; the hem of her skirt decorated with horse blanket pins. An electric battery taillight decorates the bustle of her black dress in imitation of a car or bicycle. She also used live animals as part of her street performance[s]: a wooden birdcage around her neck housing a live canary; five dogs on her gilded leash as she promenaded up Fifth Avenue. [...] With each new day, she added new twists to her repertoire of makeup, headdresses, and costumes that were frequently made from junk objects collected in the streets. Like her body, her art was androgynous: feminine in attracting the viewer's gaze to the female body, masculine in producing an unexpected shock effect.[22]

Unravelling the history of New York Dada, Jones argues that, in contrast to her male contemporaries, Baroness Elsa *lived* Dada for she 'performed a kind of unhinged subjectivity' clearly at odds with bourgeois social behaviour that the rest 'only examined or illustrated in their work'.[23] Wandering the streets with her disruptive appearance, pretty much constructed by found urban junk and organic materials, Baroness Elsa turned her body into a 'readymade in action' integrated with public space and untouchable by institutional assimilation (Figure 1.4).[24] It is the correlation of public space with everyday reality, Jones maintains, that grants performances like those by Baroness Elsa their radical and destabilizing effect outside of conventional spaces deemed fit for cultural practice. A performance on the street can thus become powerfully disruptive and even dangerous without the artistic conventions in place that assign the action its meaning as art.

An anecdotal incident that Sue Tilley describes and (similarly to Baroness Elsa) led Bowery to his arrest in 1989 involves him walking down Charing Cross Road in the late hours of night on his way to Heaven practically naked: with a bare ass and his genitals strategically covered, he wore only a sequined bra, an elaborate headdress and platform shoes.[25] His spontaneous performance in situ entailed high kicks in the middle of the road with the car headlights serving as lighting effects amid frantic honking and traffic chaos. Bowery was arrested and taken to the police station where he allegedly refused to remove his full-face covering. He was set free without charges a few hours later and after the duty sergeant had called in all his officers to have a laugh at the strange sight.

Unable to make a living from her art, Baroness Elsa led a marginal life in poverty, with her highly transgressive embodiments that conveyed an aggressively ultramodern vision fading away in visual and cultural history during a time when, paradoxically, the expanding field of art publishing was thirsty for vanguard images and stories of modern life. While *Vanity Fair* (launched in 1913) hosted a plethora of artists' portraits, their writings and cutting-edge works: from Henri Matisse and Pablo Picasso to Man Ray and Duchamp, who posed in a sleek dark suit and a fancy bow tie, traces of Baroness Elsa's outrageousness were assimilated into the publication in a less threatening mediated form. Gammel describes how an elegant photograph of caricature artist Clara Tice that was published in one of the issues was clearly inspired by

Figure 1.4: Baroness Elsa von Freytag-Loringhoven working as a model, New York, 1915. Photographer unknown. Bettman/Corbis photo agency at Wikimedia Commons.

Baroness Elsa's unsettling public presence at the same time 'wild Baroness herself was silenced and labeled insane'.[26] Fashion as art was formally consolidated years later through the refined creations of couturiere Elsa Schiaparelli, whose unconventional designs and collaboration with artists such as Salvador Dalí granted her a position among the most important fashion figures of the interwar period.

Her vanguard performances of experimentation aside, Baroness Elsa was a poet and visual artist who made sculptures of found objects (most of which have only recently been assigned to her) before Duchamp's readymades broke through as revolutionary masterpieces. Putting forward convincing evidence, Gammel claims that *Fountain* was most likely Baroness Elsa's conception and not Duchamp's, with whom she shared a close friendship after he had politely declined her sexual advances. This alternative scenario has been widely supported by historians who see the piece as more in line with her style, demeanour and scatological preoccupation than Duchamp's early abstractions. The fact that it was André Breton in 1935 who attributed the urinal to Duchamp, with the latter taking credit for it long after Baroness Elsa's death, intensifies the suspicion and raises questions about the male-dominated canonical discourse of art history, including that of the historical avant-garde.

Recovering Baroness Elsa's long-ignored legacy, both Jones and Gammel view her practice as archetypal of postmodernist ideas that disrupt the conventional model of modernist art history and shatter the heroic narrative of the historical avant-garde genius. Her irrationality, for Jones, appears more related to late-capitalist concerns surrounding feminism and contemporary art practices like body art than the idealized approach of the readymade as a point of departure for later developments in art. For Gammel, similarly, her body-centred interventions as well as her hybrid practice that extends across mediums and genres render Baroness Elsa a figure evidently ahead of her time.

Perhaps one of the main reasons that performance art remained in obscurity for so long is its intangible ontological condition that allowed it to only exist in the present and, without substantial documentation, possibly live through oral histories before eventually disappearing into memory. Its nonreproductive quality is what hindered its participation in the circulation of capital for quite some time and it is for this reason that performance art, especially in non-theatrical settings, was deemed so revolutionary among radical historical avant-garde artists, with Peggy Phelan famously describing it as 'the runt of the litter of contemporary art'; albeit this argument has by now been repeatedly debunked for it appears no longer relevant in a late-capitalist era, which has more or less configured new ways to commodify even the most vanguard of artistic expression.[27]

Radical artists whose complexities cannot be easily digested into the art canon and exist on the periphery of art history are not a strictly historical phenomenon nor necessarily bound up with anti-capitalistic views, as Bowery's example indicates. Their exclusion or difficulty is registered rather as a consequence of a certain alienation and disenchantment with normative cultural values that are often translated into a durational life performance of a dissonant subjectivity that exceeds easy categorization and discursive analysis. Such is the case arguably for the eccentric Jack Smith who is best remembered as the underground filmmaker of the scandalous *Flaming Creatures* (1962–63), but very little is known about his erratic street interventions against the art establishment and landlordism dressed in 'exotic' robes and feathers or his experimental multimedia performances in the various lofts he lived in New York. Nonetheless, this is largely due to the fact that Smith was consumed by a sort of self-sabotaging mania for he was deliberately inadequately promoting or documenting his performances as if to 'preserve his cryptic marginality', Dominic Johnson writes.[28] Closer to Baroness Elsa's and Bowery's performative practice, Stephen Varble's 'gutter art', which involved public interventions in blue-chip galleries and upmarket stores in New York during the 1970s wearing genderqueer costumes made of junk and stolen objects, has only recently been rediscovered.[29]

Despite its postmodernist character, Bowery's practice follows a long tradition of under-documented and profoundly ignored perpetual performative costuming that can be traced as far as the historical avant-garde if not earlier, and which likely gained more visibility and artistic acclaim – while still retaining its subversive edge – due to the enthusiastic reception of heterogeneity and interdisciplinary crossover that came to dominate the cultural production of his times. Unfolding the murky past of the practice, it is hard not to view Bowery's contemporary body as a sort of reincarnation of Baroness Elsa's resourcefulness, striking make-up and scandalous self-fashioning, except that her materialist appropriation of found objects that transformed her into a walking readymade is in his case replaced by the appropriation of styles and ideas that adhere to the postmodernist ethos.

Performative Costuming as Postmodernist Provocation

By approximately the mid-1950s, the allure of modernism and the avant-garde hunt for innovation and originality appeared to be frayed and exhausted as a post-war late-capitalist era, determined by broad scepticism, subjectivism, and a more flexible approach to art and cultural production, started to take shape. The emergence of Pop Art and Minimalism was viewed as a reaction to the formal visual language of Abstract Expressionism, pushing essentially modernism to its conclusion and opening new possibilities for art production that were certainly not met with enthusiasm by some prominent supporters of formalism and medium purity. Greenberg was unconvinced by Pop Art's playful mashup of styles and techniques, which he encounters as a superficial trend unable to arouse 'an authentically new episode in the evolution of contemporary art'[30]; and Michael Fried, in his now-famous essay 'Art and Objecthood' (1967), renounces Minimalism for its focus on space and the viewer's experience – its 'theatricality' as he puts it – that compromises the sublime autonomy and internal coherence that works of art should deliver. As he warned, '*Art degenerates as it approaches the condition of theatre*'.[31] Whether it does or not has been debated extensively, but indeed in further developments that established a postmodernist phase in visual arts the so-called autonomous art object has been repeatedly challenged and replaced by contextual or relational works and meanings.

A broad and slippery term, postmodernism in art can be either perceived historically as 'a bundle of styles superseding modernist ones' or sociologically as 'a radical change' towards a post-industrial society that brought forth a new and very different kind of art, critic and art historian Irving Sandler writes.[32] Either way, since the postmodernist style first manifested in architecture in the late 1960s as a vivid reference to various past styles against modernist boxlike structures, it quickly transferred to the visual arts, reflecting its intense opposition to all the things modernism stood for. Autonomy and the idea of universal 'high' art were slowly but decisively replaced by a growing emphasis on relevance and social context, making formalism appear obsolete through an array of progressive visual languages and strategies. Provocative appropriation became emblematic of a manifold postmodernist style that first and foremost sought to shatter the tyranny of originality and the normative association of art with unique precious objects. Once condemned, kitsch returned triumphant as many artists started to recycle imagery and styles taken from a wide range of sources, following the lead of Andy Warhol who had famously used advertising logos and celebrities for his Pop Art, infiltrating the art world with everyday banality, Hollywood glamour and underground experimentation. The employment of mixed media gestured at the staleness of the traditional art object and the use of alternative spaces discredited institutionalization at the same time an expanding field of ephemeral art involving performativity or the environment repudiated the commodification of art. The turbulent socio-political circumstances that defined the end of the 1960s led to an increasingly ironic and politicized art production, culminating in the decades that followed into an artistic response to urgent issues surrounding feminism, racism, homophobia, ecological destruction or other contemporary concerns.

If Bowery 'represents the cult of pure artifice and pure alienation [in] a culture which has become obsessed with authenticity', as Michael Bracewell claims, he owes it to his disorderly practice and multifarious style being deeply immersed in the charmingly chaotic postmodernist ambience of his times, which was for the most part met with suspicion if not utterly rejected by some theorists.[33] Fredric Jameson, whose thinking on postmodernism and cultural production has been influential, paints a rather bleak picture of postmodernism as a dominant hysteric condition pertaining to the expansion of late capitalism.[34] For Jameson, the surge in new technologies and mixed media, the collapse of the distinction between 'high' art and 'low' culture and the perpetual nostalgic appropriation of styles in the form of pastiche replaced the organic work of art with a depthless fragmented superficiality for easy consumption, resulting in emotional alienation from cultural production and the displacement of the traditional hermeneutic model in favour of a contemporary theory of intertextuality. His pessimistic perspective is challenged by Linda Hutcheon who does not deny the strong link between postmodernism and multinational late-capitalism but argues that in renegotiating the polarity between 'high' and popular culture, postmodernist cultural works can effectively engage in political critique often through the power of parody offered by pastiche.[35]

Irrefutable and vast in scope, postmodernism's influence swept through the arts and creative fields, from architecture and industrial design to cinema, music, dance and fashion, muddling their distinct boundaries and establishing a contemporary hybrid visual language. Glenn Adamson and Jane Pavitt, curators of a major exhibition on postmodernism held at the Victoria and Albert Museum in London (2011–12), summarize the postmodernist ethos in a few lines:

> Modernists devised new windows on the world; postmodernists offered a shattered mirror. Modernism dreamt of utopian visions, which would transform society; postmodernism threw together a new look for a night on the town. [...] Instead of authenticity, postmodernism celebrated hybridity. In place of truth, postmodernism had attitude.[36]

In many respects, postmodernism can be seen as a promising revival of the lost avant-garde. It is under this diversity of expression and creative freedom that Bowery's practice was nurtured, motivating his performative costuming as an art form.

Still rare and elusive, crafting a dissonant subjectivity through dress as art had only been superficially explored, such as in the early work of duo Gilbert & George who in 1969 performed *Underneath the Arches* as singing sculptures in a railway arch in East London, sharply dressed in suits and covered in metallic make up; or the *Transformer* self-portrait series of Jürgen Klauke in 1973 where the exploration of identity and changing visions of self-definition are conveyed through quirky costuming. Nonetheless, Bowery is perhaps the only known artist in recent years to have grounded his entire practice in such extreme costuming aligned perfectly with the postmodernist spirit. Never abandoning his desire to stimulate and shock, Bowery often resorted to provocative strategies and the ironic appropriation of offensive or sensitive symbolisms in his costumes: 'There had to be a sick element, there had to be something that was distinctly off in order to get it right', notes Bowery's friend and artist Cerith Wyn Evans.[37] His highly sexualized queer embodiments and abject performances aside, which could possibly cause embarrassment or even revulsion to certain viewers, Bowery often created controversial ensembles with politically charged symbols, deliberately challenging political correctness and precariously balancing between creative licence and vulgarity. Swastikas, allusions to the racist tradition of blackface, religious and cultural iconography, and language that is considered obscene and demeaning were engaged in a perpetual game of intertextuality and ambiguous interpretation in Bowery's performative costuming.

'A Cunt'

One of Bowery's most sculptural costumes is a white, faceless, phallic-shaped Lycra construction that covers every inch of skin and totally distorts the human silhouette. Once submerged in it the legs appear bulky and boxlike, a protruding lump under the stretched fabric accentuates the front and another big round bulge takes the place of the head and the shoulders. Only the hands retain their form, giving the impression of an anthropomorphic gigantic dildo with a beer gut. On its head, big black letters read 'A CUNT' (Figure 1.5).

The costume purportedly became a bone of contention between Bowery and collaborator Clark when the latter, although dubbed the bad boy of ballet for his unconventional productions, refused to use it as one of Bowery's costumes in *Mmm ...* (1992), a show based on Igor Stravinsky's *Rite of Spring* (1913), as it would cross the line. Bowery ignored Clark's objection and in one evening's performance he wore it anyway. Dancer Matthew Hawkins recalls how during a sequence with entrances that involved dancers in costumes with emblazoned key words on them 'the audience were flashed: "should"; "would"; "could"; "can"; "CUNT"' as Bowery 'lumbered on' at the end as a walking penis.[38] Allegedly that was Bowery's last tour with Clark's company, which also signalled the end of their ten-year creative collaboration.

In a gesture that brings to mind punk's 'confrontational' T-shirts, emblazoned with hand-painted or stitched slurs, Bowery put on a rather plain costume one of the few remaining words in the English language with a genuine power to shock in order to shake the establishment and challenge people's inhibitions. The amorphously phallic shape of the costume adds an extra sexual innuendo to its already audacious tone, which could be critiqued

Figure 1.5: Fergus Greer, *Leigh Bowery: Session VI, Look 32*, 1992. © Fergus Greer. Courtesy of the artist and the Michael Hoppen Gallery, London.

as 'exhibiting misogynist overtones' for 'trading on the offensive implications of using the word in place of an ability to exhibit female genitalia', Karantonis comments.[39] Bowery's attempt to shock by means of a taboo word that happens to literally refer to female anatomy and, as feminist writer Germaine Greer notes, is also considered 'the most degrading epithet' someone can be called seems highly problematic from a feminist viewpoint that cannot overlook the sexism and misogyny of patriarchy lurking behind its offensiveness.[40]

Tracing the etymological origins and meaning of 'cunt', Jane Mills points out that during the nineteenth century the term turned into a pejorative when it was first used either to sexually objectify women and as a 'dysphemism' for sexual intercourse or to describe 'a particularly unpleasant, stupid or disliked person of either sex'.[41] Its continuous use as an abusive slur, according to the *Slanguage of Sex*, 'reflects the deep fear and hatred of the female [...] and leaves women with few positive words to name their own organs'.[42] As a result, the word became a battlefield between radical feminists who renounced it as irrevocably problematic and those who tried to reclaim it in an attempt to shift its negative connotations. In the context of her battle against pornography during the 1970s, which was viewed by some feminists as degrading to women for assuming rather than undoing male supremacy, radical feminist Catharine MacKinnon condemns 'cunt' for adding to the dehumanization of women by reducing them to mere body parts.[43] At the opposite end, Greer, who is equally not sympathetic towards pornography, firmly defends the inculpability of the term from its offensive gist in an empowering article titled 'Lady Love Your Cunt' (1971).

In an attempt to replace its negative associations with a neutral descriptive meaning and reclaim the power of their sex, many feminists started using the term openly. Linguist Ruth Wajnryb calls this process the 'numbing effect', which occurs when a taboo word is constantly used in a different context losing its shock value.[44] When 'cunt' is thus reclaimed by women 'it is not used in anger or hurled as abuse' but 'denotatively, descriptively, deliberately stripped of its emotional connotations' in order 'to neutralize the power of the oppressor's language by using it liberally themselves'.[45] This emancipating strategy was translated into visual arts in the form of 'cunt art', a feminist art movement initiated in the early 1970s by a group of women at Fresno State College undertaking an art programme led by Judy Chicago. In exploring female experience and identity, they celebrated womanhood and sexual liberation through symbolic representations of female genitals, employing the taboo term with the goal of transforming it into a positive descriptor. A pioneer of feminist art, Chicago cites patriarchal oppression as one of the main reasons behind the decision: 'I use [...] "cunt" deliberately, for it involves society's contempt for women. In turning the word around, I hope to turn society's definition of the female around and make it positive instead of negative.'[46] Their excessive focus on female anatomy, however, was criticized as reductive and essentialist for locating the female essence simply in anatomical markers of biological sex and for establishing a fixed generalizing iconography for women as a consistent whole, disregarding their varied personal experiences or bodies.

In response to its enthusiastic adoption, radical feminist Andrea Dworkin argues forcefully that 'cunt' cannot be successfully reclaimed until hatred of women is removed from society. For Dworkin, 'power [...] determines the meaning of language'; as such, 'dirty words' will continue to remain obscene as long as what they name retains its 'low value'.[47] Exploring the relationship between feminism and linguistic theory, Deborah Cameron also views the reclaiming of 'cunt' as problematic and naive, not only in terms of its content, which uncomfortably reduces women to body parts, but also due to the unstable parameter of intent that hinders any effort for a permanent change of meaning.[48] Therefore, although reclaiming can have an impact on meaning and cultural beliefs, it essentially leads to a constant struggle.

The heavily charged slur has been a concern among theorists from the early days of second-wave feminism and its bold manifestation in art and visual culture, bravely and critically enforced by women artists, is viewed as an empowering act of solidarity in asserting gender equality and sexual liberation. It is unlikely that behind Bowery's costume lurks a feminist agenda, rather his interminable desire is to shock and mock bourgeois taste by all means. Brushing aside any hesitance to touch on delicate matters (in this case also contentious), Bowery inappropriately appropriates 'cunt' and exchanges the central core imagery that adheres to it since the 1970s with phallic allusions. Apart from unsettling sensitive prudes, his costume could in all likelihood be met with some serious feminist outrage and his motives with suspicion, for Bowery does certainly not identify as a woman who's suffered from oppression and exclusion nor necessarily as an ally.

The costume in action, as captured in documentary *Kinky Gerlinky* (2004) by Dick Jewell, presents an amusing sight: a cartoonish penis-shaped, self-proclaimed cunt bounces clumsily holding a can of beer amidst a dancing crowd. It is a funny scene and Bowery's costume was likely conceived as humorous and hopefully offensive, depending on the context and one's sentiments. Yet, the effect that Bowery anticipated, whether that is laughter, shock or embarrassment, is essentially premised on the use of a term whose strong implications derive from a deeply embedded patriarchal hatred for women that may render the costume politically problematic.

'Nazi Dominatrix'

In 1991, Greer photographed Bowery in a rather modest outfit compared to his usual, flagrant, kaleidoscopic garments. He is depicted in black-and-white wearing a classic long-sleeve white shirt with a leather harness worn over the shoulder across his chest and a belted dark pencil skirt on top of a black latex catsuit that leaves no skin exposed. The whole head is stiflingly enveloped in black latex, with a dark ponytail sticking out from the top, and the pose is not bubbly for once but stiff and militant, with the body in profile like a parading soldier. One leg stands on a shiny high-heeled ankle-strap pump and the other is hidden inside a padded construction that blows it out of proportion. In conjunction with the exaggerated hips and unreal set of pointy breasts, the ensemble makes him a monstrous commanding figure. A red armband with the unnerving symbol of Nazism decorates his outstretched arm and leads to specific lines of interpretation. The atrocious symbol of the swastika, which became inextricably associated in the West with the horrors of Nazism during the Second World War, and the obvious military and sadomasochistic references turn Bowery into a grotesque Nazi Schutzstaffel dominatrix (Figure 1.6).

Firm materials like leather, rubber and vinyl tend to signal power, heightened masculinity and kinky sadomasochistic tendencies. A leather subculture, most visible in gay communities of the 1970s, grew out of an expanding post-war biker culture in

Figure 1.6: Fergus Greer, *Leigh Bowery: Session IV, Look 25*, 1991. © Fergus Greer. Courtesy of the artist and the Michael Hoppen Gallery, London.

which the leather jacket, as a marginal and not yet fashionable accessory, came to signify adrenaline, independence and rebellion against mainstream values. Marlon Brando in his perfecto jacket and muir cap as tough Johnny in *The Wild One* (1953) exemplified and disseminated this hypermasculine ideal of dissidence that turned him into a cultural icon and fodder for butch gay fantasies. Initially used for raincoats and wetsuits, rubber and its derivative latex similarly gave rise to an underground fetish community, stealthily taking pleasure from the skin's contact with the material after John Sutcliffe, whose attachment to leather had been previously diagnosed as a symptom of mental illness, designed in 1957 the first waterproof motorbike outfit for women, revolutionizing the unthinkable and taboo until then use of leather, rubber and vinyl in tailoring. Marianne Faithfull's iconic catsuit in the erotic drama *The Girl on a Motorcycle* (1968), which titillated fetish enthusiasts, was conceived and designed by Sutcliffe, who later founded the seminal mail-order magazine *AtomAge* (1972–80) as a platform for promoting his new designs and sustaining a scattered community of fetishists. Appropriating the highly sexual visual codes of rubber fetishism, infused with a strong dose of Nazi militarism, Bowery provocatively enacts the fantasy of a hardcore queer sadist of sorts about to crush anything in their path, ensuing it seems from a well-fixed cultural cult obsession with Nazi pornographic titillation.

Despite the widespread condemnation of Nazism for the appalling crimes against humanity associated with the Holocaust, a curious aestheticized sexualization of Nazis started to appear during the 1970s in certain visual culture and literary genres pulling together pornography and horror. These 'postmodern figurings of fascism', which, according to literary critic Laura Frost, are rooted in lecherous innuendos found in First World War propaganda, follow earlier 'modern fictions of eroticized fascism' that were invested in 'prohibition, fetishism, and sadomasochism', cementing its cliché correlation with deviant sexuality and perversity.[49] Nazi insignia, military uniforms and concentration camp narratives have been regularly employed in visual culture to communicate a forbidden aesthetic of authority in transgressive erotic representations of power and submission. In Don Edmonds's *Ilsa: She Wolf of the SS* (1975) – a prominent example among Nazisploitation films involving Nazi roles and torture porn – the main character is a hypersexual Nazi dominatrix carrying out sadistic experiments on her prisoners; while in the more sophisticated and widely discussed psychological drama *The Night Porter* (1974), directed by Liliana Cavani, a twisted sadomasochistic relationship between a SS commandant and a teenage concentration camp prisoner revives years later. Writing about postmodern cultural works dealing with the sensitive subject of the Holocaust, Jörg Heiser encounters a shared sardonic attitude that is translated sometimes as 'a mindlessness at work that tries to pass itself off as productive ambivalence', and proceeds to describe Cavani's film as 'a playground for Nazi chic' and 'a melancholy soundtrack' over scenes of violence: 'Yet these kinds of oversimplifications and distortions have perhaps been inevitable in the development of a deeper understanding of how contemporary art can productively use simplification and distortion as an aesthetic tool', he writes.[50]

There are indeed plenty of examples of provocatively fetishized Nazi narratives in visual culture but more intricate appears to be the assimilation of fragmented Nazi aesthetics and symbols that – severed from their original lexicon – have suffered an existential crisis as floating signifiers of hardcore desire in depictions of sexual fantasy and expressions of dissident subjectivity. Without necessarily being tokens of anti-Semitic or other fascist sentiments, but also without escaping criticism, Nazi paraphernalia is to be found in subcultural milieus and the art works emerging from them, such as Kenneth Anger's experimental short film *Scorpio Rising* (1963), in which a gang of leather-clad bikers prepares for a race as rock 'n' roll tunes merge with sadistic and occult flash images; and the homoerotic drawings of Tom of Finland, in which beefed-up men with tumescent crotches engaging in sexual activities are sometimes depicted in early works in tight Nazi uniforms.

The robust sexual impact of the SS uniform is addressed by Susan Sontag who locates its outset in the masculine embodied ideal of the SS officer and his right to assert total power by brutally treating others as inferiors. The well-made, highly stylish Nazi uniform (designed and manufactured by Hugo Boss) and the heavy leather boots gave their wearer a stately posture, dramatizing violence to certain aesthetic standards. In the eyes of younger post-war generations that were lucky enough to not bear witness to its horrors, Nazism, Sontag maintains, 'represents the exotic, the unknown' at the same time 'the SS has become a referent of sexual adventurism', fuelling sadomasochistic desires and bestowing sexualized rituals of domination and enslavement a theatrical quality.[51]

As the ultimate emblem of fascist ideology, the swastika met a similar fate even though it is permanently stigmatized in the West as a symbol associated with genocide and brutality. It acquired the status of a universal taboo following the legal restrictions applying to the use of the German Third Reich flag in a number of European countries. The appropriation therefore of such a heavily charged symbol, whether in fashion or art, results almost always in frustration and endless debate. Apart from its explicit use in the costume under study, Bowery also employed the swastika as a decorative pattern on other occasions, causing surprise and irritation to those who found it hard to come to terms with the idea of a gay man utilizing a symbol like that. Possibly enjoying the attention, he insisted that the swastika is an ancient Indian symbol and ignored the criticism. Indeed, as Steven Heller writes, the swastika had existed as a benign symbol since prehistory in various ancient civilizations and derives from the Sanskrit word *svastika*, meaning 'well being, good fortune, and luck'.[52] However, since it was adopted and adapted by the Nazis as a nationalist emblem its symbolism in the West continues to prompt terror and repugnance, collapsing any attempt at producing ambiguity.

Bowery's offensive political references are viewed by Karantonis as variations of the punk subcultural mentality of the 1970s that saw the incorporation of disturbing political symbols and fetish wear in their highly artificial self-fashioning as a vital tactic for parody, transgression and shock: 'The creative effort there was one that was cognizant of the unacceptability of such content to audiences within progressive, politically-aware democracies.'[53] Theorized by Dick Hebdige as the subculture that most drastically induced semantic disorder with its anarchic sense of dress and appropriations, punk became notorious for its shocking, initially inassimilable style that typically included tattered T-shirts with threatening slogans, junk accessories, bright dyed mohawks, spiked hair and safety pins in facial piercings.[54] Matching the equally aggressive sound of punk music, this attitude was part of what punk style pioneer Vivienne Westwood called 'confrontational dressing', understood as a sort of visual protest against the frustration and anxiety sparked by the unstable socio-political circumstances in the United Kingdom at the time. Her infamous boutique SEX, co-owned with Malcolm McLaren at 430 King's Road in London, shaped the transgressive ethos of punk and co-opted and marketized its aesthetics. It was under this philosophy of disobedience and provocation that fetish and bondage wear, with their perverse pornographic connotations, were soon in stock at SEX before being fervently espoused by punks. In the same vein, the swastika started appearing regularly as a punk motif on t-shirts, armbands or painted on faces, causing often a strong reaction from the public but defended by punks like Siouxsie Sioux and Sid Vicious as a strategy of breaking taboos and demystifying its symbolism.

In his detailed history of the emergence of punk, Jon Savage recounts McLaren's and Westwood's obsession with Nazi memorabilia for their alleged power 'to positively confront people with the past'.[55] The troublesome and ambivalent appropriation of the swastika, which was adopted by many punks during a dangerous time of social unrest and increasing right-wing sympathy, exists at 'the heart of punk polysemy: the erosion of meaning itself', Savage writes.[56] Hebdige similarly notes that, even though punks 'were not generally sympathetic to the parties of the extreme right', the swastika was appropriated for its guaranteed shock quality and to signify 'enemy', resulting in an intertextual play that defies any authoritative interpretation.[57] This was a playful but risky attempt to extract the swastika from its totalitarian context and reorganize its meaning as bricolage – a variant of the Dada 'cut-up' technique – in which a text is hacked and rearranged to create new meaning.

In fact, punk as a cultural rebellion of anarchic aesthetic and nonconformist character has been often compared to certain leftist movements and anti-capitalist practices of the historical avant-garde. Cultural critic Greil Marcus connects the lines between punk and Guy Debord's Situationist International, an intellectual formation in the late 1950s driven by libertarian Marxism and Dada, suggesting that their propagandistic practice of *détournement*, which entailed 'phrases and images cut from their contexts [...] to change into metaphors or go blank', can be found in the 'cut and paste' style that later manifested in punk fashion and graphics; not coincidentally, considering McLaren's educational background in art.[58] Yet, the failure of the swastika to respond positively to the intellectual and philosophical premises of semiotics, for the sake of which it was ambitiously and naively been modelled as a punk accessory for its shock value and possible revival, is best summarized by Heller who anticipates the dangers of recycling a symbol with such strong attachments to extremist ideologies:

> For every naive rock-and-roller who thinks the swastika can be used with irony, there is a fervent neo-Nazi who uses it with malice. For every well-meaning artist who thinks the swastika can be tamed, there is a devout racist who embraces it.[59]

Albeit short-lived and justifiably misunderstood sometimes, punk performed a severe cultural break and dispersed its relentless influence in music, fashion and visual culture of the years that followed. As a true postmodern phenomenon, it constructed a highly visible artificial identity built on irony and ambiguity, offered by the recycling and restructuring of visual signifiers stemming from youth culture, urban decay, sexual fetish wear and, occasionally, extremist politics. Even though the swastika in the 'Nazi Dominatrix' look is clearly not used ambiguously but consciously and deliberately within a well-orchestrated Nazi narrative, it nevertheless reflects Bowery's desire to provoke as a departure from punk sensibilities and tactics: 'If Nazism was shocking then Leigh would do Nazism', his friend the artist Donald Urquhart stated.[60] His amalgam of disturbing cultural references and subcultural aesthetics signals sadomasochistic thrill and sexual arousal by control and power through the politically troubling representation of a fetishized Nazi torturer. Evidently more skilful than punks' attempts, Bowery's embodiment can unambiguously take pride in its share of potentially offensive sickness and perversion.

'Pakis from Outer Space'

The very first imaginative look Bowery created and instantly put him on the map as a spectacular club freak came about in 1983 and was provocatively dubbed 'Pakis from Outer Space'. As he was hesitant to wear it in public at first, Bowery let his friend and painter

Trojan debut it in the nightclubs they frequented. It was the positive attention Trojan started to attract that ultimately liberated him from his second thoughts and he followed suit. The rather complicated look, which across various images appears slightly modified, yet firmly attached to its concept, is a highly kitsch pastiche of traditional South Asian styling, allusions to Hindu iconography and fragments of high art put together in a distinctively postmodernist manner soaked in glittery queerness and clownish colourful excess. It was documented by many photographers in different versions and appeared briefly in Wyn Evans's experimental film *Epiphany* (1984) and Atlas's *Hail the New Puritan* (1986).

The look consists of garments that blend the feminine and the masculine in clashing patterns and textures, hats decorated with sequins and rhinestones, vibrant face paint, various *faux bijoux* and fingers loaded with cheap-looking rings that are emphasized even more by pointy manicures. In a portrait of Trojan and Bowery by David Gwinnutt, the multiple ornaments and their placement replicate South Asian body decoration that has been favoured by both men and women since antiquity to signify the wearer's identity, beliefs, community, caste or family status. The nose ring, or *nath*, they both wear is a popular ornament among Indian women and a symbol of marital felicity, while the *bindi*, the distinctive small forehead ornament, is known as a religious symbol in most South Asian cultures. A Sanskrit script on Bowery's face, which, according to Tilley, was copied from a box from a greengrocer, translates as 'Fresh satsumas from Nepal', while Trojan's face sports misplaced painted lips and a suggestive outline of a nose in profile, evoking the style of Picasso's cubist portraits of the 1930s (Figure 1.7).[61]

Bowery's and Trojan's visual cacophony illustrates a fundamental postmodernist tendency that Jameson calls 'pastiche' and signals the displacement of the modernist artist as a centred subject as well as his distinctive individual style as a token of authenticity. It is an amalgam of clashing visual elements and an endless appropriation of past styles, refraining, however, from the desire for satire and parody, a novel mishmash of dead styles and borrowed texts suggesting 'speech through all the masks and voices stored up in the imaginary museum of a now global culture', Jameson writes.[62] Still, there is a liberating power behind postmodernist pastiche that Hutcheon relates to the repudiation of the restraining notions of 'artistic

Figure 1.7: David Gwinnutt, *Trojan; Leigh Bowery*, c.1983.
© David Gwinnutt/National Portrait Gallery, London.

originality and uniqueness' that traditionally troubled artists and the challenging of 'capitalist notions of ownership and property'.[63] But most importantly and against prevailing views, she insists that pastiche can be used effectively as a valuable vehicle for irony, serving to politicize representation and provide artists with a new purpose of questioning accepted beliefs and ideologies. If Bowery's 'Space' look can be read as an ironic gesture and not just an empty decorative self-fashioning, what remains open to question is the subject of parody.

As a mere fashion statement, the 'Space' look fits well with postmodernist sentiments witnessed in fashion design at the time. Fashion historian Bonnie English writes that many designers during the 1980s similarly strived to contradict the modernist ideal of 'good taste' and beauty through a critical 'anti-haute couture or anti-fashion' attitude expressed through unconventional dress-making techniques that embraced the imperfect and the diverse.[64] For example, Jean-Paul Gaultier, the *enfant terrible* of Paris fashion, whose collections in the early 1980s included body-shaping futuristic bodices and skirts for men, drew inspiration from a wide spectrum of visual culture and the arts, such as Dada, 1950s glamour and London's club scene. Pastiche in fashion was similarly expressed via the appropriation of past styles, cross-cultural references and the diversity of sources and materials, constructing a 'visual paradox', which through humour, irony or parody intended most of the time to make a statement and stand in opposition to conventions of the past.[65]

Like Bowery, many commercial fashion designers indulged in cultural appropriation during the 1980s under the rubric of postmodernism. John Galliano's collection *Afghanistan Repudiates Western Ideals* (Spring/Summer 1985); Yves Saint Laurent's 'exoticizing' of non-Western cultures; Ralph Lauren's Indian reservation chic inspired by New Mexico; Rifat Ozbek's designs influenced by Turkish dress, dancewear and clubbing are some notable examples. However, what differentiates Bowery's South Asian-inspired look from catwalk collections with visual elements extracted from non-Western cultures is the fact that his served primarily as a performative device. Bowery *became* the look, which he kept modifying by adding more explicit references until he created a sort of walking caricature so remote from his Western identity that it ran the risk of being perceived as racist mockery.

Inhabited by a variety of ethnic groups, the region of South Asia is unified by manifold dress and body decoration codes that were shared, assimilated or transported across nation-states. Bowery's apparent fascination with South Asian style and culture derives from Brick Lane, a neighbourhood in London's East End with a predominantly British Bangladeshi population that was known for its vibrant textile shops and was proximate to his council flat in Ronald Street; hence, he named the look as a tribute (paradoxically) to the area, disregarding perhaps the offensive appellation in its title. As fetishization of the cultural other, Bowery's look projects the constantly frail relationship between the Western intelligibility of non-Western populations and their sociocultural reality by the politically troubling representation of a generalized Asian identity. In his extensive postmodernist appropriation of arbitrary South Asian elements and iconography, which becomes more explicit as the look evolves, Bowery falls into the political trap of orientalism that is broadly defined as a body and tradition of Western representations of the 'orient', namely the signs associated with fantasies of unfamiliar non-Western cultures. When applied to fashion, orientalism refers to 'the character, quality or style associated with the philosophies, expressions and fashions of Eastern nations' that expand from Türkiye to Japan, signifying the 'unknowable, mysterious, threatening, and exotic' and becoming synonymous with colonialism, Jennifer Craik writes.[66]

In later photos of Bowery in the look he is depicted posing awkwardly against a white background in a green, short ass-less bodysuit with a discreet decorative pattern, cuffed batwing sleeves and an extremely low-cut neckline that leaves his chest exposed. Three artificial-looking pearl chains connect his pierced nipples and fall loosely across the front of his body while his legs are covered in dark striped tights. He wears the usual headgear, a good deal of accessories and long red nails. This time every exposed inch of his body and face is painted light blue and the script is nowhere to be seen. Instead, two strands of cheap-looking pearls protrude from his hat across the left side of his face, seemingly inspired by *mauli*, a traditional ornament favoured by Indian women. Bowery's unusual posing and particularly the stiffness of his fingers and the way his extended arms explore the space can be read as a reference to Indian dancing and religious iconography. Indeed, certain Hindu deities (most notably Kali, Shiva, Vishnu and others) are customarily depicted with vibrant blue skin, overly adorned bodies and make-up that emphasizes the eyes. In these depictions, the deities' bodies appear rigid, either in a meditation posture or wild and triumphant, often with multiple arms and expressive hands. Bowery's face reveals his flawless make-up in all its splendour: his blue skin looks smooth and matte, his eyes are thickly lined with dark make-up, referencing the kohl-smudged eyes of South Asians to repel evil, with little tinsel stars, echoing *barwat*, glued underneath and a bigger one in the middle of his forehead, reminiscent of the traditional *bindi*. A yellow stripe above his red lips gives the impression of a well-groomed moustache, a preferable type of facial decoration in stereotypical representations of South Asian men (Figure 1.8).

Figure 1.8: Sheila Rock, *Leigh Bowery*, c.1983. © Sheila Rock.

Bowery's queer pastiche in reconstructing an 'alien other' inevitably led him to assimilate some of the most cliché traits of South Asian culture, which in reality is wide and complex, frustrating both generalization and simple definition. This may reinforce the central conception of the orient that Edward Said describes as nothing less than 'a set of references, a congeries of characteristics' originating from 'a quotation, or a fragment of a text, or a citation from someone's work on the Orient, or some bit of previous imagining, or an amalgam of all these'.[67] Constructed as the adverse of Western culture and representing Europe's greatest colonies, the orient is perceived as a place of the voluptuous and the mysterious, bearing all the fantasies and desires concerning the experience or identity of 'the other' that has been instilled in the European imagination, material civilization and culture. The hegemony of European culture both in and outside its geographical territory finds its voice in the discourse of orientalism as a performance of cultural strength that is conditioned by the collective delusion of European identity being 'superior' to 'all the non-European peoples and cultures', Said argues.[68]

Bowery's experimentation towards a transcultural whole can be seen as exemplary of the impact of orientalism in contemporary visual culture. His look might not portray a realistic representation of South Asian people (Bowery's version comes 'from outer space' after all) but has still slipped into cultural stereotyping and ethnic generalization, two common issues associated with orientalist representation and cultural appropriation. Bowery incorporated a bunch of distinctive signifiers of South Asian culture without necessarily acknowledging their symbolism or cultural significance. His artistic gesture, like orientalism itself, is premised 'upon exteriority', to use Said's words, and his perception, similar to that of the orientalist, is distant from the social and cultural reality of non-Western peoples.[69] His repertoire of contemporary elements and floating South Asian cultural references discredits, one might say, the cultural, social or religious specificities within the geographical territories of the region. The ornaments, make-up as well as the script he copied on his face are evidence of his depthless approach, with the look shifting their status from cultural, functional or religious to art. Although such an approach is typical of postmodernism, the 'Space' look sharply corroborates the complexities and danger of political slippage that cultural appropriation begets, particularly when performativity is involved and enacted from a dominant position of privilege. This diminishes any attempt to critically view the look in a positive light, especially when it comes to the relationship between postmodernist parody and minority identity politics within a postcolonial framework. Correspondingly, the 'Cunt' and 'Nazi Dominatrix' looks can hardly sustain their radicality just by embracing shock tactics and controversial symbolisms without considering the nuances and implications of their political ambivalence.

Its occasional shortcomings in politics aside, Bowery's is a progressive art practice for numerous valid reasons. Exquisite, spectacular and often awkward or utterly problematic, Bowery's imaginative performative costuming elucidates the high art of being one's own artificial creation and underpins a unique artistic identity operating at the limits of fashion, performance and life. In his phenomenal embodiments of highly crafted dissonant subjectivities – and in those by other artists who before him similarly treated their lives as ongoing art projects but remained obscured or in those by contemporaries who are already following in his steps – the avant-garde ideal of art indistinguishable from life finds its best expression. Anarchic and unpredictable as it is, living as art might not be confined to sterile gallery rooms where art traditionally participates in shaping dominant histories. Instead, it infiltrates public spaces of everyday life, it can be unexpectedly encountered on the street or the train and thrives in nightclubs. Not unreasonably, the latter, as a relatively unrestrained playground of subcultural freakishness, became Bowery's natural habitat, informing and defining his adventurous artistic journey substantially.

Notes

1. Leigh Bowery in *South of Watford*, ITV, 25 April 1986. Author's transcription.
2. See Pamela Karantonis, '"Punk's Dead, Michael": Artifice, Independence and Authenticity in Leigh Bowery's Self-Fashioned Post-Punk Performative', *Punk and Post-Punk*, 4.2–3 (2015), 205–22.
3. Anne Marsh, 'Einhorn unter Tauben', in *Leigh Bowery: Verwandlungskünstler*, ed. by Angela Stief (Vienna: Piet Meyer Verlag, 2015), pp. 161–82 (p. 169). A script in English was provided by the author. Emphasis in original.

4. See Ernst H. Gombrich, *The Story of Art* (Oxford: Phaidon, 1978).
5. Clement Greenberg, 'Avant-Garde and Kitsch', in *Art and Culture: Critical Essays* (Boston: Beacon Press, 1961), pp. 3–21 (p. 9).
6. Günter Berghaus, *Theatre, Performance, and the Historical Avant-Garde* (New York: Palgrave Macmillan, 2005), p. 36.
7. See Peter Bürger, *Theory of the Avant-Garde* (Minneapolis: University of Minnesota Press, 1984).
8. Bürger, p. 51.
9. Hal Foster, *The Return of the Real: The Avant-Garde at the End of the Century* (Cambridge: The MIT Press, 1996), p. 58.
10. Bürger, p. 57.
11. Before Kaprow, it was art critic Harold Rosenberg who first saw the action on Pollock's paintings and interpreted the dissolution of the pictorial subject as a deeply personal existential gesture that brings to the fore the artist's subjectivity and experiences, gravitating towards the merging of art and life. Hinting at Paul Cézanne's modernist compositions of still life, Rosenberg assertively claims: 'The apples weren't brushed off the table in order to make room for perfect relations of space and colour. They had to go so that nothing would get in the way of the act of painting.' See Harold Rosenberg, 'The American Action Painters', *Art News*, 51.8 (1952), 22–50 (p. 23).
12. Allan Kaprow, 'The Legacy of Jackson Pollock', in *Essays on the Blurring of Art and Life,* ed. by Jeff Kelley (Berkeley: University of California Press, 2003), pp. 1–12 (p. 7).
13. See Allan Kaprow, 'The Real Experiment', in *Essays on the Blurring of Art and Life,* ed. by Jeff Kelley (Berkeley: University of California Press, 2003), pp. 201–18.
14. See Rosalind Krauss, 'Sculpture in the Expanded Field', in *The Anti-Aesthetic: Essays on Postmodern Culture*, ed. by Hal Foster (New York: The New Press, 1998), pp. 35–47; and Douglas Crimp, 'On the Museum's Ruins', in *The Anti-Aesthetic: Essays on Postmodern Culture*, ed. by Hal Foster (New York: The New Press, 1998), pp. 49–63.
15. Jean-François Lyotard, *The Postmodern Condition: A Report on Knowledge* (Minneapolis: University of Minnesota Press, 1984), p. xxiv.
16. Matthew Weinstein, 'Trojan and Leigh', in *Leigh Bowery*, ed. by Robert Violette (London: Violette Editions, 1998), pp. 40–41 (p. 41).

17. Charles Atlas, '1990–2010: Video Shorts; Video Collages; Video Featurettes', in *Charles Atlas*, ed. by Lauren Wittels (Munich: Prestel, 2015), pp. 144–79 (p. 164).
18. See John Mitchell and Vincent Trasov, *The Rise and Fall of the Peanut Party: Journal: Twenty Days in November* (Vancouver: AIR, 1976).
19. See RoseLee Goldberg, *Performance Art: From Futurism to the Present* (London: Thames & Hudson, 2011).
20. Amelia Jones, *Irrational Modernism: A Neurasthenic History of New York Dada* (Cambridge: The MIT Press, 2004), p. 22.
21. Jones, p. 3.
22. Irene Gammel, *Baroness Elsa: Gender, Dada, and Everyday Modernity* (Cambridge: The MIT Press, 2003), p. 183.
23. Jones, p. 5.
24. Jones, p. 143.
25. See Sue Tilley, *Leigh Bowery: The Life and Times of an Icon* (London: Hodder & Stoughton, 1997).
26. Gammel, p. 203.
27. Peggy Phelan, *Unmarked: The Politics of Performance* (Oxford: Routledge, 1993), p. 148.
28. Dominic Johnson, *Glorious Catastrophe: Jack Smith, Performance and Visual Culture* (Manchester: Manchester University Press, 2012), p. 16.
29. See Janet Werther, 'Discovering Stephen Varble', *PAJ: Performing Arts Journal*, 41.3 (2019), 17–27.
30. Clement Greenberg, 'Post Painterly Abstraction', in *The Collected Essays and Criticism: Modernism with a Vengeance, 1957–1969*, ed. by John O'Brian (Chicago: The University of Chicago Press, 1993), pp. 192–96 (p. 196).
31. Michael Fried, 'Art and Objecthood', in *Art and Objecthood: Essays and Reviews* (Chicago: The University of Chicago Press, 1998), pp. 148–72 (p. 164). Emphasis in original.
32. Irving Sandler, *Art of the Postmodern Era: From the Late 1960s to the Early 1990s* (Colorado: Westview Press, 1998), p. 4.
33. Michael Bracewell in *The Legend of Leigh Bowery*, dir. by Charles Atlas (London: BBC4, 2008).
34. See Fredric Jameson, *Postmodernism, or, The Cultural Logic of Late Capitalism* (London: Verso Books, 1991).
35. See Linda Hutcheon, *The Politics of Postmodernism* (London: Routledge, 2002).

36. Glenn Adamson and Jane Pavitt, 'Postmodernism: Style and Subversion', in *Postmodernism: Style and Subversion, 1970–1990*, ed. by Glenn Adamson and Jane Pavitt (London: V&A Publishing, 2011), pp. 12–97 (p. 13).
37. Sue Tilley and Cerith Wyn Evans, 'Conversation Between Sue Tilley and Cerith Wyn Evans', in *Take A Bowery: The Art and (Larger than) Life of Leigh Bowery* (Sydney: Museum of Contemporary Art, 2003), pp. 40–53 (p. 44).
38. Matthew Hawkins, 'Member of the Thinking', in *Michael Clark*, ed. by Suzanne Cotter and Robert Violette (London: Violette Editions, 2011), pp. 298–307 (p. 307).
39. Karantonis, p. 213.
40. Germaine Greer, *The Female Eunuch* (London: Flamingo, 1999), p. 287.
41. Jane Mills, *Womanwords: A Vocabulary of Culture and Patriarchal Society* (London: Virago, 1991), p. 59.
42. Brigid McConville and John Shearlaw, *The Slanguage of Sex: A Dictionary of Modern Sexual Terms* (London: Futura, 1985), pp. 45–46.
43. See Catharine MacKinnon, *Feminism Unmodified: Discourses on Life and Law* (Cambridge: Harvard University Press, 1987).
44. Ruth Wajnryb, *Language Most Foul* (Crows Nest: Allen & Unwin, 2004), p. 45.
45. Wajnryb, pp. 50–51.
46. Judy Chicago, *Through the Flower: My Struggle as a Woman Artist* (New York: Authors Choice Press, 1975), p. 55.
47. Andrea Dworkin, *Intercourse* (New York: Basic Books, 2006), p. 216.
48. See Deborah Cameron, *Feminism and Linguistic Theory*, 2nd edn (New York: Palgrave Macmillan, 1992).
49. Laura Frost, *Sex Drives: Fantasies of Fascism in Literary Modernism* (Ithaca: Cornell University Press, 2002), p. 153.
50. Jörg Heiser, 'What Is Appropriate: The Role of Art in Responding to the Holocaust', *Frieze*, April 2010, 92–97 (p. 94).
51. Susan Sontag, 'Fascinating Fascism', in *Under the Sign of Saturn* (New York: Vintage Books, 1981), pp. 73–105 (pp. 101, 102).
52. Steven Heller, *The Swastika: Symbol beyond Redemption?* (New York: Allworth Press, 2000), p. 20.
53. Karantonis, p. 212.
54. See Dick Hebdige, *Subculture: The Meaning of Style* (London: Routledge, 1988).

55. Jon Savage, *England's Dreaming: Anarchy, Sex Pistols, Punk Rock, and Beyond* (New York: St. Martin's Press, 1992), p. 189.
56. Savage, p. 242.
57. Hebdige, p. 116.
58. Greil Marcus, *Lipstick Traces: A Secret History of the Twentieth Century* (London: Faber & Faber, 2001), p. 359.
59. Heller, p. 157.
60. Donald Urquhart in *The Legend of Leigh Bowery*.
61. Tilley, p. 196.
62. Jameson, p. 18.
63. Hutcheon, p. 89.
64. Bonnie English, *A Cultural History of Fashion in the 20th and 21st Centuries: From Catwalk to Sidewalk* (London: Bloomsbury, 2013), p. 91.
65. English, p. 92.
66. Jennifer Craik, *Fashion: The Key Concepts* (Oxford: Berg, 2009), p. 332.
67. Edward W. Said, *Orientalism: Western Conceptions of the Orient* (New York: Vintage Books, 1979), p. 177.
68. Said, p. 7.
69. Said, p. 21.

Chapter 2 The Subcultural Freak: Narcissism and the Disruption of Normativity

The stage musical *Taboo* (2002) narrates the partly fictionalized story of some of the most prominent figures of the subcultural club scene that flourished in London in 1979 and became known as the New Romantics. Although Leigh Bowery had just missed this short-lived phenomenon and historically is not considered part of the scene, he is among those portrayed in the play, with its title being a tribute to his subsequent legendary club night Taboo that sprung out of the club culture the New Romantics had propagated several years earlier.

Like many spectacular post-war youth subcultures that preceded them, from Teddy Boys to Punks, the New Romantics shaped a social identity that set them apart from the homogeneous representations and norms of dominant culture via shared activities, material artefacts, music, mannerisms and especially clothes. More than anything, sartorial style provides the most immediately recognizable identifier of subcultural membership; hence, it became a focal point among cultural theorists early on due to the intricate ways subcultural identities are constructed before being usually exploited by the mass media and the mainstream. According to John Clarke, a pioneering researcher of British youth subcultures, distinctive subcultural styles define the group's visual identity not only in response to a standardized dominant aesthetic but also often against similar subcultural groups of apparently conflicting tastes and values.[1] Recognized as the first fully fledged post-punk youth cult to come out of London, the flamboyant New Romantics performed their own refusal towards the uncertainty of a seemingly bleak future but also towards punk, which by 1977 had become exhausted and monotonous.

Incarnated by Boy George, who was one of the initiators of the scene before exploding into stardom as a pop music idol and trendsetter, the character of Bowery in *Taboo* makes an ostentatious entrance on stage. Dressed in a costume that almost perfectly resembles one of Bowery's most distinctive looks, the often called 'Spot' look, he emerges vehemently from what supposedly is a toilet cubicle (perhaps a hint at Bowery's adventurous cottaging habit) and rhetorically addresses the audience with pride: 'Mirror mirror on the wall, who's the biggest freak of all?'[2] As captured by Fergus Greer, the look consists of a long, softly A-lined, double-breasted blazer with gold buttons in pastel mint colour patterned with big orange polka dots, matching cropped straight trousers with crocheted ends and matching high socks worn over a pair of mid-heel shoes. Every exposed bit of skin is also painted pastel mint and bears the spots; his lips are bright red and his head is covered with a short ash-blonde wig. A similarly patterned scarf, wrapped tightly around the neck in the style of a cravat, turns Bowery in his elegant pose into a postmodern, freakish incarnation of Beau Brummell that erupted from the gaudy and deliberately tacky aesthetic of London's clubbing arena in the 1980s (Figure 2.1). Bowery's bizarre narcissism, his hyperbolic and often grotesque manipulation of his body and his transgressive performances have rightly granted him the privilege of a self-proclaimed freak; 'the biggest of all' as Bowery's character declares.

Loaded with heavy historical baggage and charged with negative connotations over time, 'freak' has obtained a nuanced cultural aura. The term, which was once used to broadly describe those individuals with an unusual appearance (mostly due to a congenital condition) or with a mental and behavioural anomaly who were traditionally exhibited in so-called 'freak shows' a couple of centuries ago, turned during the 1960s into 'an honorific title by the kind of physiologically normal but dissident young

Figure 2.1: Fergus Greer, *Leigh Bowery: Session IV, Look 19*, 1991. © Fergus Greer. Courtesy of the artist and the Michael Hoppen Gallery, London.

people', literary critic Leslie Fiedler observes.[3] In his pioneering study, he explores the figure of the freak as a mythical monstrous creature whose powerful otherness, invoking awe and fascination since antiquity, has relocated into contemporary culture via those metaphorical freaks who seek to contest conventional boundaries and values. This shift in the meaning of 'freak' followed the rise of an anti-establishment counterculture in the West and, as cultural revolutions often tend to have an impact on language and expression, 'freak' was reclaimed as a badge of deliberate otherness and has since turned into a widespread slang catchword.

Writing about the New Left movements in the United States at the time, which were particularly active on the West Coast and became synonymous with the hippie lifestyle, sociologist Daniel Foss was perhaps the first who entered this updated version of 'freak' into discourse by using it to describe '*visibly* members of middle-class youth subcultures' whose appearance and reality aim at diverging completely from conventional conduct. He elaborates:

> Freaks are walking counter-environments who [...] come to assert the right to total control over their physical appearance and outward behavior – to the total irrelevance of the culture and informal norms of those who dwell within conventional reality [...] except insofar as it is desired to stimulate *disorientation* among the cultural enemy.[4]

Although the so-called 'freak scene' of the 1960s has long passed and an array of subcultural movements with their distinctive fashions, lifestyles and politics have come to inspire generations throughout the decades, the term 'freak', now rejected and condemned by the kinds of anatomically different individuals to whom it had initially been applied, adheres to the visually extravagant, the rebellious nonconformist and the subcultural other.

The New Romantics performed their own distinctive freakishness, defining a vivid point in British cultural history, even though they were often viewed as a lavish scene of vanity preoccupied with surface rather than substance. Departing from the pre-punk glittering androgynous aesthetic of glam rock and experimenting with vintage fashion and theatrical make-up in the late 1970s, the New Romantic freaks constituted a threshold for both the creative club scene that erupted soon after in London and Bowery's lifestyle, performative costuming and artistic identity.

Bowery elevated their ethos of excess and *éclat* in dressing up to a deep investment in extreme body manipulation and aesthetics of deformity that distinguish his freakish embodiments from the mere performance of an ordinary subcultural subjectivity.

Enfreakment as an Aftereffect of the New Romantics

Simon Reynolds describes London at the time Bowery relocated there in late 1980 as 'a fellowship of freaks' and 'the place where people [went] to shed their past and invent a fantastical future self'.[5] This still remains the case in many ways as after the explosion of punk, which caused an abrupt cultural shock entwined with British rebellion, London was permanently registered in the consciousness of restless youth as a progressive metropolis of multiple opportunities and became the epicentre of all sorts of subcultural creative endeavours, fostered by a DIY ethic and boundless ambition. The buzzing post-punk mise en scène of London in the late 1970s and early 1980s, with its thriving nightlife, cutting-edge fashions and the reputation of the New Romantics that had spread quickly, was, for Bowery, pivotal in his decision to settle in the city and to initially attempt to pursue a career in fashion.

In retrospect, the exclusive and rather small scene of the New Romantics provided the cultural stimulus and image for the mainstream synth-pop that broke out shortly after, defining the sound of the 1980s in Europe, but above all it galvanized a vigorous and diverse club culture that persists to this day. It can be seen as a key instigator of a short transitional phase from punk to a rapidly forming post-subcultural era where the classic notion of youth subculture was replaced by what Sarah Thornton termed 'club culture', namely the 'youth cultures for whom dance clubs [...] are a symbolic axis and working social hub'.[6] Indeed, the 1980s have been registered in the minds of many as the decade of nightclubbing.

The New Romantic scene reportedly kicked off in the autumn of 1978 when – disillusioned with the quick commercialization and macho aggressiveness of punk – club entrepreneur Steve Strange and DJ Rusty Egan (who both later gained international chart success as members of synthpop band Visage) set up a David Bowie-inspired regular event at Billy's, a languishing basement nightclub in Soho. Withdrawn from punk, both musically and aesthetically, Strange and Egan favoured instead a blend of

European electronica infused with a nostalgic turn to glam rock.[7] Breaking through in the early 1970s until it was overshadowed by the outburst of punk, glam rock left its distinctive mark on contemporary visual culture and proved inspirational for the stylistic experimentation of the New Romantics. It was the elements of glamour and gender fluidity – generally absent from punk at the time but abundantly displayed through the theatrical glittery excess and cross-sexual artifice of glam rockers like Bowie and Marc Bolan – that made the New Romantics turn to the then-recent past.

Totally disinterested in hippie countercultural ideals of naturalness and authenticity, glam rockers took on flashy lurex jumpsuits, feather boas, platform boots, glittery make-up and bold hairstyles to affirm the constructedness of their performing personas. Although their lustrous excess has been dismissed by some Marxist cultural theorists as superficial, pretentious and politically elusive, it foregrounded, according to Georgina Gregory, pressing issues around gender and sexuality to challenge prevailing representations of heterosexual masculinity in popular music culture and naturalized to some extent the uninhibited embodiment of dissonant subjectivities.[8] As Philip Auslander similarly notes: 'The demand for the freedom to explore and construct one's identity, in terms of gender, sexuality, or any other terms, is glam rock's most important legacy.'[9] Following in the footsteps of glam and in order to comply with Strange's strict door policy, which required exquisite styling to maintain the event's subcultural identity, the crowd at Billy's experimented with vintage fashion and dramatic glamorous make-up, soon forming a bold movement of androgynous dandies and femme fatales in future-oriented styling.

Struggling to accommodate the crowds at Billy's, Strange moved the club night to the more spacious Blitz wine bar in nearby Covent Garden, running there until 1980. It was at the Blitz when the tag 'Bowie Night' was dropped as the scene gained notoriety and solidified its own identity, with the media granting the label 'New Romantics' to the attendees of the club. These were a rather small network of creative individuals and socialites, many of whom were fashion and art students, aspiring to fame and celebrity status amid a troubled time of deep recession and hopelessness about to be intensified by Thatcherite politics. Since 'club cultures are *taste cultures*', for Thornton, a shared interest in creative fields, aesthetics and new wave music bonded the community, with the club providing a platform for all sorts of artistic expression and the performance of eccentric subjectivities that undoubtedly sowed the seeds for Bowery's club night a few years later.[10] Exhibitionism and posing, which were much cherished among the New Romantics who deep down were competing for attention, turned into public performances where everyone could potentially become a self-made art piece, with the dancefloor serving as a stage or an unofficial catwalk for London's emerging creatives; Stephen Jones, Kim Bowen, David Holah and Stevie Stewart are only a few of the notable habitués of Blitz (also known as Blitz Kids) who shaped the New Romantic vision and later became established figures in the fashion industry. Hence, the brisk 1980s club scene of London is highly praised in fashion discourse as a ground-breaking territory for the evolution of British style.

The androgynous influence of glam, the electronic sounds and the club experience as a fundamental social nexus stood in diametrical opposition to early sensibilities of punk, but several aspects of it had been valuable in constructing the scene's so-called 'New Look'. Dave Rimmer maintains that the daring mix n' match approach to fashion and the audacious exhibitionism that punks had resorted to a few years earlier were elevated by the New Romantics to highly creative levels and enriched with a variety of aesthetics, deriving from pre-war Berlin cabaret decadence, drag and futuristic robots to style ideas from the whole history of fashion (with a strong preference in elements associated with seventeenth and eighteenth-century dress) picked up from jumble sales and charity shops.[11] Strange recalls how heterogeneous the fashions at Blitz were: he would be at the door dressed often as a punk dandy with his hair high and carrying a silver-ball cane, whereas Boy George, who was working in the cloakroom for a while, would be in a white-faced kabuki make-up and kimono, and Egan would be playing his records in 1950s-style suits.[12]

Pinpointing the New Romantic look thus does not come easy, but in a general sense it was characterized by a vibe of theatrical grandeur, blending the past and the future through the unisex adoption of lace and frills, puffy blouses, pill-box hats and heavy accessorizing combined with layers of bold make-up (sometimes unattainably imaginative) and often teased or structured haircuts.

Vivienne Westwood's and Malcolm McLaren's boutique, which was always a hotbed of cutting-edge trends, changed its name at the time to 'Worlds End' and embraced the new ethos and style that had just originated in nightclubs before disseminating it to the market with their *Pirate Collection* in 1981, solidifying a certain New Romantic look in widespread pop culture that ultimately became a caricature and was witnessed more splendidly in the image of pop band Adam and the Ants.

The thriving club culture of the early 1980s and the postmodernist approach it conveyed to styling a crafted persona served as the impetus for Bowery's gaudy practice, which grew out of his ambition to outshine with his performative costuming any devoted club enthusiast. The aggregation of visually conflicting elements and the fusion of impossible futuristic forms with retro details in Bowery's work, along with his creative make-up and the skin as a canvas, are manifest in most – if not all – of his early looks. More than any youth cult that has assumed for its members the insignia of freak for dissociating from the mainstream, the shock tactic of the New Romantics was one 'of total artistic effect', Rimmer writes.[13] One could argue by all means the same for Bowery's looks, although his costuming, which he increasingly approached as a form of contemporary art rather than simply an imaginative fashion *mélange*, clearly surpasses any New Romantic's creative feat. Steadily and meticulously, Bowery indeed turned into the biggest freak of all. Unlike most of his clubbing contemporaries, he challenged the idea of fashion significantly and blurred the boundaries between costume, art and performance. As Michael Bracewell observes:

> Bowery's costuming and make-up have usually taken the form of extending the appearance to a limit which would be unacceptable – and inaccessible – to the imagination of fashion [...] Thus his outfits are unique to his ideas. The results can be grotesque or disarmingly pretty, but they never correspond to any orthodoxy already apparent in pop, fashion or art.[14]

To refer to this creative process of fashioning a subcultural subjectivity through the dissonant presentation of self, it seems fitting to borrow the term 'enfreakment' from David Hevey who first used it in disability discourse to argue that it is the mechanism of representation that renders the strange or unusual individual a freak and not the form of the body itself.[15]

The flamboyant enfreakment of the New Romantics that built the bedrock for the evolution of similar subcultural styles, which later Bowery took to extremes, echoes the long tradition of the carnival, the ethos and imagery of which often correlate with practices of performance art. In a short exploration of confrontational carnivalesque art, Roger Malbert contends that 'extremes of [body] decoration [...] are perceived as denaturing the body, reducing it to a playground for shallow effects: at best, frivolous, at worst, blasphemous'.[16] For the members of spectacular subcultures like the New Romantics as well as for Bowery, it is the embodiment of visual cacophony, one that becomes manifest through their incongruous dress codes and negates mainstream sensibilities of style that, I maintain, fuels their enfreakment and renders them cultural aliens. 'For the rebellious, fashion-conscious young, the body often becomes a site of contestation', Malbert writes; likewise, for Bowery and his milieu, the enfreakment of self turns into the main strategy of denouncing bourgeois values.[17] Nonetheless, Bowery does not occupy the position of the freak solely due to his outrageous looks, eccentric lifestyle and subcultural status 'as an underground social celebrity', to use Bracewell's words.[18] It is through his art and performances that Bowery actively engages with a peculiar monstrous aesthetic by manipulating and visually distorting his body beyond accepted norms and fashion standards, appropriating the grotesque and uncanny appearance of circus freaks whose bodies often strike a balance between the unremarkable and the extraordinary.

Bowery's disfiguring costumes are described by Gertrud Lehnert as 'fundamentally subversive, contradictory and hybrid' creations that often 'worked in opposition' to his body.[19] Beyond the extremely padded costumes, layers of make-up and body paint that gave him a monstrous figure of implicit physical difference, Bowery also experimented with the human body and the way it can be changed, with flesh turning often into his favourite raw material. Some of his embodiments from 1990 onwards appear far more minimal in terms of fabric, albeit equally striking for the viewer. Barely covered and by manipulating the fat of his corpulent body and accentuating specific areas – especially those that are considered unflattering in mainstream fashion when bulging, such as the abdomen – or by creating the illusion of femaleness by convincingly concealing his genitals, Bowery performs bizarreness to unsettle prevailing body ideals and normative expectations of gender display. His unique queer visual language, undeniably a key aspect of his work, often turns him into a self-fashioned 'hermaphrodite', considered by Fiedler 'the most grotesque of all side show Freaks'.[20]

Bowery's published works and archival material are saturated in emblematic freakishness, but a particular black-and-white image of him in a fairly conservative outfit reveals his subtle expertise in enfreakment. He is depicted in a leather waisted blazer that is quite conventional and makes his silhouette rather bulky but feminine: hip-length and dark in colour with fur cuffs that match his fluffy hat. His pose is strong and emits confidence, with his hands resting on the hips and the legs slightly apart. The viewer's attention is immediately drawn to Bowery's disfigured face. Enclosed tightly in a bright stretchy fabric with a hole exposing the lips and (possibly) small openings for the eyes, his face resembles that of a swollen sex doll or a beautified monster with a circular mouth, excessively prominent cheekbones, intense eye make-up and an absent nose. It is the conflict between Bowery's ordinary clothing and his monstrous face that constitutes this particular image as visually strong and eminently freakish. Blending the human and the alien, the natural and the artificial, the familiar and the uncanny, Bowery frustrates commonly perceived binaries with splendour, inducing horror and fascination (Figure 2.2). Examining the figure of the freak as an ambiguous being on the verge of human subjectivity, Elizabeth Grosz writes:

> Freaks cross the borders that divide the subject from all ambiguities, interconnections, and reciprocal classifications, outside of or beyond the human. They imperil the definitions we rely on to classify humans, identities, and sexes – our most fundamental categories of self-definition and boundaries dividing self from otherness.[21]

Bowery's appropriation of a freakish glamorous aesthetic questions the widely accepted codes of fashion and normality, assisting him in crafting and establishing a unique subversive subjectivity. His desire to shock and deride bourgeois taste by enacting the freak is rooted not only in his repulsion from the monotony and unrealistic perfection of the fashion industry but also in a general dissatisfaction

Figure 2.2: Fergus Greer, *Leigh Bowery: Session VII, Look 36*, 1994. © Fergus Greer. Courtesy of the artist and the Michael Hoppen Gallery, London.

with normative standards and cultural values. By deliberately becoming what Rosemarie Garland Thomson calls a 'stareable sight', that is a person whose unusual appearance attracts attention, Bowery as well as the less spectacular New Romantic freaks who laid the groundwork for his monumental embodiments violate the rules of mainstream culture and the social conventions that rigidly regulate the way one looks and acts.[22] The impact of the New Romantic scene on Bowery's freakishness in terms of style experimentation is irrefutable, but that influence alone would be fragmentary, to say the least. The significance of the nightclub as a cultural space of unrestrained expression and the launch of niche media that sustained and regularly reported on club scenes contributed greatly to Bowery's enfreakment and incipient artistic vision.

Re-Shaping Freakishness: Nightclubs and Media

The nightclub played perhaps the most integral part in the formation of the New Romantics for it became the driving force behind their imaginative self-stylization, maintaining and cultivating the practice of enfreakment to a great extent. It is almost impossible to imagine the booming of such an exclusive manifold scene without the space of the nightclub serving as a social hub and regular meeting point where dress-up fantasies could be epically (and safely) acted out. Indubitably, music halls and ballrooms (hosting masquerade parties occasionally) had been for centuries a popular form of entertainment that in the course of time morphed into the modern concept of the nightclub.

Just before Bowie Nights started running at Billy's, the options available for a night out in London were restricted at the time to small suburban discos or sophisticated elitist clubs, both catering to a more mature and conventional clientele. The weekly events at Billy's disseminated a diverse model of nightclubbing that persists to this day where different club nights for a variety of scenes constantly spring up, restructuring the urban subcultural landscape. In the immediate post-Blitz era after 1980, a number of club nights with a similar ethos started to appear, many of which developed their own identities, such as Le Kilt with funk overtones, the notorious fetish club Skin Two and most notably The Batcave, which started as a dark glam rock and new wave club night, establishing the goth subculture. The broad spectrum of club cultures witnessed in the post-punk epoch during the 1980s was marked by a spirited carnivalesque aura of enfreakment or what Silvia Rief calls 'virtual otherness', reinforced by the expressive and mimetic practices that take place in clubs, such as dancing and dressing up for the occasion:

> Virtualization propels performative notions of identity, in which identity is understood as the result of aesthetic and prosthetic stylization or manipulation. [...] The demarcation of identity, however provisional [...] is also informed by a 'sense of possibility', of who or what one could be or might become.[23]

The opportunity for transient becomings afforded by the club experience allows for playful experimentation with identity, during which transgressive bodies take centre stage and are celebrated. It comes as no surprise therefore that Bowery, who enjoyed transforming himself and craved the spotlight, not only hosted his own club night, Taboo, but also utilized club spaces in general as the main outlet for his subversive performative practice, elevating the act of being a club freak to an art form.

Apart from club spaces being an impetus to bonding club cultures and enabling enfreakment, various niche media have equally been important to the process of constructing and solidifying subcultural identities. Writing about acid house and rave in the United Kingdom, the pinnacle of club cultures that evolved into a massive movement at the end of the decade, Thornton finds that media have been central to club subcultural formations. Contrary to past theorists who either dismiss their role or demonize them for inducing the end of subcultures, she argues that the moral panic traditionally spread by the national press and the tabloids when subcultures begin to get noticed is crucial in validating and authenticating youth cultures: 'Ironically nothing proves the originality and inventiveness of subcultural music and style more than its eventual "mainstreaming".'[24] Her focus, however, shifts from the national press to a broad spectrum of so-called 'niche media', which can be described as 'consumer magazines [that] operate in *subcultures*', constructing them as much as documenting them.[25] In 1980, the heyday of the Blitz club, newly established niche magazines *BLITZ* (1980–91), *i-D* (1980–) and *The Face*

(1980–2004; 2019–) embraced the New Romantic ethos until they discovered the next soon-to-be big thing. Their early engagement with the thriving club scene shaped their identities as publications and simultaneously assisted in cementing and sustaining the identity of the New Romantic scene as well as the legend that surrounded Taboo and Bowery's club persona.

BLITZ, *i-D* and *The Face*, which started as humble entrepreneurial ventures by young creatives before establishing a broad following internationally, explored a wide range of lifestyle topics and culture that aimed explicitly at the expanding youth market. With cutting-edge design, striking visuals, innovative fashion stories and unconventional journalism, they turned their attention to London's club scene from the beginning. *BLITZ* is mostly remembered as an iconic style magazine of the 1980s that drew inspiration from the club scene and often included subcultural references in its alternative (but delicately orchestrated) fashion editorials. *i-D* and *The Face* were arguably more invested in scrutinizing and recording authentic subcultural street styles as they 'roamed around "clubland"', in Thornton's words, 'celebrat[ing] posing and elaborat[ing] a subcultural ideology'.[26] From their early issues they were regularly reporting on the scene of the New Romantics, using various titles to describe it, such as 'Cult with No Name', 'Blitz Kids' and 'Now Crowd'. This tendency of niche media to categorize and pigeonhole social groups is, according to Thornton, what 'give[s] definition to vague cultural formations', turning them into 'subcultural homologies'.[27] Nonetheless, the plurality of dress styles the New Romantics employed to celebrate individuality may have been in this instance the reason why the scene became so hard to label. However, this also became a key factor in cultivating the attention of niche media, which the scene embraced (Figure 2.3).

Recorded as the first post-war subcultural scene obsessed with celebrity and glamour, the New Romantics flaunted a collective, though varied, fashion-conscious identity leveraged by media exposure. An innovative and regular section that became emblematic of *i-D* and was later imitated by other magazines included photographs of interestingly dressed people and subcultural freaks spotted on the street with a few lines about themselves. They became known as 'Straight-ups' and were head-to-toe portraits (black-and-white in the early issues

Figure 2.3: 'A Day in the Life of Steve Strange', *The Face*, October 1980. Photographs by Janette Beckman. Courtesy of the Central Saint Martins Special Collections, University of the Arts, London.

and subsequently in colour) against a plain wall with a short informative caption about the subject and their clothes. Being featured in the pages of *i-D* during the 1980s provided a sort of confirmation of subcultural membership; for the club habitués in particular it meant that they were officially accepted in the scene.

Bowery first appeared in *i-D* in September 1984, roughly three years after the closure of Blitz and the beginning of the decline of the New Romantic scene, which in the meantime had managed to propagate its clubbing ethos and inspire the plethora of alternative club nights the publication favoured. He and Trojan are pictured in separate photographs in their 'Space' look at Do-Do's, a monthly club night held at Busby's in Charing Cross. Fully embodying his crafted persona, Bowery presents himself campily in the caption as a designer who is 'very spiritual' and 'one' with 'the cosmic', while in his company is a 'fashion entrepreneur newly arrived from Colombia', Victoria Fernandez, now an established figure in high fashion.[28] Subsequent issues of *i-D* and *The Face* dedicated short illustrated articles to the outrageous duo, introducing their

PENTHOUSE

LEIGH BOWERY is a 23 year old clothes designer and Trojan is a 19 year old male prostitute and painter. Trojan got his name from the old reggae record label. They live together in a 2-bedroomed council flat on the 11th floor of an estate in Stepney. Push the plastic daisy doorbell and a variety of noises announce the arrival of a visitor at the standard olive-coloured front door from a 'Halloween' screaming tape loop to a loud knocking on hollow wood sound to a sex film soundtrack. The sex tape wasn't very successful – Leigh: "Everytime someone pressed the bell and I heard all the gasping and moaning, I just thought it was Trojan having another asthma attack in his room so I never bothered to answer the door".

The whole flat is UV lit (£17 per lightbulb from the Edgeware Road light shop) – Trojan blew a £99 dole cheque on them. Four different shades of purple Regency-style flocked wallpaper line the hallway and cover the bathroom and toilet doors Clumps of plastic flowers on wire stalks poke out of the skirting board and other unexpected places. Trojan's paintings (2D mixed with 3D) blend in with the decor, particularly because he uses the flocked wallpaper and patterned bed sheets as his canvas.

'Star Trek – The Movie' wallpaper covers the walls and speakers whilst '70's Silver Woman' on the ceiling reflects in the black tiled floor. A few art books, photo albums and bondage mags fill the small, as yet, conventional kitchen (white, Hygena units), the silver painted fridge is well-stocked with rum, lemons, eggs and bottles of 'Bolts' poppers. After moving into No.43 in January, Leigh and Trojan have been very selective about the contents and decoration, prefering to wait until they can afford the things they want instead of making do with an ugly, aesthetically unpleasing kettle or chair. Leigh: "All the wallpaper comes from 'Dee Jay Decor' in Watney Market. The '70's Silver Woman' and the 'Star Trek' wallpaper came from there, so did the flock wallpaper – it's £6.99 a roll, any colour, good quality. They cater for the Paki sort of clientele, which suits our tastes as well. Some of the stuff they have is so gross that even the Pakis turn their noses up at it, I think they're really grateful when we go in there. The wallpaper in my bedroom is very strange, that sort of bubbly aluminium stuff, it's quite expensive and I didn't buy it at first, but because my room's the smallest in the flat – I felt it well worth it. Weekly rent: £29.15; electricity and phone bills: High; Cleaning: By Sandra.

i-D: Does the interior of your home match the interior of your mind?
Leigh and Trojan: Yes, it's an extension of what we wear.

8

Figure 2.4: 'Penthouse', *i-D: The Inside Out Issue*, October 1984. Photograph by Steve Pyke. Courtesy of the National Art Library, Victoria and Albert Museum, London.

deliberately garish flat and dubbing them 'The New Glitterati', respectively (Figure 2.4). Although by late 1984 Bowery had gained substantial recognition in London's subcultural circles and niche media as a talented experimental designer, it was his club night Taboo (co-hosted with entrepreneur Tony Gordon at Maximus in Leicester Square during 1985–86) that established him as an iconic freak in the city's club scene.

Favouring an anarchic style in music and dress, Taboo was held weekly in a small basement disco with a particularly passé décor of red velour banquettes, lots of mirrors and a dance floor with several cheap light effects and a glitter ball. The music video of trans artist Lana Pellay's Hi-NRG hit 'Pistol in My Pocket' (1986) that was filmed on the premises offers a glimpse of the flashy interior (which admittedly could not be more suited for the mischievous lyrics: 'I got a pistol in my pocket, baby. I got it pointed at you') and features some of the most prominent figures of Taboo, including Bowery. He is shown in full masquerade welcoming the viewer at the entrance before being lost in the dancing crowd of freaks that surrounds Pellay. Perhaps the only extant footage of an actual Taboo club night is that broadcasted in *South of Watford*, which supposedly presents a day in the showy life of Bowery, with the narrator appointing him a contemporary reincarnation of the dandy.[29] There, we see him arriving by car at the busy club at night and walking confidently straight inside all dressed-up, with dripping paint on his shaved head. He lip-kisses his friends, with the camera following him around, before socializing with a fancy cocktail in hand and dancing in the frenzied crowd. In the meantime, long queues of partygoers wait patiently outside the club in the hope that overdressed doorman Mark Vaultier will let them in.

Following the ethos of Blitz, in which emphasis was given on exquisite appearances, Taboo adopted a similarly strict door policy and the catchphrase 'Dress as though your life depends on it or don't bother.' became its motto, encouraging deep experimentation with style and subjectivity and promoting a strong sense of theatricality. In his thorough account of modern British nightclubbing, Dave Haslam remarks humorously that regulars at Taboo 'didn't just wear mad outfits; they became new people' and goes on to assert that 'Bowery replaced the post-Blitz mainstream version of "gender-bending" with something more hardcore and outsider'.[30] Being the public face of Taboo, a role that inevitably entailed being in the spotlight, demanded that Bowery re-invent himself stylistically each week. His desire to show off and attract attention led him to push the boundaries and surpass himself constantly, even though at the time he had not yet started experimenting with his body shape and his club outfits could be described as fairly normal. Taboo is arguably a milestone in Bowery's art and life; its tawdry disco dancefloor, which would turn into Bowery's stage, was potentially the perfect stimulus that culminated in him permanently shifting his focus from fashion design to art and performance.

Just a couple of months after the opening of Taboo, *i-D* published a piece titled 'Slap: Leigh Bowery's All-Gay Family'. The main picture of the spread depicts Bowery in the foreground lying down in his clubbing apparel while some of his friends (likewise creatively attired) pose behind him in what looks like a nightclub setting. In the accompanying text, Bowery, fashion designer Rachel Auburn, Trojan and Vaultier talk about their make-up inspiration and their beauty products of preference (Figure 2.5). Regardless

VIDEO

If black and brown be the colours of cloth this winter, what be the colours of make-up this spring? Are the greasepaint gang on the rampage again, or are the talcum teen varnishing themselves for action? Mascara, rouge, eyeliner, khol, lip-gloss and ...

SLAP

i-D started building on a strong foundation and went in search of some of the cosmetic delights of the month. Made UP? Of course we were...what with Caroline Baker, Barbara Hulanicki, Mitzi Lorenz, Ray Petri, Jally Bakke, Helen Whiting, Mary Quant, Phyllis Cohen and Kay Montano... Make-up always allows for role-playing supreme, so we start off with one player living out their fantasy...

COCO – Is she or isn't she?: Dancer waiting to be nominated for fame school of performing arts. Wearing her Issey Miyake top for the occasion. Insecurity hiding beneath her eager anticipation. Confidence? Mark says no trouble, Coco says time is so long. The V.I.P.s say this girl doesn't wear No.5.

SPOT ON

LEIGH BOWERY'S "ALL GAY FAMILY"

"It's genetic really – I mean we're all equally attractive and we're all equally famous. I spend most of my time with these people so I suppose it's only natural that I call them my family. . . I like them and I like to be seen with them." Is there anyone that he would like to have in his family tree? "Not at all. . . if there is anyone, then they'll be in it soon enough, I'm sure. By the way, I must stipulate that we do *not* all take drugs."

MAKE-UP TIP (A)

MAKE-UP TIP (B)

MAKE-UP TIP (C)

MAKE-UP TIP (D)

30

LEIGH BOWERY'S ALL-GAY FAMILY 31

Figure 2.5: 'Slap: Leigh Bowery's All-Gay Family', *i-D: The Flesh & Blood Issue*, April 1985. Photographer unknown. Courtesy of the National Art Library, Victoria and Albert Museum, London.

of whether the particular article in *i-D* contributed in any way to establishing Bowery's club night as one of the most eminent in the months that followed, it certainly signifies the close-knit and mutually beneficial relationship between the rather exclusive club scene and niche media. The fashionable subjects' endorsement of make-up brands and clothes (many of which came from independent labels at Hyper Hyper, a retail space on Kensington High Street populated with stalls run by emerging fashion designers) assisted in consolidating the scene's identity by carving out a space for commercializing – and eventually mainstreaming to some degree – its subcultural aesthetics. As is the case with wider subcultural formations, the extravagant style of Bowery and his milieu that became synonymous with Taboo acquired its status through the process of being brought to light by niche print (and to some extent broadcast) media.

At the time Bowery's club night had become what his close friend Richard Torry describes as 'the pinnacle of deranged, decadent expression', *i-D* published a sequence of super-8 stills shot in Taboo with a few words hinting at its outrageous style etiquette.[31] Some of the stills focus on Bowery's shapely hairy legs and his white briefs, sneaking out of a patterned super mini skirt, and others depict a girl dancing in a frilly blouse and a pair of Y-front knickers. In bold lettering below, we read that 'flesh becomes this season's choice for the bold and brazen "Bowery Bums"' and that nylon, frills and showing a bit of skin are the way to go among Taboo's boozy 'kitschmaniac regulars'.[32] Associating its content with club scenes, *i-D* put a spotlight on Taboo's fashionably kitschy crowd from early on, communicating the scene's temperament by publishing sensational visual material and adopting a distinctive slangish language.

Traditionally, the largest part of the mainstream media is proven to be not sympathetic to divergent cultural expression. Like most subcultural movements and scenes that eventually suffer from the effect of moral panic, Taboo closed down in 1986 after its hedonistic ambience reached *YOU*, a magazine distributed for free with the conservative tabloid *Mail on Sunday*. The article made explicit allegations of extensive drug use, alcohol abuse and indecent behaviour taking place on the premises and, as a result, the management decided to suspend the club night. When the fuss subsided a few weeks later and Bowery was approached to resume the club night he declined and that way the legacy of Taboo as 'London's sleaziest, campest and bitchiest club' was preserved intact before turning into a corny attraction to outsiders due to mainstream media attention.[33]

Just like with Blitz and its instigator Strange a few years earlier, the publicity Taboo gained during its course established Bowery as the quirkiest figure of London's subcultural club scene in the mid-1980s. Furthermore, it cultivated an ongoing interest in Bowery who never abandoned clubbing but moved from his role as a regular club host to more explicit performance-related activities, such as his own art projects, performances in clubs in Europe and New York and his collaboration with Michael Clark's dance company both as designer and performer. Following an extensively illustrated cover article about Bowery in 1987, *i-D* continued to include pictures of him in its clubbing pages every now and then. In February 1995, almost a decade after his first appearance in the magazine as an aspiring designer, it announced Bowery's death in a short obituary, describing him as 'a performer, artist, dancer, walking art piece and more'.[34]

A Freak at the Gallery

In the long run, Bowery's freakish performative costuming proved salient in gaining permission into the elite establishment of art galleries as an artist. Pivoting on his mastering of freakish embodiments, Bowery's performances at the prestigious Anthony d'Offay Gallery in Central London – which were part of a series of shows dedicated to emerging British artists – constitute his first and only solo show to take place in an institutional art space. During the performances, Bowery would exhibit himself as a living installation attired in some of his most embellished looks, submitting his presence to the visitors' scrutinizing stare. As the most striking club figure in London at the time, Bowery at d'Offay's gallery, Malbert writes, made a spectacle of his 'grotesquely exaggerated looks' like a 'freak in a fairground side-show'.[35] While Bowery's exhibition does not explicitly reproduce the cultural and aesthetic specificities of the traditional freak show, it does restage its politics and sociological implications, resonating with Robin Blyn's concept of the 'freak-garde', a distinctive avant-garde tradition in the arts of the twentieth century that drew inspiration from the freak show to generate and promote distinctive modes of being under liberal capitalism: 'Like any avant-garde worthy of the name, this freak-garde is devoted to revolutionary change, to emancipation', writes Blyn.[36]

The modern freak show, the politics of which unintentionally Bowery mirrored in his performances at the Anthony d'Offay Gallery, is defined by sociologist Robert Bogdan as 'the formally organized exhibition for amusement and profit of people with physical, mental, or behavioral anomalies, both alleged and real'.[37] Those involved a wide range of human curiosities, but arguably some of the most popular exhibits were those with – what are now recognized as – congenital anomalies or disabilities, including individuals who were diminutive or extremely tall, obese or skeletal, albinos, gender-ambiguous, conjoined twins, armless or legless, with extra limbs, excessive body hair or various skin disorders. This kind of widely acceptable popular entertainment appealed to individuals across social classes and had its golden era from around 1840 through 1940 mostly in the United States and Western Europe where dime museums, circuses, fairs, amusement parks and carnivals often hosted freak shows as respectable family-friendly spectacles. For maximum appeal to the paying audience, the bizarreness and irregularity of the 'freak' were accentuated through special costumes, crafted visual and textual representations and stylized performances that determined understandings of freakishness and established perceptions of normality. Bogdan's ground-breaking materialist analysis of the freak show approaches it for once as an institution essentially upheld by the labour of people with disabilities (albeit at the time they were not being perceived as such) and provides a social constructivist reading of the freak, arguing that it was not the anomalous body that made one a freak but the variety of representational tactics that framed their exhibition.

Bowery's performances at the Anthony d'Offay Gallery ran from 11 to 15 October 1988 and the idea centred on Bowery exhibiting himself for two hours daily in a different look each day (except from the last day in which the performance lasted for four hours and included two looks). The installation involved a seemingly simple set with a chaise-longue placed at the centre of a gallery room, transformed so that a two-way mirror separated

Bowery on the chaise-longue from the audience. The lighting was designed to illuminate Bowery's space while the observers were in relative darkness, allowing him to be able to see only his own reflection on the glass. In addition, the sound of traffic was transmitted from the gallery's speakers and the visitors' sense of smell was stimulated by a different pleasant scent each day.[38] In terms of action, the performances were quite static, resembling the stylistic attributes of *tableaux vivants*, a fact that was undoubtedly made up for by Bowery's grandiose presence (Figure 2.6).

Cerith Wyn Evans's video *Leigh Bowery* (1988) offers a glimpse of the daily performances and Bowery's apparent narcissistic desire: he is shown attired in six of his most iconic looks spending most of the time observing his own reflection. Produced with basic means and minimal editing, the video (which starts with Bowery in his signature 'Spot' look) is focused on the performances and neglects the overall conditions and the audience without providing a complete narrative and a thorough account of the event. This documentary approach can be viewed

Figure 2.6: Leigh Bowery performing at the Anthony d'Offay Gallery, London, 1988. Photograph by Nils Jorgensen. © Nils Jorgensen/ Shutterstock.

perhaps as a consequence of Bowery's captivating presence that overshadows the surrounding circumstances or as an accentuation of his performed egomania. During the impromptu performances, Bowery would rest stretched out on the chaise-longue checking himself in the mirror, striking odd poses and moving around from time to time. When he is not posing gracefully, grimacing, adjusting his outfit or playing sensually with his tongue, he just lies on the chaise-longue in a meditative state reminiscent of Édouard Manet's *Olympia* (1863) in a queer interpretation. There is a sense of dramatic calmness in Bowery's shots as he abides in darkness under a spotlight all dressed-up. The viewer's gaze is unavoidably fixed upon his arresting outfits and the freakish styling as he enacts a disparate fashion mannequin of sorts posing for an invisible photographer. Fashion practices and art converge in a distorted way in Bowery's performances. However, in opposition, for instance, to the sleek tableaux performances of Vanessa Beecroft who often employs professional models for her living installations and has collaborated with numerous high fashion houses, projecting a glamorized aspect of conventional beauty, Bowery glorifies subcultural freakishness and complicates both the stereotypical notion of haute couture elegance and the grandeur of institutional art.

By disturbing the visual status quo with his 'baroque beauty', an expression Garland Thomson came up with to describe the 'irregular, exaggerated and peculiar', Bowery demands to be stared at, offering interminable voyeurism to the astonished spectators.[39] Unlike Wyn Evans's footage that is obsessively focused on Bowery, Dick Jewell's *Leigh Bowery – What's Your Reaction to the Show* (1988) deals only with the impressions that Bowery's performances left to the visitors and reveals their mixed responses. Shot during all five days of the exhibition, it includes clips of Bowery's performances along with statements of gallery visitors who were confronted with the title question upon exiting the gallery. Beyond the most predictable responses, which range from the performance being just 'interesting', 'fantastic' or 'extraordinary' to 'boring', 'static' and 'crap', some insightful and engaging comments associate Bowery's relatively motionless presence with *tableaux vivants* or the living sculptures of Gilbert & George. The feeling of attending a peep show or watching a strange animal at the zoo, which some mention, correlates with the voyeuristic gaze the confined freak induced in spectators during the nineteenth- and early twentieth-century sideshows and brings Bowery's performances closer to the spirit of freak-garde. The conceptual affinity between his performances at d'Offay's gallery and those at a traditional freak show can hardly be ignored.

Viewed in the context of freak shows, Bowery's artifice suggests the embodiment of a self-made freakish persona. The way human curiosities were promoted through stylized presentations and the way they acted as part of their performances were imperative in the construction of a freak. The main exhibited categories that Bogdan distinguishes were not limited to 'born freaks', namely people with visible 'real physical anomalies' usually due to a medical condition, but also 'made freaks' who, like Bowery, 'do something to themselves that make[s] them unusual enough for exhibit' as well as 'novelty acts', which refer to 'an unusual performance or ability'.[40] Circassian beauties (white women with dark big frizzy hairstyles supposedly originating from the Caucasus region), heavily tattooed people and fabricated 'wild' men and women are some of the most typical examples of self-made freaks who acquired their freakishness for the purpose of the show, while the broader category of novelty performers includes the likes of fire eaters, sword swallowers, snake charmers, anatomical wonders and contortionists. Fictional biographical narratives relating to their freakishness to spark the imagination of the audience and appropriate costuming to emphasize their bizarreness were equally important in their process of enfreakment.

Tracing, for example, the social history of the densely tattooed ladies who worked in travelling circuses as freaks in the United States, Amelia Klem Osterud points out that they deployed 'a variation of a standard captivity narrative' to excite the spectators, confirming at the same time their stereotypical ideas about 'primitive' civilizations and Indigenous cultures.[41] The most common stories involved the idea of a helpless Westerner captured by a 'savage' tribe on an 'exotic' island and turned into a freak after being forced to endure the painful traditional ritual of tattooing. The fictitious tales that accompanied the lightly clothed, tattooed freak turned the regular working-class subject into a victim whose body 'had been brutalized by savages' and carried 'permanent symbols of torture'.[42] The exhibition of human oddities was thus premised on the construction of dissonant characters and their public performance of freakishness, displaying, essentially, a sort of theatrical selfhood.

Bowery's flaunted extravaganza corresponds to what Bogdan defines as an 'aggrandized' performance of freakishness, which along with the 'exotic' category constitute the two prevalent modes of presentation, that is 'the standardized set of techniques, strategies, and styles that showmen used' to contextualize freaks.[43] In contrast to the exotic mode – in which non-Western persons (or those who passed as such) were exhibited as cultural others, stigmatizing certain ethnic and racial identities and solidifying colonial imperialist stereotypes of Western superiority – the aggrandized mode suggested that, beyond the anomalous body, the freak was an eminent person of a prestigious social class with remarkable skills. Accordingly, impressive tales about the freak's descent and status and relevant props of opulent taste (including refined clothes and elaborate accessories) were necessary.

In the same fashion, the gallery's press release for Bowery's performance series praises him for his 'extraordinary presence' and 'exceptional talents' and presents him as a 'cultural icon', a 'design phenomenon' and a celebrity of sorts of 'the alternative and new cultural scene in London'.[44] His impressively crafted costumes and phenomenal styling of self, which exceed all modes of mainstream and subcultural representation, establish his image in the eyes of spectators as that of nightclub freak royalty. By means of a similar methodology, Bowery's performances implicitly recast the long-gone voyeuristic mentality of the historical freak show, which by the late 1930s had lost its glory and was considered by many a distasteful and vulgar spectacle where disability, illness or ethnic traits were being exploited. This shift was ascribed to the production of knowledge brought especially by rapid developments in scientific and medical fields, which pathologized freaks and demystified their otherness, turning them into intriguing case studies for medical consideration rather than wondrous creatures for public speculation and consumption.

During its course, the freak show served as a persistent site of representation that attached a damaging and enduring meaning of otherness to the extraordinary bodies of those being atypically formed or non-Western. In a critical investigation of the cultural history of freak shows in relation to the ways bodily difference was framed, Garland Thomson underlines that freakishness was constructed through tactics of presentation that cultivated a mutually defining relationship between the 'abnormal' freak and the normative spectator, rendering the freak a voiceless passive object: 'Freaks are above all products of perception [shaped by] those who control the social discourse and the means of representation [...] to claim the center for themselves and banish others to margins.'[45] In the context of the ardent American egalitarian democracy of the nineteenth century that Garland Thomson grounds her observations, the freak acts as the physical opposite of an idealized middle-class American selfhood determined by the normative markers of masculinity, whiteness, heteronormativity and able-bodiedness. As the antithesis of this embodied ideal of docility claimed by the average man, and which is a highly valued requisite in a democratic society to function smoothly, the 'unruly' body of the freak represents, for Garland Thomson, a potential threat of individuality and anarchy against national unity and conformity that is, nevertheless, safely and symbolically contained and mastered within the boundaries of the freak show.

The allure of the freak operates simultaneously on two different levels for their extraordinariness 'reassured audiences of their commonality' but for some also 'symbolized a potential for individual freedom denied by cultural pressures towards standardization'.[46] Those belonging to the second category include either disabled subjects who identified with the inherent individuality of the freak or 'banal democrats', as Garland Thomson puts it, with a deep-rooted desire for non-conformity; as emblems of physical and cultural anarchy, freaks remained 'creatures who embodied freedom's elusive and threatening promise of not being like [everybody] else'.[47] This influential reading resonates with the resurgence and cultural reformulation of 'freak' during the 1960s by those who – becoming disillusioned with the tactics of American contemporary democracy – chose to retract in a collective state of self-induced disidentificatory freakishness, which since then kept adapting accordingly to the desires and challenges of those who felt excluded from dominant discourses or sought alternative modes of being.

The fascinating ambiguity of freaks, their 'ontological indeterminacy', as Blyn calls it, is what has similarly motivated many artists throughout the twentieth century to repeatedly revisit the freak show, turning its exploitative residue into a politically charged freak-garde driven by a desire for new subjectivities.[48] As in Tod Browning's controversial cult film *Freaks* (1932) (which was interestingly rediscovered and appreciated in hindsight during the countercultural 1960s) where a troupe of circus freaks resort to brutal revenge to defend their dignity, all sorts of self-proclaimed contemporary freaks continue to pop up in the history of performance with a vengeance to assert the right to self-identification and haunt the myth of normalization.

As 'extensions of his own ritual of studying himself in the mirror', Bowery's performances at the Anthony d'Offay Gallery were his 'last laugh at the expense of formal art', Bracewell notes.[49] In a downright Duchampian manner, Bowery positions his freakish-looking persona straight from the nightclub into the gallery as an art object, disrupting the formal conventions of art that traditionally distinguish the artist as an active subject from the produced artwork. The fact that the following month he repeated the performance with a few adjustments in the shop window of Parco (a department store in Tokyo) complicates further the already problematic terrains of authenticity, exclusivity and the 'high/low' polarity that prevail in art institutions and sustain the art market.[50] Most importantly, however, it is the infiltration of an anticipated high art space with subcultural freakishness that challenges the conventional apparatus of art and at the same time demands to reconsider notions of selfhood and difference by bringing to the fore the powerful dynamics of staring and objectification. As an instance of freak-garde, Bowery's relocation of the historical freak figure into a gallery setting as a subcultural other consolidates in postmodernist sharpness Bogdan's argument about the freak being no more than 'a frame of mind, a set of practices, a way of thinking about and presenting people. [...] [T]he performance of a stylized presentation'.[51]

Negotiating the Stare: Agency and Narcissistic Desire

It only took a couple of decades after the decline of the modern freak show for the freak to be revived during the 1960s as a promising allegorical figure of difference and liberation in progressive consciousness. Towards the end of the century its aesthetic conventions, too, were resurrected and appropriated for the sake of a radical freak-garde that insists on political reform through alternatives to the oppressed and disciplined subject of a society of normalization. This turn to freakishness is fleshed out by artists who, like Bowery, claim the position of a postmodern self-made freak by means of extreme body modification and risky practices in favour of a politically charged art, tackling issues around identity and their representation; or by those artists who identify as disabled and specifically seek to confront deep-rooted assumptions about non-normative bodies through explicit references to freak show practices that are now considered by many dehumanizing at least.

A certain antipathy for the institution of the freak show as exploitative and demeaning started to solidify after the rise of the disability rights movement that triggered clamorous criticism from scholars and activists who condemned its stigmatizing of corporeal difference and discrimination against 'deviant' embodiments.[52] In response to those arguing otherwise, those who view the freak as a historical performer in charge of their act versus a pitiful 'cripple' and their commercial exhibition as a conscious choice and a fortunate opportunity to make a good living (and indeed that was often the case, with some freaks obtaining wealth and gaining fame outside the freak business, most notably the diminutive Charles Sutton and conjoined twins Chang and Eng), they still remained vulnerable to a cultural and economic system of objectification and ableism that offered few other alternatives for survival.

By today's standards of politically correct terminology, 'freak' is widely perceived as offensive when applied to individuals with physical or mental impairments. Nevertheless, as with many other derogatory names that have gradually broken free from their negative meanings, a collective tendency to embrace 'freak' has been developed among some disabled people that functions, according to Grosz, 'as an act of defiance, a political gesture of self-determination'.[53] Apart from those disability activists who wish to vocally assert their difference against a normalizing society, a robust confirmation of this tendency lies in the fact that even to this day being a performing freak sits comfortably with some people with unusual bodies who proudly flaunt their 'freakishness' alongside contemporary self-made freaks carrying out their novelty acts in the handful of active freak shows that still exist mainly in the United States. Far from the spectacular allure their predecessors once held, these postmodern enterprises venture into nostalgia determined to keep the anachronistic spirit of the freak show alive. The same spirit – from the viewpoint of disability studies – has arguably shaped the reception of disability enormously by establishing a damaging ongoing association between unusual bodies and freakishness.

Disability performance scholar and artist Petra Kuppers remarks that the freak show along with the medical amphitheatre aggregate disabled people's history of oppression for they constitute the sole historical territories where disabled people routinely surrendered their bodies to curious stares, whether for the public's entertainment or the specialists' medical examination.[54] It is the power of staring, which Garland Thomson describes as 'an interrogative gesture' seeking a narrative, that traditionally validates the unusual body's freakishness. This has become the matter in hand for many contemporary disabled artists working with performance who seek to challenge negative representations of disability and negotiate their social position.[55] Their cultural alienation and objectification 'depends upon looking as an act of domination':

> When persons in a position that grants them authority to stare take up that power, staring functions as a form of domination, marking the staree as the exotic, outlaw, alien, or other. The colonizing look marks its bearer as legitimate and its object as outsider.[56]

Traditionally confined by the material structures of the stage or medical platform, the irregular body of the freak is fixed. It is looked at, examined and named. The same effect was successfully reproduced by Bowery at d'Offay's gallery. Detached from the club, his 'natural' surroundings, and confined within the gallery space, consumed by his narcissism with no interaction, Bowery with his self-made freakish appearance turns himself into a voiceless human oddity, a strange sight for the eyes of the 'normal' spectators. This tactic of passive enfreakment and his turning into the silent object of the stare is at odds with certain performance strategies employed by disabled artists who prioritize the interrogation and interruption of the problematic stare through its critical appropriation, invigorating a vivid disability arts movement.

Spawned from the formation of an alternative disability culture that insists on differentiating itself from the mainstream, which systematically excludes the disabled, the disability arts movement offers a critical response to pressing issues, such as accessibility in the arts and the broader social experience of disability. Most importantly it seeks to undo the pervasive negative stereotypes surrounding disability in cultural and media portrayals, making the prospect of a confident group identity palpable. Mat Fraser and Mary Duffy are two contemporary artists associated with the disability arts movement. Their conscious engagement with the historical freak show and its objectifying tactics seeks to actively challenge the oppressive mechanism of normative identity formation and the ableist ideologies historically promoted and sustained by such displays, confronting at the same time the spectators' intrusive act of looking. The main strategy for shifting the colonizing stare into dynamic agency (a decisive quality that Bowery's performance lacks) is the *critical* appropriation of the freak show as a historical and cultural apparatus that has stigmatized and marginalized disabled subjects followed often by a sort of autobiographical verbal testimony concerning their unusual bodies and personal experiences.

Mat Fraser, a man of many talents but best known as an actor (he appeared in the television series *American Horror Story: Freak Show*), embarked on an art project with the freak show and cultural heritage of the disabled performer as a point of departure to explore the ways in which disability in drama is still received within the stereotypical context of freakishness. Born with a noticeable physical impairment fixated on his underdeveloped arms that resemble those of a seal (explained as a type of phocomelia in medical terms), Fraser has performed as a freak for a number of seasons at Sideshows by the Seashore in the iconic fairground at Coney Island in New York, re-enacting the historical act of Stanley Berent. Known in the freak business as Sealo, Berent had the same condition and performed mundane activities with his short arms, like shaving or rolling a cigarette, in various freak shows throughout the United States until his retirement in 1972.

Fraser's attraction to the cultural history of freak shows and his investment in disability politics culminated in *Sealboy: Freak* (2001), a one-man play juxtaposing the uncomplicated life of Sealo, who had accepted and relished his position as a performing freak, and that of a fictional contemporary character with the same impairment (perhaps Fraser's alter ego) whose ambition for an acting career is regularly hampered by the narrow way his unusually formed body is read.[57] Engaging with freak tactics and utilizing a brutally honest monologue that addresses the audience without avoiding taboo subjects, Fraser revokes the passivity of the freak and transforms it into a powerful agent opened up to the sensationalist gaze of the non-disabled audience that prevents him from being viewed as other than a freak. In her detailed examination of the performance, Kuppers concludes that Fraser's strategic appropriation of the freak show explicates the continuing difficulty of the disabled body to be seen as active in social performance (and by extension in drama), for freaks, as 'strange foreparents to today's disabled performers', were not seen as performing an act but as non-human others, just like with Sealo who attracted the audience to be seen carrying out ordinary activities with his differently formed arms or clapping his hands like a seal.[58]

Fraser's investigation of the freak show as a catalyst for the reception of disability on stage today and his personal journey from a performing freak in Coney Island to the stage of Edinburgh's Fringe festival, where he presented *Sealboy: Freak*, are the subject of a penetrating television documentary titled *Born Freak* (2002). An extended close analysis of the film by disability scholars David Mitchell and Sharon Snyder is acute and categorical in its research findings: not only is the disabled actor inextricably bound to the degrading legacy of the freak show as an exploitative spectacle, but even its systemic critique strikes as inadequate in eradicating the firmly fixed modes of objectification it bears. Being a born 'freak' cannot be simply equated or compared with the metaphorical enfreakment of gender, race and sexuality and thus any ambitious attempt at converting the freak show into 'a vehicle of disability reappropriation, resistance, or reclamation' proves scanty and futile.[59] To shatter the dominant representation of the freak as an idle existence that barely stares back, disability artists undertake performative tactics powerful enough to confront and respond to the dehumanizing stare by asserting their unique subjectivities, as Fraser does as his vocal alter ego in *Sealboy: Freak*.

While Fraser experimented comfortably with freak show performances, many disabled people were horrified by the idea. A painter and activist born without arms who has worked with the medium of performance in the past, Mary Duffy came to terms with her identity as a disabled woman and focused her work on her experience with disability after a major life crisis she faced as a young adult when she was offered (and declined) a job at a circus that involved shaving men from the audience using her feet. Her performance *Stories of a Body* (1990) as a *tableau vivant* Venus is typical of the type of work produced by some female disabled artists who engage with dynamic self-display to denounce dominant narratives about disability and femininity. In a setting of total darkness followed by enigmatic visuals and sounds, Duffy emerges naked and spotlit from the front as an enactment of the classical figure of the *Venus de Milo*, the ancient Greek statue attributed to Alexandros of Antioch that was unearthed with both its arms shattered, becoming over the years emblematic of the evolution of what Tobin Siebers calls 'disability aesthetics' in visual arts.[60] Aligning her disabled body with the iconic statue of female beauty in Western tradition – the same body that was once sensationally displayed in freak shows and later forced into invisibility – Duffy turns it into a critical art object to radically call attention to the cultural reception of unusual bodies and redefine disability.

Demanding and welcoming the stare, her body presented as such evokes fascination, curiosity, bewilderment and awe, but it is when she addresses the audience and turns into a speaking subject, Garland Thomson tells us, that she decisively upsets the dynamic of starring, dismantling her objectification. In her short monologue she talks openly about her unusual body and the feelings that stem from the hurtful language and medical terms used, silently or not, to describe her condition. She recalls all the stereotypical questions she frequently encounters and the assumptions people make of her appearance and finally dwells on her body being 'whole, complete, and functional'.[61] By exposing her body and appropriating the words others use to describe her – staring right back at the audience – Duffy employs a sort of 'stare-and-tell ritual' that vigorously uncovers the process of her enfreakment, criticizing the oppressive politics of appearance that renounce distinctive subjects as non-normative towards an 'act of self-making'.[62] It is this combination of narrative and visual, prominent in both Fraser's and Duffy's performances, that creates the dynamic exchange of agency between performer and audience and permits the stareable subject to stare back. Unlike Bowery's body, which appears at d'Offay's gallery as a spectacularly manipulated object exclusively to be viewed, the unadorned body in disability performance, serving as the medium and the content of the performance, becomes 'an object both to be viewed and to be explained'.[63]

Bowery's dramatic mannerisms and 'extravagant clothing' emit 'an extreme egocentrism' seemingly far removed from critical engagement: 'It was all about him and his body. The audience is secondary', René Zechlin writes.[64] Similarly, for Martin Engler, the mirror effect that obstructs any kind of dialogue between Bowery and the observers allows him to 'create an existential, almost iconic image of narcissistic loneliness and self-inflicted isolation'.[65] The performance, which seemed natural for Bowery who consumed a considerable amount of energy daily posing and studying himself in the plethora of mirrors in his flat, can potentially be dismissed as mere exhibitionism, a superficial act of vanity to serve his narcissistic ego. Not to mention that narcissism had turned into a dirty word in art discourse as a recurrent accusation of artistic self-obsession by those art critics belligerent to the postmodernist propensity for uninhibited self-display. It was not until the 1990s, John Welchman argues, when narcissism cropped up in the terrain of institutional fine art as a promising strategy for negotiating subjectivity and identity, having until then been through a tempestuous cultural journey: '[F]rom a classical myth to a clinical condition, and then from a metaphor for cultural introspection to a significant condition of representation.'[66] In this canonical climate of restored narcissism, masquerade constitutes, for Welchman, the most complicated mode in the representation of self, with its postmodern parents being the master of transformative self-photography Cindy Sherman and the versatile appropriation artist Yasumasa Morimura – both highly valued in the art market.

Despite the adverse overtones attached to narcissism (mostly associated with feminist body art for the ease with which the usually female nude body takes centre stage, risking fetishization), the potential to function as a liberatory act of politicized self-expression is contemplated by Amelia Jones. In defence of the condemned self-objectifying strategies of postmodernism, she suggests that, as 'the exploration of and fixation on the self', narcissism essentially leads to the projection of the individual's 'internal structures of identification and desire outward', having an impact on the other; it can be regarded, therefore, as a strategy not only for permitting one's deepest desires to surface but for communicating and relating one's self to the other.[67] It is not coincidental that this kind of body-focused work emerged at a moment in history (in the late 1960s and early 1970s) when the fragmentation of the self was becoming increasingly visible via the prominence of various social movements that gave voice to those traditionally disenfranchised. What Jones considers genuinely subversive in regards to the 'fundamentally intersubjective' quality of narcissistic body art is that most of the times it intensifies the deconstruction of the domineering and highly problematic figure of modernism: the white, non-disabled, heterosexual male.[68]

The disclosure of the inner self, facilitated by narcissism, can potentially unsettle the authority of normalization that forces the individual to fulfil certain stereotypical standards through particular socially acceptable identifications. By failing to do so, they create an array of new possibilities of embodiment that would otherwise remain in the margins; in Jones' words: they 'may access the domain of *abject* beings':

> It is this domain of abject beings that I believe the most interesting body art projects to be enacting: women as (provisional) subjects, men who are openly ambivalent in their relationship to the phallus and particular in spite of their privileged masculinity, subjects who are otherwise not normative.[69]

Enacting his inner self by bringing a domestic ritual into the public realm queerly attired, Bowery at the Anthony d'Offay Gallery embodies an abject subject who disrupts or complicates the authority of normalization in multiple levels with his 'irregular' masculinity, freakish appearance, and 'aberrant' attitude. In the same manner that the restrictive cultural norms of ableism are disputed in disability performance art by exposing the raw realism of the unusually formed body, seizing control of one's appearance – like Bowery does by inscribing his inner desires on the body and letting them surface through his narcissistic impulse – can also be an effective strategy of resistance and visibility against normative societal ideals of equally oppressive nature.

As the absolute embodiment of the climax of the New Romantic ethos, Bowery answers to those condemning the scene for superficiality and lack of political and social gist: 'Politics, when you were dressing like Lord Byron [...] came fairly low down on your list of social responsibilities', Bracewell asserts.[70] What, however, is overlooked in this line of argument is the radical potential of dressing up as cultural intervention at a time of heightened political depression and lurking homophobia. For the marginalized freaks of the 1980s, including Bowery, dressing like Lord Byron becomes a political scream, an audacious mix of narcissism and defiance, proclaiming 'We're here, we're queer and we look fabulous!'.

Especially within the context of the public health crisis during the 1980s, the decade that experienced the threat of a 'gay plague' (the casually homophobic label given to AIDS when it was initially believed it could only spread among promiscuous male homosexuals), Bowery's narcissistic excess acquires further significance. Heather Warren-Crow, for instance, argues that Bowery's signature spot pattern, which was used widely in his looks and his designs for others, is indicative of 'the dissident mobility of queers' and conveys 'an aesthetic of community acquisition' against the attempts to eradicate queer networks during the AIDS crisis.[71] Acknowledging that blots are historically linked to disease and infection, she translates Bowery's spots as the aestheticization of Kaposi's sarcoma (a skin cancer closely associated with AIDS) and as a means of 'hypervisibility' of the sick queer body.[72] Confined at the Anthony d'Offay Gallery with spots all over him and being the best representative of the nightclub – the most prevalent but also the most vilified locus among queer networks – Bowery's glamorous enfreakment can thus be viewed as a metaphor for the marginalization and stigmatization of HIV-positive bodies. Furthermore, his gloriously self-assured narcissism and excessive artificiality unsettle common assumptions surrounding the failing queer body and its inevitable death due to a depraved lifestyle.

Looking at Bowery as a queer freak suggests that there is more to the comparison with disabled performers than it seems in the first place for both disability and queerness stand in contrast to the hegemony of 'normative' identities. Departing from the premise that heterosexuality and the gender binary are constructed as the natural order that produces queerness as deviation, Robert McRuer argues that disability too is a product of a compulsory able-bodiedness that under neoliberal capitalism appears to be woven together with compulsory heterosexuality, crystallizing the subordination of those identities that do not qualify as heterosexual or able-bodied.[73]

The video performance *Leigh Bowery* (2006) by The Disabled Avant-Garde (disabled artists Aaron Williamson and Katherine Araniello), which Warren-Crow describes as 'one of the most unusual tributes' to Bowery, fleshes out in a humorous way this peculiar alliance between queerness and disability as two marginalizing carriers of contemporary freakishness.[74] The short video features the duo surrounded by trippy effects, produced by greenscreen technology, watching Bowery's performance at the Anthony d'Offay Gallery on a small television screen. They are attired queerly with wigs and various eccentric accessories (with Williamson bearing Bowery's spot pattern on his face) while dancing now and then to upbeat jazz music and imitating some of Bowery's movements amid grunting noises and chicken clucking cries (Figure 2.7).[75] 'This video makes a clear, queer connection between two contemporary performance artists

Figure 2.7: The Disabled Avant-Garde, *Leigh Bowery*, 2006. Video stills. © The Disabled Avant-Garde. Courtesy of the Live Art Development Agency, London.

who identify as disability activists and Bowery [...] who claimed not to identify', Warren-Crow writes, implicitly outlining their apparent difference.[76] She goes on to assert that by 'aestheticizing and re-materializing the stigma' with his widely embraced spot aesthetic, Bowery challenges their nature, 'reminding us that the marks affecting both queers and people with disabilities are not stable and natural but mobile and cultural'.[77] His performed freakishness and devotion to artificiality give space to the emergence of alternative embodiments of otherness, constantly questioning the gravity of the alleged normative physical body.

Bowery's living installation at the Anthony d'Offay Gallery is a glorification of his self-induced freakishness, an imperative aspect of his performative costuming sparked by the carnivalesque ambience of club culture in the 1980s and fed on media exposure. From aspiring fashion designer to master of subcultural freakishness, Bowery brought himself in replete theatricality and grandeur from the dancefloor to the gallery to be gladly scrutinized as a rare nocturnal specimen, a contemporary freak who dares to be different with no further explanation. His performance of spectacular freakishness in an exaggerated and self-absorbed manner is certainly not looking to speak back or provide a lesson, as is the case with disability performance art that represents the oppression and anxieties of those whose difference was not a choice and who have suffered their unwilling objectification and the stigma of the freak the most. Yet, in contextualizing freakishness and presenting it in a positive light, Bowery turns it into a political act of difference by highlighting the cultural and social constructiveness of the freak, signifying splendidly Susan Stewart's much-cited claim that the assumed 'freak of nature' is instead a 'freak of culture'.[78]

Notes

1. See John Clarke, 'Style', in *Resistance through Rituals: Youth Subcultures in Post-War Britain*, ed. by Stuart Hall and Tony Jefferson (Abingdon: Routledge, 2002), pp. 175–91.
2. *Taboo: The Boy George Musical* (London: Blackhorse Entertainment, 2004) [DVD]. Author's transcription.
3. Leslie Fiedler, *Freaks: Myths and Images of the Secret Self* (New York: Simon & Schuster, 1978), p. 14.

4. Daniel Foss, *Freak Culture: Life-Style and Politics* (New York: E. P. Dutton, 1972), p. 132. Emphasis in original.
5. Simon Reynolds, *Totally Wired: Post-Punk Interviews and Overviews* (London: Faber & Faber Limited, 2009), p. 401.
6. Sarah Thornton, *Club Cultures: Music, Media and Subcultural Capital* (Cambridge: Polity Press, 1995), p. 3.
7. Although Strange's and Egan's regular event at Billy's is credited as the most significant, there were similar club nights popping up around the same time in venues throughout England, such as at Pips in Manchester, the Adelphi pub in Leeds and most notably the Rum Runner in Birmingham.
8. See Georgina Gregory, 'Masculinity, Sexuality and the Visual Culture of Glam Rock', *Culture and Communication*, 5.2 (2002), 35–60.
9. Philip Auslander, *Performing Glam Rock: Gender and Theatricality in Popular Music* (Ann Arbor: University of Michigan Press, 2006), p. 234.
10. Thornton, p. 3. Emphasis in original.
11. See Dave Rimmer, *New Romantics: The Look* (London: Omnibus Press, 2013).
12. See Steve Strange, *Blitzed!: The Autobiography of Steve Strange* (London: Orion Books Ltd, 2002).
13. Rimmer, p. 64.
14. Michael Bracewell, 'Leigh Bowery's Immaculate Conception', in *The Space Between: Selected Writings on Art*, ed. by Doro Globus (London: Ridinghouse, 2012), pp. 126–33 (pp. 129–30).
15. See David Hevey, *The Creatures Time Forgot: Photography and Disability Imagery* (London: Routledge, 1992).
16. Roger Malbert, 'Exaggeration and Degradation: Grotesque Humour in Contemporary Art', in *Carnivalesque* (London: Hayward Gallery Publishing, 2000), pp. 74–97 (p. 94).
17. Malbert, p. 94.
18. Bracewell, p. 130.
19. Gertrud Lehnert, 'Die Kleider des Leigh Bowery', in *Leigh Bowery: Verwandlungskünstler*, ed. by Angela Stief (Vienna: Piet Meyer Verlag, 2015), pp. 73–94 (p. 78). Author's translation.
20. Fiedler, p. 33. The mythological term 'hermaphrodite' was once used to refer to intersex persons, but it is now considered offensive.
21. Elizabeth Grosz, 'Intolerable Ambiguity: Freaks as/at the Limit', in *Freakery: Cultural Spectacles of the Extraordinary Body*, ed. by

Rosemarie Garland Thomson (New York: New York University Press, 1996), pp. 55–66 (p. 57).

22. Rosemarie Garland Thomson, *Staring: How We Look* (Oxford: Oxford University Press, 2009), p. 32.
23. Silvia Rief, *Club Cultures: Boundaries, Identities, and Otherness* (New York: Routledge, 2009), p. 9.
24. Thornton, p. 128.
25. Thornton, p. 151. Emphasis in original.
26. Thornton, p. 153.
27. Thornton, p. 151.
28. *i-D: The Money Issue*, September 1984, p. 47. PP.22.J, Periodicals, National Art Library, Victoria and Albert Museum.
29. See *South of Watford*, ITV, 25 April 1986.
30. Dave Haslam, *Life after Dark: A History of British Nightclubs and Music Venues* (London: Simon & Schuster, 2015), p. 315.
31. Richard Torry in *The Legend of Leigh Bowery*, dir. by Charles Atlas (London: BBC4, 2008).
32. 'Newsflash–', *i D: The Spectator Issue*, November 1985, pp. 22–23. PP.22.J, Periodicals, National Art Library, Victoria and Albert Museum.
33. Alix Sharkey quoted in Sue Tilley, *Leigh Bowery: The Life and Times of an Icon* (London: Hodder & Stoughton, 1997), p. 58.
34. Paul Hunwick, 'Leigh Bowery – Obituary', *i-D: The New Faces Issue*, February 1995, p. 78. PP.22.J, Periodicals, National Art Library, Victoria and Albert Museum.
35. Malbert, p. 94.
36. Robin Blyn, *The Freak-Garde: Extraordinary Bodies and Revolutionary Art in America* (Minneapolis: University of Minnesota Press, 2013), p. xix.
37. Robert Bogdan, *Freak Show: Presenting Human Oddities for Amusement and Profit* (Chicago: The University of Chicago Press, 1988), p. 2.
38. Alexander McQueen reproduced the same mirror effect in the catwalk show for his collection *Voss* (Spring/Summer 2001) where the models paraded in a reconstructed room with glass walls unable to see the audience on the outside. In the finale, an enormous dark glass box placed in the middle of the room shattered to reveal writer Michelle Olley reclining nude on a chaise-longue covered in moths and wearing a full-head alien mask attached to a breathing tube.
39. Garland Thomson, p. 189.
40. Bogdan, p. 8.

41. Amelia Klem Osterud, *The Tattooed Lady: A History* (Golden: Speck Press, 2009), p. 52.
42. Klem Osterud, p. 53.
43. Bodgan, p. 104.
44. Anthony d'Offay Gallery, *Leigh Bowery* (press release) (1988). 261830-1001, Ephemera, Tate Library, Tate Museum.
45. Rosemarie Garland Thomson, *Extraordinary Bodies: Figuring Physical Disability in American Culture and Literature* (New York: Columbia University Press, 1997), p. 63.
46. Garland Thomson, *Extraordinary Bodies*, p. 68.
47. Garland Thomson, *Extraordinary Bodies*, p. 69.
48. Blyn, p. xix.
49. Bracewell, p. 131.
50. Bowery performed as a live mannequin in the shop window of Parco department store in Tokyo for three days in November 1988. The shop window included only an old-fashioned chaise-longue and Bowery posed for approximately twenty minutes in a different look each day. The shows were part of his *Ruined Clothes* exhibition that took place in the same premises.
51. Bogdan, p. 3.
52. See Lennard J. Davis, 'Crips Strike Back: The Rise of Disability Studies', *American Literary History*, 11.3 (1999), 500–12.
53. Grosz, p. 56.
54. See Petra Kuppers, *Disability and Contemporary Performance: Bodies on Edge* (New York: Routledge, 2003).
55. Garland Thomson, *Staring*, p. 3.
56. Garland Thomson, *Staring*, p. 42.
57. See *Devolving the Mutant, Mat Fraser's Live Art 1999–2011: From Societal Oppression to Personal Succession* (London: Live Art Development Agency, 2011) [DVD].
58. Kuppers, p. 47.
59. David Mitchell and Sharon Snyder, 'Exploitations of Embodiment: *Born Freak* and the Academic Bally Plank', *Disability Studies Quarterly*, 25.3 (2005), <https://dsq-sds.org/article/view/575/752> [accessed 27 February 2025].
60. See Tobin Siebers, 'Disability Aesthetics and the Body Beautiful: Signposts in the History of Art', *Alter*, 2.4 (2008), 329–36.
61. Quoted in Rosemarie Garland Thomson, 'Staring Back: Self-Representations of Disabled Performance Artists', *American Quarterly*, 52.2 (2000), 334–38 (p. 337).

62. Garland Thomson, 'Staring Back', p. 338.
63. Garland Thomson, 'Staring Back', p. 334.
64. René Zechlin, 'Introduction: The Human Body as an Artwork', in *Leigh Bowery: Beautified Provocation*, ed. by René Zechlin (Heidelberg: Kehrer Verlag, 2008), pp. 31–32 (p. 31).
65. Martin Engler, 'The Multiple Bodies of Leigh Bowery', in *Leigh Bowery: Beautified Provocation,* ed. by René Zechlin (Heidelberg: Kehrer Verlag, 2008), pp. 55–60 (p. 59).
66. John C. Welchman, *Art after Appropriation: Essays on Art in the 1990s* (New York: Routledge, 2001), p. 185.
67. Amelia Jones, *Body Art/Performing the Subject* (Minneapolis: University of Minnesota Press, 1998), p. 46.
68. Jones, p. 47.
69. Jones, p. 50. Emphasis in original.
70. Michael Bracewell, *England is Mine: Pop Life in Albion from Wilde to Goldie* (London: Flamingo, 1998), p. 207.
71. Heather Warren-Crow, 'Acquired Community: Leigh Bowery and *Hail the New Puritan's* Mise-en-Scène of AIDS', in *Different Bodies: Essays on Disability in Film and Television*, ed. by Marja Evelyn Mogk (Jefferson: McFarland & Company, 2013), pp. 39–54 (p. 41).
72. Warren-Crow, p. 41.
73. See Robert McRuer, *Crip Theory: Cultural Signs of Queerness and Disability* (New York: New York University Press, 2006).
74. Warren-Crow, p. 52.
75. See *The DAG: Bite the Hand that Feeds* (London: Live Art Development Agency, 2012) [DVD].
76. Warren-Crow, p. 52.
77. Warren-Crow, p. 53.
78. Susan Stewart, *On Longing: Narratives of the Miniature, the Gigantic, the Souvenir, the Collection* (Durham, NC: Duke University Press, 1993), p. 109.

Chapter 3 Fabulously Painful: BDSM and the Performance of Extremity

One of Leigh Bowery's less-known club performances that caused controversy took place in 1993 at Industria in Hanover Square in London. The club was reputed to be frequented mostly by lesbians and Bowery's performance was set to inaugurate the opening of SMact, a supposedly sadomasochistic club night. Unlike his usual spontaneous solo dance spectacles, Bowery's performance at Industria included a narrative and two other performers: a woman named Barbara and Berkeley the club host. The performance, which is only documented in passing in Sue Tilley's biography of Bowery and captured in a few photographs by Gordon Rainsford, involved the enactment of a ritualistic surgery of sorts carried out by Bowery and Barbara. Dressed in his 'Nazi Dominatrix' look, Bowery was joined on stage by Barbara who sported a total white outfit with an apron, a surgical face mask and an armband with a swastika. At some point, Berkeley, playing the role of a Holocaust victim, entered the space lightly dressed in what appears to be a hospital gown and laid on a table with various medical paraphernalia in sight where a simulated castration took place. The action involved a dildo – Berkeley's penis – being grotesquely cut by the other two performers, spraying the audience with fake blood. Reaching higher levels of abjection, Tilley writes that fake shit (in fact dog food) also sprayed the audience and that for the grand finale 'Berkeley [...] gave the dildo a blow job and then, to finish off, Leigh pushed it up the patient's arse'.[1] Typical of Bowery's twisted humour, the gory spectacle and its highly provocative innuendos, with explicit references to Nazi doctor Josef Mengele and his tormenting medical experiments, was not found amusing by a substantial part of the audience and was received with lukewarm applause. Bowery was called a racist and was no longer welcome in the nightclub after the performance (Figure 3.1).

From an art-historical perspective, Bowery's grotesque staging of mutilation and Nazi connotations evoke the spirit of some of the pioneering works of the Viennese Actionists, four radical avant-garde Austrian artists – Günter Brus, Otto Muehl, Hermann Nitsch and Rudolf Schwarzkogler – who produced art collaboratively and individually during the 1960s. Their transgressive works are frequently interpreted as a repercussion of the fragile socio-cultural circumstances in post-war Austria, which

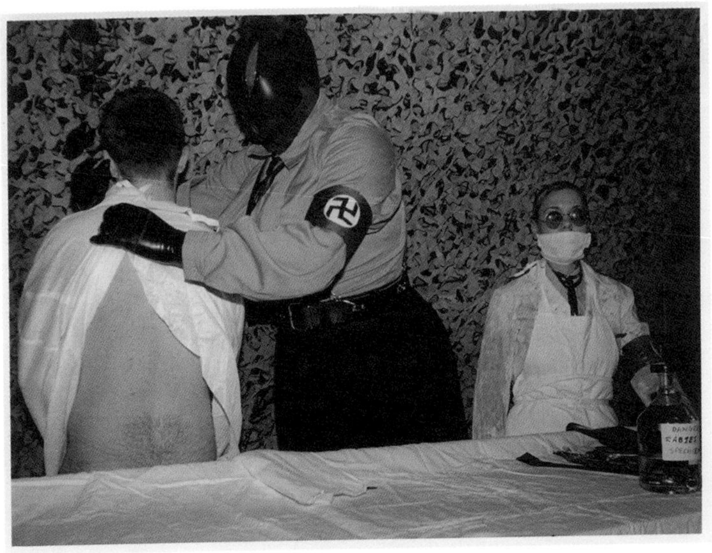

Figure 3.1: Berkeley, Leigh Bowery and Barbara performing at Industria, London, 1993. Photograph by Gordon Rainsford. Courtesy of the Bishopsgate Institute, London.

for decades retained many post-fascist elements, and as a violent response to the largely conservative climate that still dominated the Austrian art scene. In line with the general shift from the art object to the process of art-making witnessed during the second half of the twentieth century, the experimental work of the Viennese Actionists, Hubert Klocker notes, 'speaks of an aesthetic whose whole impetus [...] encompasses a libertarian spirit of radical protest'.[2] By moving away from traditional mediums and incorporating performativity for the possibility of an 'immediate, uncompromising, and also political' art, the body acquired a central position in their practice.[3]

The Viennese Actionists became widely known for performing actions, both in private and public spaces, that were deemed aesthetically repellent and violent, often involving nudity, scenes of self-torture, allusions to rape, the use of bodily fluids and the entrails of animals in quasi-religious ritualistic ceremonies. Thomas McEvilley suggests that such works should be viewed within the wider context of cultural history and locates their origins in ancient ceremonial activities that surfaced as a response to modern civilization in the 1960s and early 1970s through various channels, such as dream material and experimentation with psychedelic drugs.[4] The themes of self-injury, cross-dressing and the performance of taboo acts in public, which are heavily featured in most performances by the Viennese Actionists, reflect, for McEvilley, shamanic practices of magic and ancient initiation rites. Being in the margins of international developments in the field of performance art and excluded for some time from English-speaking discourse, the Viennese Actionists, Philip Ursprung observes, 'were performing their own ambivalence to modernity' as a challenge to the apolitical character of traditional art.[5] By defying its boundaries as well as what constitutes public decency, their activities, which often mobilized the police and the mass media, drew attention to the oppressive mechanisms of the state that largely regulated public spaces in conservative post-war Austria.

In the United Kingdom, the shock tactics of the Viennese Actionists were fervently espoused by live art and experimental music pioneers COUM Transmissions (1969–77), an art collective founded by Genesis P-Orridge that gained notoriety with their retrospective exhibition *Prostitution* (1976) at the

Institute of Contemporary Arts in London (ICA). The rarely seen short film *After Cease to Exist* (1977), which premiered the following year in an experimental film festival in the Netherlands, includes scenes performed by prominent COUM members Cosey Fanni Tutti and Chris Carter that graphically simulate castration.

Whether Bowery had ever encountered the significant work produced by COUM is unknown, but he appeared to be genuinely fascinated by the Viennese Actionists and especially Rudolf Schwarzkogler's actions and the myth that surrounded his death. Klocker notes that Schwarzkogler was the only one in the group 'to make any explicit statement about the relationship to the performative event [...] and its transposition into a "staged photograph"' since his performative work, which includes only six actions in total carried out in private during 1965–66, was conceived to be executed exclusively in front of the camera.[6] The visual language of his 'action photography' evokes strong images of injury, mutilation, bandaging, digestion of fluids and frequently castration, communicating 'the idea of marked sadomasochistic destruction', Klocker remarks elsewhere.[7] His *Action 2* and *Action 3* (1965), in particular, contain images hinting at castration, a recurring theme in Schwarzkogler's work that very likely inspired Bowery's performance at Industria. Photographed by Ludwig Hoffenreich, both actions include sequences of black-and-white photographs that construct a specialized visual repertoire consisting of nudity, dead fish, razor blades, bandages, tubes, syringes and other medical paraphernalia. Many of these images depict a close-up of a nude male groin that belongs to artist Heinz Cibulka and is either covered by the mangled flesh of a fish or blooded bandages.

Schwarzkogler's limited oeuvre, the fact that his staged actions were performed privately and exist only in photographs as well as his apparent suicide at the age of 29 granted him 'a place somewhat similar to that of the unknown hero of legend', Klocker characteristically writes.[8] His legacy was further intensified when in an article condemning postmodernist art as 'a sluggish descent into entropy', published in *Time* magazine, art critic Robert Hughes erroneously reported that 'poor Schwarzkogler', who was 'mad as a hatter', had died 'a martyr to his art' due to his '[s]uccessive acts of self-amputation'.[9] The myth of his death as a result of self-castration continued to circulate for years as a factual event even among prestigious art scholars and had deeply intrigued Bowery who possibly sought to reproduce Schwarzkogler's uneasy aesthetic.[10] However, his deployment of shock tactics in his performance at Industria appears to lack the political weight and acuity of the Viennese Actionists, whose work acquires significance in the context of a conservative society with a troubled Nazi history, and it is arguably for this reason that it was rather perceived as irrelevant, superficial or offensive to some.

The obsessive emphasis on the artist's body as art material, which dominates the pioneering works of the Viennese Actionists and informs Bowery's freakish costuming and performances at large, erupted in the Euro-American visual arts during the 1960s and early 1970s. Bodily pain, manifest either through the transgression of physical boundaries or the sight of wounded flesh, corresponds to a wide range of extreme body-focused works, with Chris Burden being perhaps the first and most celebrated artist within performance art narratives to have perilously risked his physical and mental stamina in stretching art's limits. In *Shoot* (1971), probably his most iconic piece, Burden was famously shot in the arm with a rifle by a friend at the F Space Gallery in Santa Ana, California, inaugurating what is broadly marked as masochistic performance, endurance art, ordeal art or, more recently, the performance of extremity.

In contrast to the typically simulated works of the Viennese Actionists, who adopted a visual language of staged violence and fabricated bloodshed, many artists like Burden started engaging in extreme practices of actual suffering that involved injury and trauma often in an attempt to move beyond the apolitical role of the artwork as a commodity and purely decorative object. Kathy O'Dell uses the term 'masochistic performance' to describe such works that demonstrate a 'highly unconventional' use of the body in 'individual acts of bodily violence'.[11] Borrowing the term as a metaphor and stripped from its clinical definition, O'Dell points out that even though the performances of bodily extremity do not necessarily reflect the desire to suffer, they 'clearly qualify as masochistic' if one considers 'the social history of the term and its fundamental components', namely masochism as a form of sexual or social contract prompted by fantasy, suspense, demonstration and provocation.[12]

Although extremity remains vague and relative in its conception (since it can potentially encompass a broad spectrum of taboo actions and feelings), it has been commodiously used in performance discourse to accentuate ordeal, injury or self-inflicted violence. For Dominic Johnson, the performance of extremity revolves around 'extremes of too much or not enough', whether in physical, emotional or conceptual terms, without, however, constituting a solid category determined by notions of suffering and the expression of pain that might overshadow the possibility of engaging with radicality in more diverse ways.[13] Similarly, writing about endurance art, Lara Shalson moves away from its usual associations with risk or pain and focuses on the 'bodily commitment and persistence' such works involve to offer a 'more specific and broader' understanding of the term.[14] The manner in which Bowery's body plays out as art material in his flamboyant practice and his (mostly) amusing performances is at first glance distant from these manifestations of extremity that allude to actual experiences of pain, suffering and ordeal; even though some of his later looks and performances, like the one at Industria, reveal a growing fascination with BDSM aesthetics, body modification, risk and atrocity.

Empty Masochism and Modern Primitives

Bowery's engagement with freakish aesthetics and his profound dedication to the vast possibilities of corporeal metamorphosis were premised upon utilizing his body as an instrument for navigating prevailing assumptions of perversion and normality. His incongruous looks, which most of the time required copious amounts of composure not only to materialize but most importantly to be performed, are, according to Anne Marsh, 'explorations of narcissism' that 'could also be interpreted as cathartic acts in line with the experimental body art of the 1970s and beyond'.[15] Although pain and suffering are not explicitly pronounced in Bowery's performative costuming or visual vocabulary, they occupy a central position in his practice. His costuming, Robyn Healy writes, 'was an act of self-inflicted pain for the sake of fashion'.[16] Similarly, as Hilton Als puts it, '[n]o look was worth Bowery's time unless it contained some element of physical pain'.[17]

What he called the 'Black Fetish' look, for instance, is a tribute to BDSM subculture and aesthetics as well as one of his most asphyxiatingly uncomfortable outfits. Even though Bowery was not personally invested in BDSM as a sexual practice, the scene's visual codes inspired him to design a black sculptural vinyl bodysuit that put to a test his high pain tolerance: fully confining, with one padded leg, big hips and breasts, and a tight hood with a long ponytail on top. An assistant was necessary to squeeze him into it before polishing him with a multi-surface spray. It comes as no surprise that 'Black Fetish' was featured in a promotional flyer for a scheduled performance, which ultimately did not go ahead, of Bowery's group Minty at London's alternative fetish club Torture Garden (Figure 3.2). Launched in 1990, during a time in which fetishism and BDSM remained taboo subjects, Torture Garden appealed to a post-goth, industrial and hardcore crowd irrespective of sexual orientation. Since its early days, during which police forced events to be cancelled often, the club gradually achieved notoriety as allegedly the world's largest and most famous fetish and body art club. It has since grown into a top latex fetish fashion label, a production company and a performance agency. Most importantly, Torture Garden has become renowned for instilling the underground body piercing scene in a wider audience by staging alternative fashion shows and providing a platform to various performers of extremity who were otherwise broadly denied visibility: Fakir Musafar, Ron Athey, Franko B, David Hoyle as 'The Divine David' and Marisa Carnesky are some notable examples.

No amount of distress or discomfort could compromise Bowery's artistic vision: dangerously high platform shoes, claustrophobic outfits, restrictive belts and corsets, gaffer tape that cut into his chubby chest, glue on his genitals to feminize his body and facial and body piercings to accommodate his costume ideas. Pain functioned as evidence of his extreme costuming being worthwhile, fueling Bowery's excitement for transforming himself and venturing out. His 'excruciatingly painful' practices 'required incredible courage, and perhaps insanity' to endure, Healy exaggeratingly writes to highlight Bowery's devotion

Figure 3.2: Flyer (front and back) for Minty's performance at Torture Garden in London, 1994. Photograph by Fergus Greer. Courtesy of the Torture Garden Archive, London.

and perfectionism.[18] Even though not a requisite in his practice and hardly noticeable by the viewer, his silent suffering indeed implements Karen Gonzalez Rice's definition of endurance artists: '[P]ractic[ing] self-discipline by testing [one's] physical and psychic capacities, performing long-term actions or submitting to pain or hardship', she notes, are attributes belonging to endurance artists who treat their bodies as 'a material of art', renegotiating the traditional divisions between artists, artworks and audiences.[19]

Bowery's experimentation with the boundaries of the physical body is not limited to his sculptural outfits but also expands to the extended field of body modification, which includes a series of permanent or semi-permanent painful-looking procedures for changing the appearance or form of the body. These typically include piercing, tattooing, branding, cutting, binding or inserting implants. Their emergence in the West in the late 1980s, Victoria Pitts writes, took the form of a rebellious body-focused cultural movement that resonated with a growing fascination for non-Western cultures and the proliferation of gender and sexual politics. Although the movement encompassed a variety of 'subcultural groups with diverse interests', with most prominent the BDSM community, the body 'as a [postmodern] site of exploration' that needs to 'be reclaimed from culture' by bearing one's own identifications remained a shared concern among them.[20] Nonetheless, Bowery's engagement with body modification functioned as another avenue to experiment with his malleable image and costuming.

Bowery's piercings, which he considered a homage to punk's use of safety pins, were apparently far removed from their association with identity formation or sexual arousal nor were they used exclusively as cosmetic fixtures of adornment but rather to support and facilitate certain looks. One of the few times his pierced nipples were exposed was in his 'Space' look in which they were linked by two pearl chains adding to the richness of his South Asian-inspired body decoration. His facial piercings on his cheeks constitute a more splendid example of this tendency. A styling idea that included their use – but eventually deemed too unpractical and risky – was to wire a small bulb into his mouth so that the light would glow through the holes. After abandoning this plan, he invented a special head harness that supported two light bulbs, one on each side of his face, working with batteries that were hidden inside his costume. Still, Bowery created a series of plastic prosthetic lips that were secured with safety pins through the piercings, covering his mouth and giving him the appearance of an inflatable sex doll.

In a video portrait titled *Teach*, shot by Charles Atlas in 1992, Bowery attempts to lip-sync the soul song 'Take a Look' (1967) – written and produced by Clyde Otis and performed by Aretha Franklin – with his mouth covered with a series of costume lips. To compensate for his camouflaged mouth, which complicates and adds a comedic tone to his lip-syncing, he exaggerates the expression of his overemphasized eyes (Figure 3.3). His having only a few piercings may not be exemplary of a spectacular showcase of body modification enthusiasm, but at the time they were still rare and indicative of a marginal practice that was mainly encountered in subcultural settings and non-mainstream visual culture.[21]

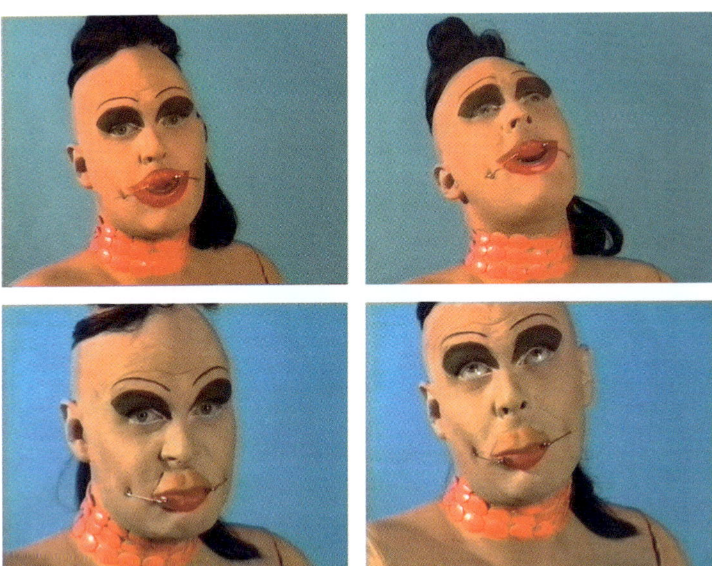

Figure 3.3: Charles Atlas, *Teach*, 1992. Video stills. © Charles Atlas. Courtesy of the artist and Luhring Augustine, New York.

Beguiled apparently by the mysticism prevailing in body modification, Bowery stated that he regarded piercing as a means of 'recognising', 'claiming' and 'transforming' his body and that painful practices had been 'like a kind of passage' that made him feel 'more connected' with it.[22] His professed turn to a more esoteric approach to the relationship between body and pain, translated aesthetically in some of his costumes as well as his performance *The Laugh of No. 12* (1994), was greatly inspired by the philosophy and ritualistic performances of Fakir Musafar. An influential and well-respected figure in the field of body modification, Musafar, a white American who renamed himself after an Iranian Sufi, was the instigator of the subcultural movement of the Modern Primitives, a resurgence of a wide range of Indigenous body-altering practices and rituals for challenging identity boundaries and discovering a more authentic selfhood away from Western ideals and culture. Musafar coined the term as early as 1967 to describe 'a non-tribal person who responds to primal urges and does something with the body' to transcend pain and master 'the expression of *pleasure with insight*'.[23] Apart from the plethora of body modification practices Musafar experimented with, he famously re-enacted extreme ceremonial rituals of intense hardship, such as the Native American *O-Kee-Pa*, the Indian *Kavadi* bearing and the *Sadhu* ball dancing ritual, cementing the mentality and visual identity of the Modern Primitives in (sub)cultural consciousness. Having grown from a confined BDSM scene into a subcultural movement of empowerment for alienated minorities, the Modern Primitives, Pitts remarks, nostalgically 'valorize tribal societies as more spiritual, communal, and environmentally sensitive than their own'.[24]

Musafar started secretly experimenting with acts of body modification and altered states of consciousness as a teenager, during the 1940s and into the 1950s, in the basement of his family house in Aberdeen, South Dakota. The self-portraits that he initially took with a small folding camera to document his activities constitute an impressive body of work on the intersection of art and body play. Although Bowery's flamboyant demeanour hardly approaches the meditative tenets of Musafar, he was most possibly captivated by the shock and awe these extreme body practices could provoke. As Pitts highlights, the kinds of '[p]ermanent, painful and non-normative adornments' did at that time come across in the West 'as forms of self-injury' associated with antisocial behaviour and mental health issues.[25]

Whereas Musafar explored his profound interest in non-Western practices by fully identifying with Indigenous people, performing their spiritual ceremonies of transcendence and mindfully copying their bodily adornment – problematically exercising, in Pitts's phrasing, a sort of 'subversive subcultural performance' – Bowery eclectically appropriated some of their visual components in line with his postmodernist ethos of pastiche.[26] It is no coincidence perhaps that Angela Fisher's *Africa Adorned* (1984), a heavily illustrated account of the diverse styles of adornment of the peoples across the continent, was among Bowery's favourite books of modernist masters and classic couturiers. Furthermore, like Musafar, he was an avid reader of *National Geographic*, which had been for decades the main source of information and imagery related to non-Western body rituals and adornment.

Undeniably, some of Bowery's costumes incorporate, consciously or not, decorative elements that hint at Indigenous body practices and styles, acting, Katharina Sykora writes, 'as barbs to an ethnocentric gaze'.[27] His avant-garde approach, she adds, makes any 'reference to ethnographic archetypes [look] second hand, underscoring its artificiality', with the 'Space' look being without a doubt exemplary.[28] Likewise, the devotion of the Modern Primitives to the appropriation of Indigenous styles and practices, which they saw as a way of differentiating from capitalist Western societies, has been broadly criticized for postmodern eclecticism, narcissistic superficiality and disseminating an essentialist view of traditional non-Western cultures. Sociologist Christian Klesse, for instance, claims that by reproducing the obsolete and highly problematic notion of 'primitivism', the primarily white subculture of the Modern Primitives (although well-intended) perpetuated 'a tradition which played a significant role in the justification of colonial rule and subordination'.[29] In their search for authenticity and in asserting an identity divergent from Western ideals, they reproduced uncritically the colonial fantasy of a homogenized racial other. As a naive and highly idealized gesture towards self-exploration, the subculture of the Modern Primitives, for Klesse, 'is deeply informed by the ambivalences of stereotyping and racialized representation'.[30]

Bowery's body work and costuming are not directly aligned with the 'tribal' aesthetics of the Modern Primitives but occasionally demonstrate elements that hint at practices and styles associated with Indigenous cultures, channelling some of Musafar's experimental self-portraits of body compression. In one of his looks, Bowery wears a striped colourful ensemble comprising a cropped top, crotch-high boots and an excruciatingly tight band around his waist that is particularly reminiscent of the traditional *Itiburi* of certain Indigenous males in New Guinea that Musafar favoured, managing to permanently fix his waist at an exceptionally small diameter (Figures 3.4 and 3.5).

Closely related to this practice appears the Western-style corset, which, apart from arduously assisting in achieving a more elegant and feminine silhouette according to Western ideas of femininity and beauty, was regarded by Musafar as inducing 'a state of permanent sexual arousal' for the wearer;

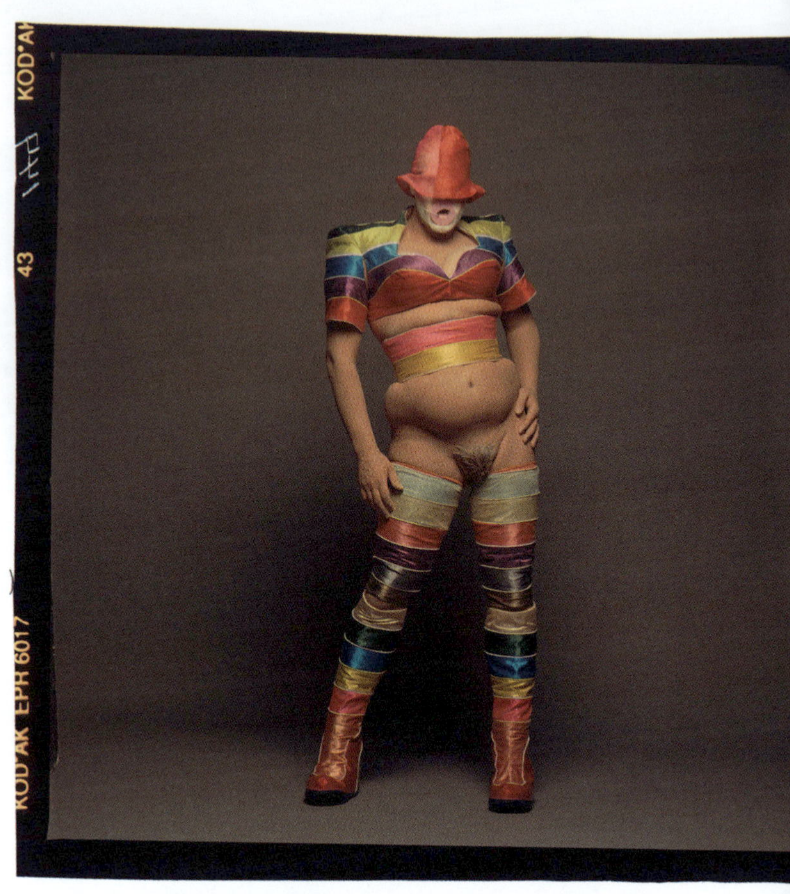

Figure 3.4: Fergus Greer, *Leigh Bowery: Session III, Look 15*, 1990. © Fergus Greer. Courtesy of the artist and the Michael Hoppen Gallery, London.

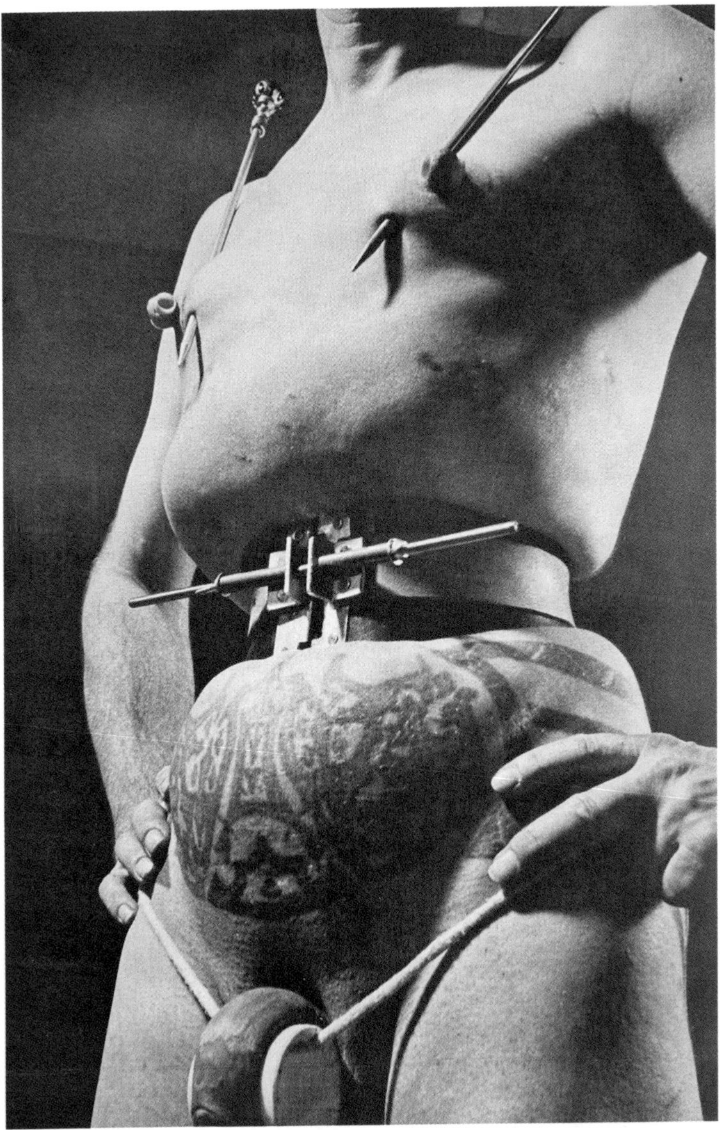

Figure 3.5: Fakir Musafar, *Ibitoe*, 1977. © The Regents of the University of California, The Bancroft Library, University of California, Berkeley.

hence, the corset was fervently embraced by the fetish and BDSM community.[31] Notably, both Musafar and Bowery were drawn to the complicated craft of corset-making, with the former establishing a business and the latter collaborating closely for a number of years with acclaimed corset maker Mr. Pearl. Alongside body corsets, Bowery and Mr. Pearl designed a series of neck corsets that can be read either as a reference to the Kayan women of Burma, who wear brass coils around their necks from an early age to make them slenderer and elongated, or Musafar, who also practised neck stretching by wearing a metal collar.

Allusions to constriction and bondage can also be found in a photograph of Bowery with Sheila Tequila and Stella Stein as Raw Sewage. The three of them pose naked with their genitals tucked between their legs, wearing white tower platform boots, black stockings and full-arm black gloves, with faces reminiscent of the racist tradition of blackface in minstrel shows and heads covered with assorted headgear. Their torsos are firmly compressed by black belts with studs and metal details that make their flesh burst stiflingly, mirroring the non-Western practice of reshaping one's limbs with tight arm and leg bands that Musafar embraced (Figures 3.6 and 3.7).

Although not rooted in an Indigenous practice, body play with wooden clothes pegs features in a series of Bowery's portraits. Posing with minimum make-up in a plastic transparent vest contoured as a female torso and his head covered by a realistic phallus-shaped cap, Bowery bears a string of clothes pegs attached to the skin along his jawline. Some of the early experiments of teenage Musafar involved a pinching ordeal with clothes pegs affixed to his face and torso. This type of body compression can be particularly uncomfortable if endured for several hours and is a fairly common practice within the BDSM community. One of Robert Mapplethorpe's photographs titled *Clothespinned Mouth* (1978) depicts, as the title suggests, a close-up of two hands parting a bunch of clothes pegs attached to swollen lips and ears. Bowery's staged portrait, despite being slightly basic in comparison to his typically excessive looks, is a far more fashionable attempt to depict BDSM than that in Musafar's documentary photography or Mapplethorpe's raw realism. The former was a passionate practitioner of risky body-focused rituals,

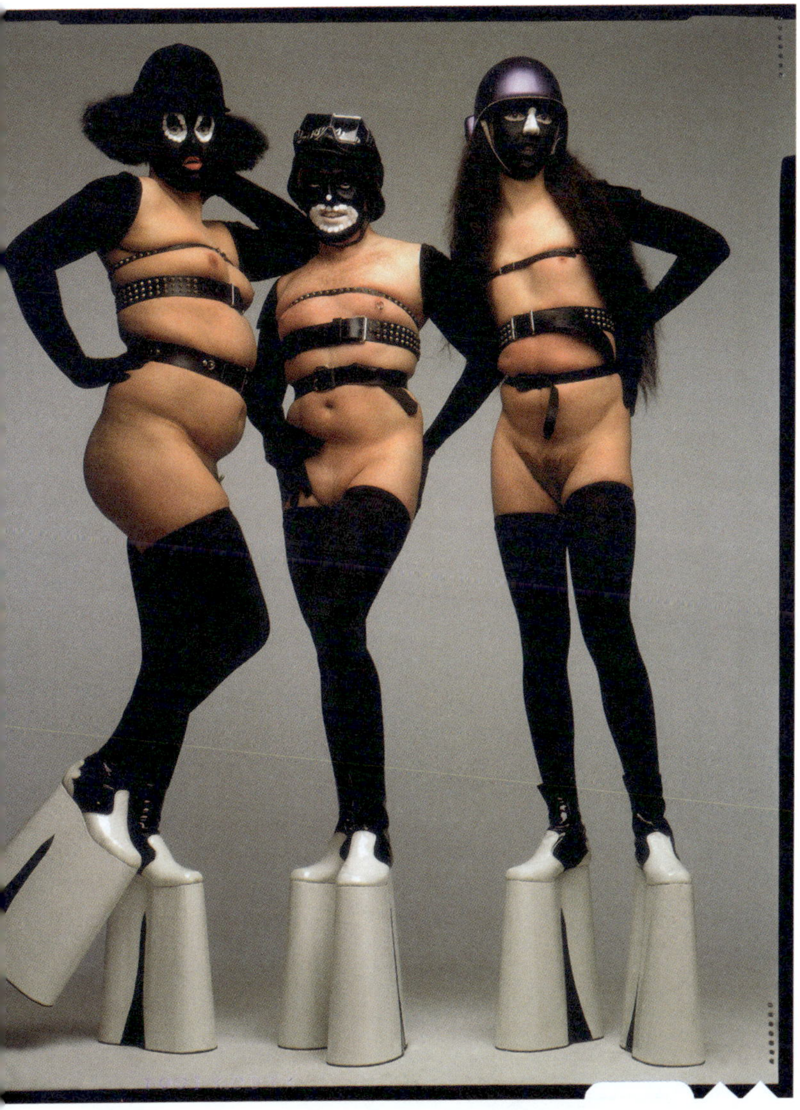

Figure 3.6: Fergus Greer, *Raw Sewage: Session II, Look 4*, 1989. © Fergus Greer. Courtesy of the artist and the Michael Hoppen Gallery, London.

Figure 3.7: Fakir Musafar untitled self-portrait, date unknown. © The Regents of the University of California, The Bancroft Library, University of California, Berkeley.

with his self-photography initially intended for personal use, and the latter a committed participant in the BDSM gay scenes of New York, which informed part of his work, causing political controversy. In comparison, these contingencies may render Bowery's sleek interpretation less threatening to the social order and less authentic a gesture, yet enigmatic and imaginative (Figures 3.8–3.10).

Following the subcultural zeitgeist of his times, Bowery became more and more drawn to the drastic effects of body modification that costuming alone could not achieve. That was mostly due to expanding his territory beyond the club and being involved with people who experimented with body manipulation, opening fresh creative avenues and possibilities for his practice. Sadly, his early death prevented the materialization of what would have been perhaps his most ambitious project: a 'major reconstruction' involving plastic surgery, he stated in an interview years before French artist ORLAN became widely known for employing surgery in her major art project *The Reincarnation of Saint ORLAN* (1990–93).[32] Further details regarding Bowery's idea were never revealed, though he was reportedly keen on a big nose extending from his forehead like in Pablo Picasso's iconic paintings. Whether Bowery would have proceeded with his seemingly impossible plan for cubist anatomy or if his statement was one of mere speculation is left unknown.

By distorting and manipulating his silhouette in such extreme ways, Bowery demolishes 'the idea of the body having any boundary at all', Alison Bancroft writes.[33] '[T]o undertake the physical endurance his costumes required', she continues, 'attests to a transcendence of ascesis that comes from negating physical pain in the pursuit of a higher purpose'.[34] In contrast to quasi-religious and mystical body practices of transcending suffering or the sexual pleasure in BDSM, Bowery's higher purpose, I maintain, is the impossibly perfect look; as he stated, pain is 'something coincidental' he just had 'to deal with' and not a prerequisite.[35] Los Angeles-based artists Bob Flanagan and Ron Athey are perhaps the most eminent figures in recent histories of performance art (albeit both in the relative margins) to engage deliberately in ritualistic BDSM or other painful practices as a means of empowerment and agency. Bowery's practice on the contrary corresponds neither to the

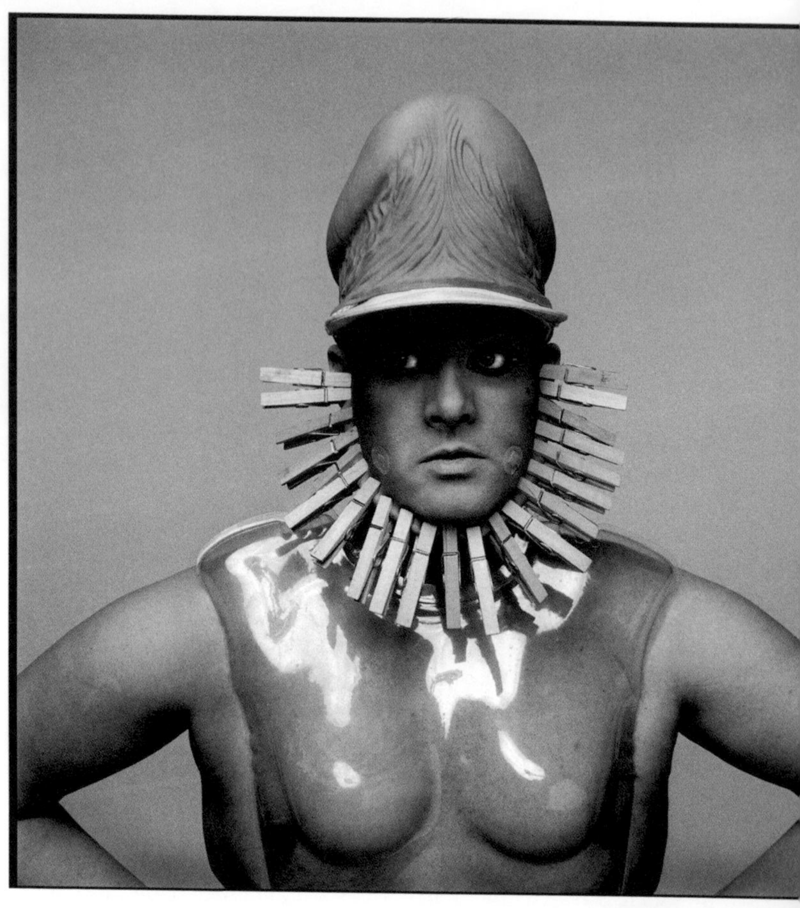

Figure 3.8: Fergus Greer, *Leigh Bowery: Session VII, Look 35*, 1994. © Fergus Greer. Courtesy of the artist and the Michael Hoppen Gallery, London.

It started in earnest the night I lashed myself against the coal bin wall. I was 17 then. I'd fasted for two days – reduced myself to an emaciated robot by dancing for hours with fifty pounds of logging chain wrapped around my legs, arms and torso. I was seeking an experience, a happening, that no other human being I knew had ever had. Even if it meant death!

Clothes Pin Fans, 1950

Figure 3.9: Spread from *Body Play: The Self-Images of Fakir Musafar*, Insight Books, 1982. Photographs by Fakir Musafar. © The Regents of the University of California, The Bancroft Library, University of California, Berkeley.

Figure 3.10: Robert Mapplethorpe, *Clothespinned Mouth*, 1978. © The Robert Mapplethorpe Foundation, New York.

sexual nor the spiritual desire to overcome pain, which rather occurs unintentionally as a side effect of his creative vigour. Bowery endured pain to be fabulous. His is a transformative gesture concerned with aesthetic criteria and less with esoteric impulses for identification and belonging. His fascination with BDSM practices, such as piercing and other body modification techniques that functioned as inspiring references, turns into a type of body play that stays on the surface: an empty masochism. Drawn by imagery and practices capable of maximum visual impact and without delving too much into their symbolism or function (as is also the case in unquestioningly reproducing the idiosyncrasy of the Viennese Actionists at Industria), Bowery favours an appropriation of style over substance that may often become discursively challenging.

Suffering in Style

The revival of so-called 'neo-tribal' body practices during the 1980s, primarily through the subcultural popularity of the Modern Primitives, was naively rooted in the dream of a better society that could possibly be attained by seizing absolute control of and letting one's desires surface on the body. The re-enactment of versions of traditional body ceremonies within a subcultural framework and their inevitable association with BDSM sensibilities thwarted their original sociocultural function in Indigenous communities and complicated their symbolisms. As Ted Polhemus accurately underlines, it is only in the case of these painful body rituals being motivated by a sexual impulse that is appropriate to be labelled as sadomasochistic:

> The concepts of sadism and masochism are western in origin (specifically deriving from de Sade and Sacher Masoch) and are inappropriate to categorize ritual practices in traditional societies. It is absurd, for example, to label a Sioux practitioner of the Sun Dance or a Nuba woman undergoing scarification as 'masochistic'.[36]

The queering of body rituals and modification in spaces like nightclubs, where they were often re-enacted to cement progressive identity politics and bolster alternative modes of sexual expression, shifted their status from traditional community-based rituals to public performances of subcultural belonging. Performance artists engaging in extreme acts of body manipulation in the 1980s and 1990s have, according to Polhemus, 'revolutionized the possibilities of our performative experience' by bringing their 'specialty acts' from freak shows, where they once might have belonged, to fetish clubs and subsequently to art spaces.[37]

The transcending of suffering and pain that anomalous body practices of risk and hardship entail has been for decades a typical attribute of performing freaks. Such is the case, for instance, of Edward H. Gibson, known as the 'Human Pincushion', whose trademark novelty act during the 1920s involved members of the audience sticking pins up to their heads into his body before he meticulously pulled them out one by one or subsequently the 'invulnerable' Mirin Dajo who became famous for penetrating his torso with swords without injury and claimed he was taught the technique from a Hindu fakir. What categorically separates these acts of pure entertainment from the performances of extremity witnessed in the 1990s – in the aftermath of a politically turbulent era also deeply marked by the explosion of the AIDS crisis – is the burning desire to confront the regulation of bodies by the law and conventional morality that characterize the latter.[38] The stigmatizing enfreakment that novelty performers and unusual-looking individuals were traditionally subjected to for profit turned into empowering performances for sexual minorities.

In 1994, Bowery was invited to perform at the opening of *The Laugh of No. 12*, a multimedia group exhibition curated by Anna Tilroe that took place in Fort Asperen in the Netherlands. The exhibition expanded over the three floors of the fort and featured works by Charles Atlas, Tony Oursler and Irene Grundel, with each artist transforming one of the three floors. In contrast to his usual performances of excess in embellished costumes, Bowery's performance at Fort Asperen, which took its title from the exhibition, signifies a radical turn towards BDSM practices and aesthetics that sustain an explicit dialogue with the ritualized body works of risk and ordeal that had started to emerge in previous years. The performance unfolded outdoors during the afternoon in a countryside setting and in front of a mixed crowd of a few hundred people. A rickety construction supporting a glass panel covered by a heavy white curtain was installed close to the fortress where the audience had gathered waiting for the spectacle.

The short performance started with heavily made-up Nicola Bateman, dressed in an impressive wide tutu designed by Mr. Pearl, walking in front of the makeshift theatre curtain and emptying two cans of air freshener while the loud sound of birds chirping was transmitted from speakers. The curtain opened shortly after that to reveal Bowery's bulky naked body suspended upside down behind the glass panel. His styling included only tower platform shoes, black latex high stockings and a neck corset; his head was covered in black paint and a finishing touch involved numerous clothes pegs attached along his penis and nipples as a tribute to Musafar's body play. Bowery's friend and collaborator Richard Torry, standing beside him naked and covered only by a cluster of blue balloons, made aggressive noise with an electric guitar. Dense vegetation, abandoned scaffold sections, scattered wooden pallets and people moving randomly in the background added to the uninhibited vibe of the performance. Still upside down and facing the audience with a microphone clutched close to his mouth, Bowery chanted the following amidst struggling groans:

This is like a dream
This is so unreal
It's ..., I can't believe this is true
It's so beautiful
We could ..., there's so much we can do
Total pleasure
It's incredible
I can't believe it, I can't believe it
We can do anything, everything, everything we want
Total pleasure
Yes, yes, yes
Nothing is taboo
I feel so released
No embarrassment at all
Oh, my God, this fantastic feeling
It's so gorgeous
This is so tense

I can't believe it, so moving
It's surreal
We can do anything
Anything is possible
Anything in the world
Total pleasure
Yes, yes, yes, yes nothing is taboo
Total pleasure
Yes, yes, yes nothing is taboo
Total pleasure, total pleasure
Total, total, total, total
Total, total, total, total
No embarrassment at all.[39]

In expressing his contentment for the beauty surrounding him and the overwhelming feelings of release he experienced, Bowery tries to reproduce the meditative effect pertinent to moments of introspection and self-actualization as popularized by Modern Primitives. Like his masochism, his re-enactment appears to be empty of any attempt to deeply engage and experiment with such altering practices and more anxious in staging a convincing spectacle on the intersection of extremity and self-reflection. After his short monologue the guitar noise gradually faded, letting the bird sounds consume the space. Bowery started to count aloud. When he reached number twelve, Torry who was by then holding Bowery's suspended body back at an angle released it, crashing violently onto the glass panel and shattering it. As a matter of fact, it was an electronic mechanism that smashed the glass before Bowery's body touched it, giving the illusion that he had passed through it. Bowery remained motionless with his body swinging and the curtain was shut quickly, signalling the end of the performance (Figure 3.11). When he walked back to his dressing space shortly after, blood was gushing out of cuts in his arms from glass shards despite the damage limitation plan. Slightly aghast by his unexpected injuries but still excited, Bowery struck a few joyful poses for the photographer who was documenting the event.

Both the exhibition and Bowery's performance were inspired by the symbolism of the twelfth card of the Tarot deck, known as 'The Hanged Man', which depicts a man being hung upside down by one

Figure 3.11: Richard Torry and Leigh Bowery performing *The Laugh of No. 12*, Fort Asperen, 1994. Photograph by Leo Erken. © Leo Erken.

ankle. Tilroe was fascinated by the rich metaphor of the card which can represent, she writes:

> [A] person whose life has run aground, who is no longer able to progress or retreat, and who must see himself and the world in an entirely new way and from a different perspective, not angry or rebellious, but accepting his situation with a smile.[40]

In the aftermath of Bowery's death from an AIDS-related illness just a few months after *The Laugh of No. 12*, Tilroe views the performance as a rite of passage with a significant symbolism of 'advancing from one state to another' fearlessly through the materiality of the body.[41] The performance as such has been limited to either speculative interpretation or valued for its significance for stretching definitions of art. Besides the oppressive social boundaries that Bowery's body metaphorically wreaks by breaking through the glass, Bancroft insists that the action further represents the limits of performance and subjectivity.[42] She views the shattering of the glass frame as a symbolic action for trashing the obsolete codes of what constitutes performance and Bowery's costumed body as a metonymy for the performance itself and for the dissolution of subjectivity, which viewers facing their own liminality can potentially identify with. Like Tilroe, Bancroft discusses Bowery's 'liminal state' as 'a negation of the self that is transcendent and transgressive' and interprets the performance as his brutal final passing towards the next stage: to the thirteenth card of the Tarot, Death.[43]

Bowery's act of transgression and apparent self-inflicted violence as a means to come to terms with his life-threatening condition can, due to its extremity, be placed alongside performances such as that of Flanagan and Athey who both addressed their personal struggles and confronted illness through art. There are certain affinities with this kind of performance of extremity, which adopts elements of BDSM, especially in terms of aesthetics and concept; but while Flanagan's deep-rooted masochism challenged mundane representations of disability and Athey's deliberate bloodletting provoked anxieties surrounding the AIDS crisis, Bowery's political efficacy seems to have been shattered along with the artificially crushed glass panel. His engagement with BDSM, which is reduced to a performance of style and a spectacle of illusion (most likely for shock purposes) and to some extent even his secretive attitude towards his illness might have deprived the work under study of the confrontational quality necessary in bolstering identity politics and constructing an effective social critique – something that Bowery consciously avoided. Alternatively, Flanagan's and Athey's performative suffering functioned not just as a mechanism to cope with their own experiences but also to form connections with other people, a prospect that Bowery's – otherwise brilliant – self-absorbed narcissism did not leave much space for.

Challenging performances (including those involving risk and injury) became more prominent during the 1990s after a period of deep censorship in the arts known as the 'culture wars' in the United States, which was fuelled by the masked homophobia that the AIDS pandemic engendered. O'Dell maintains that masochistic performance, which first emerged at the high of the Vietnam War, reappeared in the late 1980s as a response to the belligerent circumstances in culture brought by the conservative right.[44] This comeback was particularly marked by a fascination with a new type of (mostly) male sexual masochist who subverts the patriarchal codes of impenetrability, inflexibility and macho toughness inscribed onto the male body and troubles the dominant concept of the triumphant masculine hero artist of endurance that dominated the 1970s. As Marla Carlson distinctively writes, 'Burden's art may have been masochistic, but it held queerness at a distance'.[45]

Flanagan, who is perhaps most widely known for nailing his penis to a board in a Schwarzkoglerian fashion, is a unique case when it comes to wielding BDSM and performance art.[46] Arguably, his contribution as a self-proclaimed 'supermasochist' lies in the incorporation of his extensive masochistic lifestyle and his lifelong battle with disability into the art canon. Flanagan was a sufferer of cystic fibrosis (CF), an incurable hereditary disease affecting mainly the respiratory and digestive systems that finally caused his death at the age of 43. The journal Flanagan consistently kept during the last year of his life reveals that he was accustomed to a daily routine of suffering that included an extensive regimen of drugs and regular stays in the hospital.[47] The painful and distressing medical procedures he had to endure since childhood contributed in his own account to the masochistic tendencies he manifested later in life as a teenager. Flanagan's submissive fantasies as an unconscious and urgent response towards managing pain were cultivated from an early age; he recalled, for example, that rubbing against the sheets to soothe his terrible stomach aches started to culminate in pleasurable orgasms. Blending pain with sexual excitement became a strategy of survival and, as he famously claimed, he 'learned to fight sickness with sickness' (Figure 3.12).[48]

Flanagan was initially involved in the poetry scene of Los Angeles and his investment in submissive sexual activities was kept private. It was after he met his long-term partner and dominatrix Sheree Rose in 1980 when their adventurous experimentation with BDSM started to transform into artistic exploration and public performance acts. As he frequently asserted, it was never his intention to become a performance artist, but it occurred as a result of Rose's dedication to documenting their BDSM activities and 'showing them around'.[49] Her photographs depict a usually nude Flanagan with multiple genital piercings, suspended, in bondage,

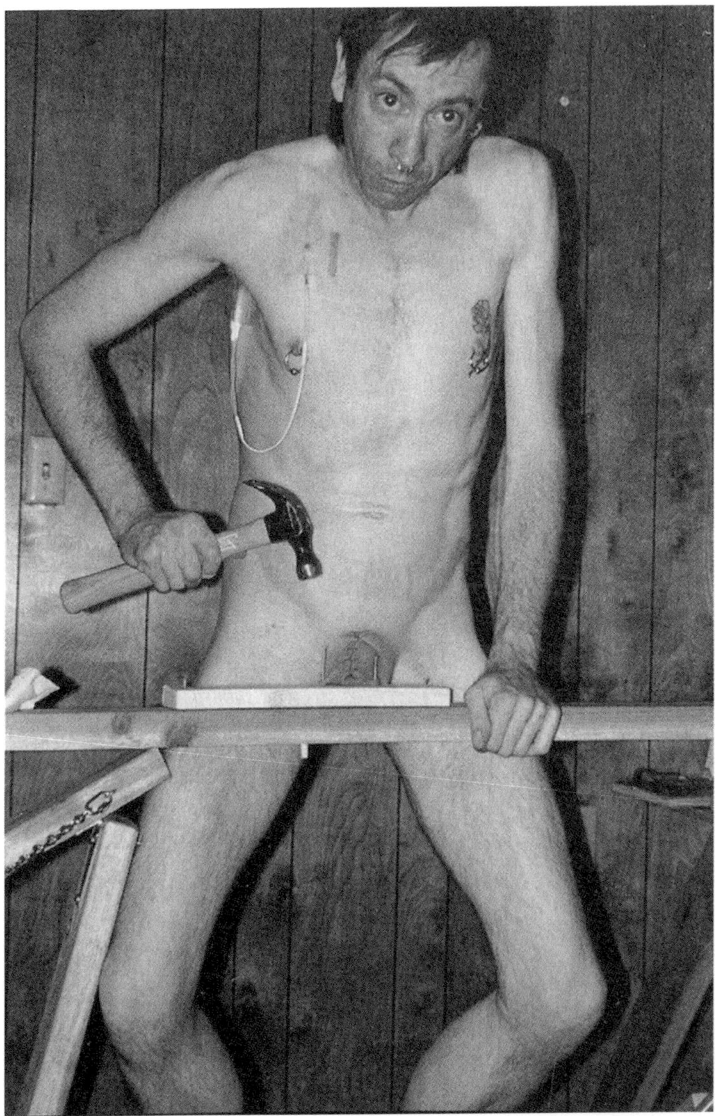

Figure 3.12: Bob Flanagan nailing his scrotum during a Threshold event on auto-erotic SM, Los Angeles, 1989. Photograph by Sheree Rose. Courtesy of ONE Archives at the University of Southern California, Los Angeles.

marked, constricted, pinched and trying out special BDSM gear. Their early performances in underground clubs and events formally associated with the Modern Primitives evolved from demonstrations the pair did for the Los Angeles Janus Society (later Threshold), an organization promoting safe BDSM practices. Notably, as their subcultural demonstrations progressed towards more refined artworks and performances for mainstream audiences, they became a subject for investigation in relation to the National Endowments for the Arts and the Humanities, without ever having been direct recipients of federal funds.

Flanagan's experience of getting older and sicker is reflected in the pair's more mature works, such as the much-discussed touring retrospective *Visiting Hours*, which opened at the Santa Monica Museum of Art in 1992. *Visiting Hours* included a selection of mixed-media artworks for which the space of the museum, Ralph Rugoff describes in his review, was 'transformed [...] into a medical clinic, replete with waiting-room furniture, potted plants and copies of *Highlights for Children* magazines. [...] In the middle of the gallery, in a re-created hospital room, Flanagan [...] was the patient'.[50] Throughout the duration of the exhibition, Flanagan was presented as an art installation resting on the hospital bed, 'his home-away-from-home' as Linda Kauffman calls it.[51] Visitors were welcome to interact with him and many took the opportunity to sit by his side and chat about the work, ask questions or share their personal experiences with illness and disability. Periodically and without notice, Rose would lift Flanagan by a rope that was attached to his ankles and a pulley and for some time he would remain hanging from the ceiling upside down, with his hospital gown sliding off, revealing his naked frail body. In concluding his review, Rugoff praises Flanagan for pointing up 'art's potentially therapeutic side effects' and for reclaiming 'the perverse bodies' that remain culturally invisible (Figure 3.13).[52]

Despite the marked differences in Bowery's and Flanagan's artistic practices, the materiality of the body signifies for both a cultural battlefield for calling attention to non-normative identities and experiences. For Tilroe, Bowery's 'extreme manipulation' in his costuming translates to 'mockery of a culture that reduces the body to an efficiency machine'.[53] Likewise, Flanagan's body, marked by sickness and pain, questions, scholar and performance

Figure 3.13: Bob Flanagan performing during *Visiting Hours* at the Santa Monica Museum of Art, Santa Monica, 1992. Photograph by Scott Boberg. Courtesy of ONE Archives at the University of Southern California, Los Angeles.

artist Martin O'Brien writes, the highly problematic modernist concept of the body as a vigorous machine, a view that excludes the complex human experiences of chronic illness and disability.[54] Whether through performative costuming or raw masochism, they both celebrate the body by transgressing its boundaries. Yet, in light of Bowery's remarkable plasticity in experimenting with visual language and role-playing, *The Laugh of No. 12* could be viewed as a spectacular showcase of extremity in which BDSM aesthetics are employed as a fitting fashion statement to serve the concept. Instead, Flanagan's investment in BDSM 'has nothing to do with style' but 'pain management and the consequences of dependence', C. Carr notes; his lifestyle appears to be 'completely unglamorous' and 'far removed from the leatherclad ideal'.[55] Powerfully affective, Flanagan's strictly autobiographical work derives from honesty; hence, he rejected the label 'performance artist' for himself.

By elevating his bedridden body as artwork, Flanagan opens a dialogue regarding the role of the museum and art more broadly as channels of personal and political agency. O'Brien, who also has CF and has collaborated with Rose numerous times, appreciates Flanagan's performance in *Visiting Hours* for its dynamic reframing of the hospital bed from an 'emblem of illness' and 'endurance' to a site of political signification.[56] Turning the museum space into a fully functioning hospital room allows Flanagan to deconstruct its conventional purpose and blurs the distinction between artist and patient. Most importantly, he collapses medicine with BDSM; the erotic body suspension above the hospital bed of pain allows him to transform his inevitable submissiveness to the medical apparatus into a kinky submissiveness to pleasure. That way, O'Brien argues, Flanagan 'redefine[s] the role of the patient, imagining his endurance as a worthwhile activity towards self-ownership'.[57]

Flanagan's performance calls attention to his perplexing relationship with disability and sexual perversity. By embodying sickness not just literally but metaphorically due to his non-normative sexual practice, he confronts stereotypical expectations surrounding sick bodies and, as Kauffman writes, 'challenge[s] society's most cherished assumptions about the body's integrity and rectitude'.[58] Carrie Sandahl expands this point further and argues that by deviating from traditional connotations of disability, which appear to be emasculating, Flanagan proposes an alternative model of masculinity that complicates the patriarchal model of male dominance and exposes gender construction.[59] Helplessness, asexuality, infantilization and other negative connotations of disability (especially the latter's permanent forms) are theatricalized and eroticized in Flanagan's empowering representation. His disability is not portrayed as an obstacle to embodying the masculine ideal but 'as exactly what made him a man, what made him a masochist', Sandahl writes, urging for a reconsideration of the meaning of masculinity.[60]

Nevertheless, the political efficacy of *Visiting Hours* is not limited to empowering subjecthood and resisting clichés about disability and masculinity, but lies in its power to generate affect, driven by realness, and in providing a space where visitors were confronted by honesty. As Kauffman maintains, spectators were forced to face their own anxieties and clashing emotions about illness, desire, voyeurism, eroticism and fear.[61] Flanagan's availability and unpretentious interaction with visitors created a sort of community platform where these emotions could surface and taboo subjects and intimate concerns about death, disability, suffering, and sexuality could be shared and discussed. Moving beyond the banality of suffering and pain, Flanagan embraces extremity in Johnson's terms, that is by 'attempt[ing] to dissolve or buckle the strictures of the category of art, hybridising it with the limits of life itself'.[62]

The Politics of Blood

Athey's highly uncomfortable autobiographical performances are possibly the best example of this kind of queer masochistic work and have been widely discussed for their association with pleasure and pain, the AIDS crisis and the unreasonable political controversy during the US culture wars. Coming on the art scene via the underground club culture of Los Angeles, Athey shares with Bowery a similar subcultural outset since the work of both sprung out of two very distinctive (yet significantly divergent) club scenes that fostered their need for experimentation and informed their aesthetics and artistic identities at large. Athey's performances date back to 1981 when he and Rozz Williams, frontman of deathrock band Christian Death, made for a brief period a series of interventions, usually in clubs, under the name Premature Ejaculation. However, it was at Club FUCK! during the early 1990s (followed by Sin-a-matic and other club nights) when Athey solidified his artistic signature and developed some of his early performance pieces after almost a decade of inactivity largely due to drug addiction.

Although short-lived, Club FUCK! was a crucial venture at the intersection of post-punk, queer nightlife and performance art at a time of immense marginalization of non-conforming queer people and alternative sexual identities largely due to the moral panic caused by the rapid spread of HIV/AIDS. The weekly club night debuted in 1989 at Basgo's Disco in Silver Lake out of a need for an inclusive space that would embrace queerness, industrial and acid house music, fetishism and BDSM, aspects that were missing from and were not well received in the sleek gay discos of West Hollywood.[63] The cramped space of Club FUCK!, which was essentially an open room with a bar and a makeshift platform, pioneered performances that celebrated a broad spectrum of BDSM expression: from whipping and bondage to live piercing by Modern Primitive enthusiasts like Athey, who as a regular go-go dancer showed off his strikingly decorated body with tribal-style tattoos or performed vignettes that culminated in his early works (Figure 3.14).

Martyrs & Saints, Athey's first fully formed performance piece since the Premature Ejaculation actions, was developed at Club FUCK! as a series of standalone ten-minute demonstrations; the full performance premiered at Los Angeles Contemporary Exhibitions in 1992 as the first part of what became known as the *Torture Trilogy* (1992–95). These premature club performances as well as the *Torture Trilogy* as a whole reflect the anxieties, stigmatization and devastation of the queer community, which in the early 1990s witnessed the highest rate of AIDS-related deaths. Coping with the loss of an immense number of friends and being HIV-positive himself, Athey was driven by 'frustration, grief, anger [and] despair', whereas the explicitly sexual nature and exhibitionism of his performances served as 'an affirmation of life'.[64] This affirmation was ardently espoused at Club FUCK! whose 'resolute agenda seemed to be: exploring how to have desire in the thick of an epidemic', Bhaskar Sarkar observes.[65] The proliferation of queer bodies on display, whether heavily adorned,

Figure 3.14: Ron Athey go-go dancing at Club FUCK!, Los Angeles, 1991. Photograph by Rush Riddle. Courtesy of ONE Archives at the University of Southern California, Los Angeles.

manipulated, marked or in crisis, conveyed the collective struggle towards visibility and the striving of the community to come to grips with the stigma attached to it. For Sarkar, who used to be a regular, Club FUCK! provided a platform for this 'new breed of "industrial-strength queers" who wanted to shake off the precarity of the AIDS crisis to re-emerge as resilient social subjects, unapologetic about the continuing centrality of atypical sexual mores in their lives'.[66]

Apart from Athey's iconic presence, Rick Castro, Fakir Musafar, Bob Flanagan, Sheree Rose, Catherine Opie and Johanna Went are some of the artists involved in Club FUCK!, which Andrew Henkes reasonably describes as 'the avant-garde of nightclubs and a nursery for art'.[67] In a similar fashion to Bowery's Taboo, its intimate ambience and sense of community started to crumble when the club night was moved to Dragonfly in West Hollywood in 1993 and attracted the attention of the press and outsiders. A few months later, Club FUCK! was forced to stop running after a worried attendee complained to the police about illegal activity upon witnessing a challenging BDSM performance that included nudity. This resulted in a police raid and the arrest of 27 individuals the following week. Although in the long run no conviction was deemed possible without substantial evidence, the club night was never revived. The threats by the authorities to revoke the liquor licence of any venue that would host the event disheartened any attempt for a resurgence.

Athey's performances of extremity were brutally informed by the harsh reality of the AIDS epidemic and served as a platform for 'exorcising cultural and social demons'.[68] Involving the participation of a group of Athey's friends as performers, the widely discussed *Torture Trilogy* includes a series of performance pieces that negotiate suffering, desire, homophobia and loss via the highly symbolic use of the dissident body in pain. *Martyrs & Saints* was followed by the much controversial *4 Scenes in A Harsh Life* (1994) and, finally, *Deliverance* (1995). The complex and deeply allegorical vignettes of all three performances blend seamlessly a variety of contradicting aesthetics and allusions soaked in blood that mainly stems from Athey's personal experiences; his frenzied religious upbringing as a Pentecostal child prodigy, his struggle with addiction and illness, tragic loss and queer desire are infused with Modern Primitivism, 'neo-tribal' rituals, BDSM, religious iconography and sexual acts.

Athey's appropriation of Christian martyrology and esoterica features heavily in the trilogy and was aided by body modification techniques and other extreme practices. Mary Richards, who parallels performances of wounding and bloodletting like Athey's to the sacrificial body in religious representations of Christianity, attests to the social critique the marked body in performance can generate as 'a moral conduit through which [others'] suffering may be memorialized and remembered'.[69] This applies quite literally to Athey who appropriates the iconic representation of the martyrdom of St Sebastian almost obsessively in many of his performances, empowering it with contemporary meanings. A third-century martyr, St Sebastian is commonly depicted as a semi-nude young man bound to a pole with his flesh penetrated by arrows as punishment by the Romans for not renouncing his Christian faith. During the Middle Ages the saint also acquired an abiding reputation as a defender against the plague, affording him a symbolism of recovery and healing that resonated deeply with Athey's existential crisis. The homoerotic imagery of St Sebastian, Richards notes elsewhere, is appropriated by Athey to enact 'a melodrama of suffering' in which the HIV-positive body is presented 'as a sort of post-modern secularised saint', denying the relinquishing of its queer identity.[70]

The martyrdom is performed by Athey and his troupe in the closing vignette of *Martyrs & Saints*, following a powerful sequence that negotiates loss, the harsh reality of AIDS patients and homoerotic desire via overstimulating abject narratives where queer bodies are allowed to be overwhelmingly vulnerable. Amidst a wild concoction of allegoric fantasy, medical procedures, religious iconography, and BDSM aesthetics and practices, the performers' bodies are brutally pierced, mummified, violated and exposed, whipped and subjected to deliberate bleeding. Towards the end, Athey, naked and trembling, with his hands tied above his head, which is pierced by a crown of thorns assembled from needles and acrylic threads, submits himself completely to one of his collaborators enacting a Roman soldier who pushes arrows made of long medical needles into Athey's tattooed body. For the finale, the soldier pulls out the needles from Athey's forehead letting blood rush out all over his face, conveying the relief of redemption (Figure 3.15).

Some typical activities across Athey's performances, such as extended body piercing, bloodletting, scarification, castration, penetration, and constriction, constitute highly uncomfortable imagery that potentially bears a shocking quality for some spectators and, due to this likely possibility, would certainly have gained Bowery's admiration. For Athey, however, these actions do not sum up 'a strategy of shock' but rather a gesture of 'generosity' in exposing the unexposed and disclosing the self in its most vulnerable state to elicit the spectators' emotional response.[71] Jennifer Doyle, who has discussed Athey's work in depth, identifies its difficulty not in the strong imagery and extreme acts but in the uncomfortable feelings that spectators may be confronted with; it is not about what will happen to the performers who carry out these acts, but what will happen to us, the spectators, in terms of emotion.[72] Athey's work can be difficult, she maintains, because of the way it spectacularly combines pleasure and pain, speaking openly to larger social experiences – most arrestingly the

Figure 3.15: Ron Athey performing *Martyrs & Saints* at PS122, New York, 1993. Photograph by Dona Ann McAdams. © Dona Ann McAdams.

AIDS crisis that spectators might identify with. Its significance, therefore, is not limited to challenging mundane perceptions of what is perceived as art but lies in its capacity to expand the debate from art discourse to the social sphere and essentially 'speak to quite fundamental aspects of being a social subject'.[73] Delving into strong feelings in performance as generators of social and political effects, Amelia Jones considers Athey's work 'among the most excessive and overtly affect-driven art practices known internationally'.[74] The indication of pain, for instance, which is so prominent in his work, may remind spectators of their own frailty and precariousness as physical and emotional beings but also the specific socio-political context it actively responds to. In Jones's words, Athey's work has caused her 'tender and often uncomfortable sadness, fear, love, longing and joy', feelings that have the power to transform into political awareness and community building in difficult times.[75]

It is this honesty and 'realness', both in aesthetic terms and intention, that *The Laugh of No. 12* lacks, undermining its political and social potential. This is by no means to suggest that Bowery's practice as a whole is a frivolous aesthetic venture unable to provoke strong feelings and substantial socio-political effects; his shock tactics, witty cultural appropriation and innovative vision in performative costuming are irreplaceable contributions to queer visual culture in their own right. Yet, the empty masochism of *The Laugh of No. 12*, even though it might have provided a challenging spectacle for some, avoids any kind of communication that directly speaks to the darkest fears of the affected community. Not that disabled or sick artists are obliged to function through their work as spokespersons or representatives of specific communities – especially when they might not identify as such – but the absence of this aspect makes *The Laugh of No. 12* appear fragile when discussed alongside performances of extremity that make use of BDSM as a form of community building or what Jones calls 'implicit activism'.[76]

Athey's work remained stigmatized in art institutions in the United States for many years due to a moral panic and a subsequent Congressional debate triggered by a misleading article falsely alleging that his performances exposed the audience to HIV-infected blood. Whether Athey's performances induce strong feelings towards social transformation or inflame veiled homophobic and AIDS-phobic sentiments, they do so by refusing to mask the reality of the sick body. The body instead takes centre stage, it is gloriously cut wide open, offering generously the spectacle of bloodletting. The deliberately bleeding body in public 'performs a refusal', Richards writes, as it frustrates the regulation forced on wounded bodies by medical or other interventions.[77] In Athey's performances, its presence becomes radical, not least because the bleeding body in contemporary culture 'has come to represent a physically weakened and potentially vulnerable sick body in a society that refuses to see these bodies'.[78] Their unapologetic visibility serves as an act of empowerment of society's neglected and cultivates awareness of suffering, posing a serious threat to the strictly policed structures of art and culture that regulate and sustain control over social and political power.

In a largely homophobic and AIDS-phobic society in which people with AIDS were expected to hide their fear and mortality, Athey's confrontational work becomes dangerous and vile 'because he does not keep these experiences of violence, self-destruction, and disease private', sex theorist and activist Patrick Califia writes.[79] By contrast, Bowery's idea of radicality in *The Laugh of No. 12* (as well as the performance at Industria) seems to be premised on the potential shock effect of BDSM and the prospect of causing embarrassment or triggering an upset response from the audience. His accidental bloodletting during the performance could possibly provide an opportunity for the kinds of imaginative or political effects Athey's work is keen to create but is anxiously hidden from view as an unexpected mistake.

What eventually distinguishes works such as Athey's and Flanagan's from Bowery's artificial extravaganza in *The Laugh of No. 12*, making the former more politically compelling and thus threatening to the social order, is their crude realness. In Athey's work 'realness' is 'a sense of being anchored, something with weight; not fantastical in origin, and definitely not strategic or polite'.[80] Unlike the so-called 'AIDS plays' of the 1980s that portrayed a carefully staged and blunted representation of the disease, Athey 'presents an uncensored version of what he understands to be the "reality" of sickness [...] and confronts the audience with his "real" HIV positive body' amid the anxieties that blood elicited at the peak of the AIDS crisis, Richards argues.[81] It is realness that makes Doyle feel 'more like a witness than a spectator' and Califia 'culpable' and 'a co-conspirator' when attending Athey's performances.[82] Commentators on Flanagan's work also stress the importance of realness in relation to his artistic BDSM play. Carr claims that 'Flanagan was all about real and shameless self-disclosure'.[83] Similarly, Lynda Hart views his work as 'unremittingly "real"' and maintains that by transferring his intimate BDSM practice to the public domain, Flanagan essentially 'recharged' those activities that had become dull from repetition, adding 'the dimension of exhibitionism'.[84]

Bowery's attachment to artifice and metamorphosis may preclude the possibility of 'realness' – which acquires political agency through the exposure of the vulnerable self – to manifest in his work. It does, however, create a breeding ground for challenging the hegemony of so-called normative bodies through freak aesthetics or troubling the binary gender system through ostentatious trans-queer embodiments. An infamous performance of his for an AIDS benefit that involved an enema douching the audience reveals an alternative strategy in dealing with difficult and sensitive issues, one that is anchored in burlesque humorous transgression. In contrast to the unconvincing extremity of *The Laugh of No. 12*, this work powerfully disrupts narratives of illness and disability in significantly different ways to Flanagan's and Athey's more politically acute BDSM tactics.

Humour of Sickness

Despite their disparate agendas and varied artistic practices, Bowery and Athey shared a mutual admiration for each other's work that influenced their aesthetics. *The Laugh of No. 12* and Bowery's broader interest in BDSM and body modification possibly came about after meeting Athey in 1994 in London, where the latter was invited to perform at the ICA, doing also a performance at a fetish party held at Milch, a radical gallery space. Vice versa, Athey embraced Bowery's artifice and deranged glamour in a short solo, *Trojan Whore* (1995), which he devised as a tribute to Bowery after his death.[85] Moreover, he acquired one of Bowery's costumes – an impressive burgundy velour gown – that he has honoured in his performances many times, infusing it with new meaning. Whereas in photographs Bowery, through his excessive styling and melodramatic posing, appears as a detached object for admiration, Athey, wrapped in the same gown, comes across as more relatable to queers' struggles by 'instantiat[ing] a very queer notion of community built on discomfort and pain', Alpesh Kantilal Patel interestingly claims.[86] This interpretation likely stems from Athey's ability to transform disaster into agency, using extremity to overcome the anxieties and harrowing experiences of AIDS that devastated the queer community. In contrast, Bowery never explicitly addressed his illness in his work and the posthumous analyses of *The Laugh of No. 12* rely heavily on speculative interpretations of his feelings about it.

Bowery kept his HIV-positive status a secret even from his closest friends (apart from Tilley) and he was embarrassed about it, although his last words in the performance were ironically a declaration against embarrassment. His determination to keep his diagnosis private stemmed from his anxiety to be remembered as a visionary rather than someone with AIDS. During his final days in the hospital he jokingly instructed Tilley to spread rumours after his death that we had suddenly relocated to Papua New Guinea to help the Indigenous peoples.

This assumption that coming out as HIV-positive would overshadow his artistic legacy was very likely conditioned by the frenzied reaction and moral panic the global epidemic generated through the regular sensationalist stories and negative representations of people with AIDS in the media. With over 2.5 million confirmed cases of HIV/AIDS by the early 1990s worldwide and coming to terms with the fact that anyone without exception could potentially be exposed to the virus – and not just gay men, sex workers and IV-drug users, as it was initially believed – the media on both sides of the Atlantic took on a shared mission of raising awareness among the 'respectable' general public (which they considered exclusively heterosexual), often misinforming it to satisfy their moralistic agenda. This strategy in combination with shocking images of emaciated people dying from AIDS complications and the extreme measures proposed by certain conservative representatives (such as quarantining, tattooing and even sterilizing HIV-positive persons) fuelled the demonization of gay men as depraved, reckless and promiscuous, leading to the irrational stigmatization, victimization and shaming of those living with the virus.[87] Remaining voiceless and inactive equated to complicity in institutional homophobia and the tragic consequences suffered by the queer community, hence, the slogan SILENCE=DEATH in the iconic poster by grassroots activist group ACT UP. Bowery's fearful denial of his illness might have precluded the possibility of creating politically engaged art as a form of AIDS activism, but under these turbulent socio-political circumstances his silence demands sympathy.

The only time Bowery was involved in any kind of politically charged venture was when he reluctantly agreed to perform at *Hearts in the Right Place*, an AIDS benefit cabaret at The Fridge on Valentine's Day in 1990. Distanced from AIDS activism, which he unfairly believed sustained a general feeling of victimhood, Bowery rehearsed ceaselessly a dance routine that involved squirting a water fountain from his bare ass using an enema, a spectacle that did not quite go as expected. His attire for the performance included a beaded corset that squeezed his chubby flesh creating a rich bosom, an elaborate headdress and glittery ankle boots. His genitals were covered by a self-made pubic wig known as a 'merkin'. To make an entrance, Bowery allegedly climbed on the shoulders of a friend – the film director Baillie Walsh – and put on a very long cloak that covered both, conveying the illusion of a queer, towering creature.

After taking the stage, Bowery clambered off Walsh's back, removed the cloak and danced around clumsily for a while until it was time for the highlight of the now-legendary performance. He bent down protruding his ass towards the spectators below and, according to Tilley's graphic account, 'a nasty stinking brown mess spurted out of his bottom' (which she puts down to his awfully tight corset), landing on the audience at the front 'who were all sitting at beautifully decorated round tables'.[88] Without losing focus, Bowery climbed back onto Walsh's shoulders, who had to endure the stench of the revolting mess smeared all over him, bringing the performance to a close (Figure 3.16). The scandalous performance was considered by some 'particularly tasteless' and offensive for an AIDS benefit and it also infuriated Lambeth Council, which tried to close the club down. Bowery defended himself by stating:

> If you've got AIDS it doesn't mean you've lost your sense of humour, does it? I didn't want to make concessions just because people were ill or dying. I was quite pleased with the hostile reaction. If anything I want to make reactions stronger. If I have to ask, 'Is this idea too sick?' I know I'm on the right track.[89]

Figure 3.16: Leigh Bowery performing at The Fridge, London, 1990. Photograph by Gordon Rainsford. Courtesy of the Bishopsgate Institute, London.

Bowery was never truly invested in gay politics, which he found dreary and depressing. Even his elaborate performative costuming functioned perhaps as a defensive mechanism or a form of escapism from bleak reality. Trapped within a meticulously crafted image of fabulousness, Bowery was terrified that revealing his HIV-positive status would lead people to pity him or interpret his outrageous behavior as mere anger stemming from his illness. Not unreasonably, however, the only scholarly reading of the performance at the AIDS benefit, posthumously by Bancroft, could not ignore the catalytic role his diagnosis might have played in the work and deciphers Bowery's scatological enthusiasm as a conduit of 'a troubled queer corporeality that is under attack' rather than just a humorous prank intended to shock.[90] As a medical procedure that can serve both as a hygienic preparation for sex and as a form of sexual stimulation within BDSM play, the enema gives emphasis to the anus both as a site of gay desire and a potential entry point for the virus via anal penetration. Bowery's body then turns into a metonymy of his personal experience with a terrible life-threatening disease, with the enema on stage culminating in a public spectacle of abjection where boundaries collapse, corporeal integrity diminishes and liminal subjectivities between life and death come to the fore, disturbing the order of things.

Abstaining from the morose, mournful or earnest tone of some forms of activism, which equally marks many works dealing with illness, Bowery's performance of extremity can be viewed as ineptly hilarious unless one found themselves in close proximity to the stage that evening. Bowery's sense of humour, which was often considered inappropriate and coarse by those close to him who endured his teasing, was most likely employed here as a strategy of survival or of anti-sentimentalism against the misery surrounding AIDS discourse. It agrees with what Gregg Bordowitz calls 'a queer structure of feeling', namely 'a set of cultural strategies of survival for queers' witnessed in AIDS media activism and art, that appreciates the ridiculous, values masquerade and adopts mockery.[91]

Sigmund Freud's assertion about the liberating power of humour as one of the great strategies of the human mind to circumvent the compulsion to suffer is useful in getting to grips with such works as well as Bowery's performance.[92] Freud theorizes humour as a rebellious tactic of the narcissistic ego for avoiding trauma and denying being negatively affected by harsh reality, which instead turns into an opportunity for pleasure. This could also be the case in the acidic, self-lacerating and absurd humour found symptomatically in some art of the same era dealing with the AIDS crisis – Jerome Caja's painting *Bozo Fucks Death* (1988) and David McDiarmid's *Rainbow Aphorisms* series (1993–95) come to mind – or, most notably, the radical low-budget zines *Infected Faggot Perspectives* (1991–93) and *Diseased Pariah News* (1990–99), created by and for queers living with the virus. Both functioned as supportive forums for coping with the reality of HIV/AIDS without victimizing those diagnosed with it and retaliated against the widespread brutal dehumanizing representations of ill (typically) gay men in the media, giving space to positive portrayals of people living with HIV/AIDS as active and in control, resilient and worthy human beings with bodies and desires. And it was this suspicion embedded in every homophobic consciousness – that 'infected' persons might still be promiscuous or at least sexually active – that media put at ease with what Douglas Crimp calls 'phobic images' of bodies wasting away.[93]

Clearly in line with this anarchic mentality, Bowery's subversive performance can be viewed as a frustrated backlash of exasperation mediated by abject humour that aims to disrupt our assumptions, emotions and perspectives. His valuable contribution as an artist who eventually died from AIDS complications, fully realized only after his unexpected death, is his perpetual lust for life and creativity that he deliberately refused to take the chance of tarnishing by coming out as sick or surrendering himself to public pity. His determination to keep up with his active lifestyle, auspiciously afforded by his overall good health until he was hospitalized shortly before he died, debunks the fantasy of haggard queer corporeality suffering as a consequence of depraved sexual habits, a popular representation that became a trite symbol in the service of veiled homophobia.

It is for this reason that Bowery's body deserves to be seen in the aftermath of his death as triumphant and glorious no matter the political slippage I sometimes detect in his performances. His narcissistic desire might have prevented him from exposing his 'realness' and the empty masochism he employed might fall affectively short in comparison to Flanagan's or Athey's brutally painful honesty, but they all point to an infinite play with an array of aesthetics and signifiers where the spectacular queer body is alive and in focus. By manipulating, altering and glamming up the body, be it in leather or glitter, Bowery performs his own resistance to normalization or the cultural politics of illness for he decisively exercises the right to be in control of one's body. Whether this right is asserted by deeply and openly engaging in BDSM as Flanagan and Athey do or by performative costuming and deranged humour, it remains in essence a shared objective among those who feel excluded from or disparaged in dominant discourses and representations.

Notes

1. Sue Tilley, *Leigh Bowery: The Life and Times of an Icon* (London: Hodder & Stoughton, 1997), p. 201.

2. Hubert Klocker, 'Viennese Actionism/Bodypolitics', in *Viennese Actionism: Günter Brus, Otto Muehl, Hermann Nitsch, Rudolf Schwarzkogler* (Seville: Ministry of Culture of Andalusia, 2008), pp. 21–30 (p. 21).
3. Klocker, p. 21.
4. See Thomas McEvilley, *The Triumph of Anti-Art: Conceptual and Performance Art in the Formation of Post-Modernism* (Kingston: McPherson & Company, 2005).
5. Philip Ursprung, '"Catholic Tastes": Hurting and Healing the Body in Viennese Actionism in the 1960s', in *Performing the Body/ Performing the Text*, ed. by Amelia Jones and Andrew Stephenson (London: Routledge, 1999), pp. 138–52 (p. 146).
6. Klocker, p. 27.
7. Hubert Klocker, 'The Dramaturgy of the Organic', in *Viennese Aktionism*, ed. by Hubert Klocker (Klagenfurt: Ritter Verlag, 1989), pp. 41–55 (p. 49).
8. Klocker, 'Viennese Actionism/Bodypolitics', p. 27.
9. Robert Hughes, 'The Decline and Fall of the Avant-Garde', *Time*, 18 December 1972, pp. 40–41 (pp. 40, 41).
10. The myth of Schwarzkogler's acts of self-mutilation is also reiterated in RoseLee Goldberg, *Performance Art: From Futurism to the Present* (London: Thames & Hudson, 2011); and Henry M. Sayre, *The Object of Performance: The American Avant-Garde since 1970* (Chicago: The University of Chicago Press, 1989). It was influentially debunked in Kristine Stiles, 'Readings: Performance and Its Objects', *Arts Magazine*, November 1990, pp. 35–47.
11. Kathy O'Dell, *Contract with the Skin: Masochism, Performance Art, and the 1970s* (Minneapolis: University of Minnesota Press, 1998), p. 2.
12. O'Dell, p. 2.
13. Dominic Johnson, *Unlimited Action: The Performance of Extremity in the 1970s* (Manchester: Manchester University Press, 2019), p. 7.
14. Lara Shalson, *Performing Endurance: Art and Politics since 1960* (Cambridge: Cambridge University Press, 2018), p. 7.
15. Anne Marsh, 'Einhorn unter Tauben', in *Leigh Bowery: Verwandlungskünstler*, ed. by Angela Stief (Vienna: Piet Meyer Verlag, 2015), pp. 161–82 (p. 168). A script in English was provided by the author.
16. Robyn Healy, 'Where the Sun Shines: Leigh Bowery the Super-Fashion Heavyweight', in *Take a Bowery: The Art and (Larger than)*

Life of Leigh Bowery (Sydney: Museum of Contemporary Art, 2004), pp. 78–85 (p. 83).

17. Hilton Als, 'Cruel Story of Youth', in *Leigh Bowery*, ed. by Robert Violette (London: Violette Editions, 1998), pp. 10–25 (p. 22).
18. Healy, p. 85.
19. Karen Gonzalez Rice, *Long Suffering: American Endurance Art as Prophetic Witness* (Ann Arbor: University of Michigan Press, 2016), p. 1.
20. Victoria Pitts, *In the Flesh: The Cultural Politics of Body Modification* (New York: Palgrave Macmillan, 2003), p. 7.
21. Bowery is shown having his cheeks pierced in *Unstitched* (1990), a short film by Baillie Walsh that was often used as a backdrop to his performances. Similarly, scenes of body piercing can be found in some of the early experimental short films of Richard Kern who was a key figure of the Cinema of Transgression, a brief underground film movement in New York's Lower East Side during the 1980s. His documentary *Pierce* (1986), in which his girlfriend at the time is getting her nipples pierced, recalls Sandy Daley's earlier film *Robert Having His Nipple Pierced* (1968), which shows Robert Mapplethorpe undergoing the procedure. Later, in *The Sewing Circle* (1992), Kern filmed Kembra Pfahler having her labia sewn up by a friend in an act of sexualized control.
22. Jack Jaeger, 'Interview with Leigh Bowery', in *Take a Bowery: The Art and (Larger than) Life of Leigh Bowery* (Sydney: Museum of Contemporary Art, 2004), pp. 152–53 (p. 153).
23. V. Vale and Andrea Juno, 'Fakir Musafar', in *Modern Primitives: An Investigation of Contemporary Adornment and Ritual*, ed. by V. Vale and Andrea Juno (San Francisco: Re/Search, 1989), pp. 6–36 (p. 13). Emphasis in original.
24. Pitts, p. 126.
25. Pitts, p. 24.
26. Pitts, p. 133.
27. Katharina Sykora, 'Ego-Abenteuer zwischen Aktion und Bild', in *Leigh Bowery: Verwandlungskünstler*, ed. by Angela Stief (Vienna: Piet Meyer Verlag, 2015), pp. 209–32 (p. 216). Author's translation.
28. Sykora, p. 216.
29. Christian Klesse, '"Modern Primitivism": Non-Mainstream Body Modification and Racialized Representation', in *Body Modification*, ed. by Mike Featherstone (London: Sage Publications, 2000), pp. 15–38 (p. 18).
30. Klesse, p. 34.

31. Vale and Juno, p. 30.
32. Richard Torry, 'What about Your Sex Life?', in *Leigh Bowery*, ed. by Robert Violette (London: Violette Editions, 1998), pp. 198–209 (p. 207).
33. Alison Bancroft, 'Leigh Bowery: Queer in Fashion, Queer in Art', *Sexualities*, 15.1 (2012), 68–79 (p. 71).
34. Bancroft, p. 71.
35. Jaeger, p. 153.
36. Ted Polhemus, 'The Performance of Pain', *Performance Research*, 3.3 (1998), 97–104 (p. 100).
37. Polhemus, p. 98.
38. See Dominic Johnson, 'Intimacy and Risk in Live Art', in *Histories and Practices of Live Art*, ed. by Deirdre Heddon and Jennie Klein (Basingstoke: Palgrave Macmillan, 2012), pp. 121–47.
39. See *Zapp Magazine #2* (Amsterdam: Zapp Productions, 1994) [VHS]. Author's transcription.
40. Anna Tilroe, 'The Laugh of No. 13', in *Take a Bowery: The Art and (Larger than) Life of Leigh Bowery* (Sydney: Museum of Contemporary Art, 2004), pp. 120–28 (p. 120).
41. Tilroe, p. 124.
42. See Bancroft.
43. Bancroft, p. 78.
44. See O'Dell. The author mentions performance artists Holly Hughes, John Fleck, Tim Miller and Karen Finley who became known as the NEA Four after they had their National Endowment for the Arts grant cut in 1990 for obscenity. Artist David Wojnarowicz, whose work was also targeted, is another well-known case.
45. Marla Carlson, *Performing Bodies in Pain: Medieval and Post-Modern Martyrs, Mystics, and Artists* (New York: Palgrave Macmillan, 2010), p. 118.
46. Contrary to popular belief, Flanagan nailed his penis only in private – including once for a video by Sheree Rose. *Nailed*, a performance in which Flanagan nailed his scrotum, was first staged at Olio performance space in Los Angeles in October 1989. A revised version was performed the following month at Southern Exposure art space in San Francisco.
47. See Bob Flanagan, *The Pain Journal* (Los Angeles: Semiotext(e), 2000).
48. Andrea Juno and V. Vale, *Bob Flanagan: Supermasochist* (New York: Re/Search Publications, 1993), p. 3.

49. Juno and Vale, p. 60.
50. Ralph Rugoff, 'Visiting Hours', *Grand Street*, 53, Summer 1995, pp. 65–73 (p. 66).
51. Linda S. Kauffman, 'Sadomedicine: Bob Flanagan's "Visiting Hours" and Last Rites', *Performance Research*, 3.3 (1998), 33–40 (p. 36).
52. Rugoff, p. 66.
53. Tilroe, p. 128.
54. See Martin O'Brien, 'Lie Back and Take It: BDSM, Biomedicine and the Hospital Bed in the Work of Bob Flanagan and Sheree Rose', *Body, Space and Technology*, 15 (2016), <http://doi.org/10.16995/bst.18>.
55. C. Carr, 'The Pain Artist', in *On Edge: Performance at the End of the Twentieth Century* (Middletown: Wesleyan University Press, 2008), pp. 321–24 (p. 322).
56. O'Brien.
57. O'Brien.
58. Kauffman, p. 40.
59. See Carrie Sandahl, 'Bob Flanagan: Taking It Like a Man', *Journal of Dramatic Theory and Criticism*, 15.1 (2000), 97–106.
60. Sandahl, p. 98.
61. See Kauffman.
62. Johnson, *Unlimited Action*, p. 15.
63. See Andrew J. Henkes, 'A Party for the "Freaks": Performance, Deviance and Communitas at *Club Fuck!*, 1989–1993', *Journal of American Culture*, 36.4 (2013), 284–95.
64. Dominic Johnson, 'Perverse Martyrologies: An Interview with Ron Athey', in *The Art of Living: An Oral History of Performance Art* (London: Palgrave, 2015), pp. 195–218 (p. 205).
65. Bhaskar Sarkar, 'Industrial Strength Queer: Club Fuck! and the Reorientation of Desire', *Media Fields Journal*, 7 (2013), <http://mediafieldsjournal.squarespace.com/industrial-strength-queer/> [accessed 27 February 2025].
66. Sarkar.
67. Henkes, p. 294.
68. Johnson, 'Perverse Martyrologies', p. 214.
69. Mary Richards, 'Specular Suffering: (Staging) the Bleeding Body', *PAJ: A Journal of Performance and Art*, 30.1 (2008), 108–19 (p. 112).
70. Mary Richards, 'Ron Athey, A.I.D.S. and the Politics of Pain', *Body, Space and Technology*, 3.2 (2003), <http://doi.org/10.16995/bst.224>.

71. Johnson, 'Perverse Martyrologies', p. 199.
72. See Jennifer Doyle, *Hold It against Me: Difficulty and Emotion in Contemporary Art* (Durham, NC: Duke University Press, 2013).
73. Doyle, p. 20.
74. Amelia Jones, 'How Ron Athey Makes Me Feel: The Political Potential of Upsetting Art', in *Pleading in the Blood: The Art and Performances of Ron Athey*, ed. by Dominic Johnson (London: Live Art Development Agency and Intellect, 2013), pp. 152–78 (p. 166).
75. Jones, p. 158.
76. Jones, p. 167.
77. Richards, 'Specular Suffering', p. 118.
78. Richards, 'Specular Suffering', p. 118.
79. Patrick Califia, *Speaking Sex to Power: The Politics of Queer Sex* (San Francisco: Cleis Press, 2002), p. 363.
80. Johnson, 'Perverse Martyrologies', p. 207.
81. Richards, 'Ron Athey, A.I.D.S. and the Politics of Pain'.
82. Jennifer Doyle, 'Blood Work & "Art Criminals"', *Art21 Magazine*, 10 December 2008, <https://magazine.art21.org/2008/12/10/blood-work-art-criminals/> [accessed 27 February 2025]; and Califia, p. 364.
83. Carr, p. 321.
84. Lynda Hart, *Between the Body and the Flesh: Performing Sadomasochism* (New York: Columbia University Press, 1998), p. 139.
85. *Trojan Whore* was the opening performance of a memorial event for Bowery held at the Matthew Marks Gallery in New York. During the performance Athey emerged in drag after he was cut free from the layers of black gaffer tape he was fully wrapped within and pulled out of his asshole a seemingly endless string of pearls.
86. Alpesh Kantilal Patel, 'Leigh Bowery Cape', in *Queer Communion: Ron Athey*, ed. by Amelia Jones and Andy Campbell (Bristol: Intellect, 2020), pp. 323–26 (p. 326).
87. See Simon Watney, *Policing Desire: Pornography, AIDS and the Media* (Minneapolis: University of Minnesota Press, 1987).
88. Tilley, p. 199.
89. Quoted in Tilley, p. 199.
90. Bancroft, p. 75.
91. Gregg Bordowitz, 'The AIDS Crisis Is Ridiculous', in *The AIDS Crisis Is Ridiculous and Other Writings, 1986–2003*, ed. by James Meyer (Cambridge: The MIT Press, 2006), pp. 43–67 (p. 49).

92. See Sigmund Freud, 'Humour', in *The Standard Edition of the Complete Psychological Works of Sigmund Freud, Volume XXI (1927–1931): The Future of an Illusion, Civilization and Its Discontents and Other Works*, ed. by James Strachey (London: Vintage, 2001), pp. 159–66.
93. Douglas Crimp, 'Portraits of People with Aids', in *Melancholia and Moralism: Essays on AIDS and Queer Politics* (Cambridge: The MIT Press, 2002), pp. 83–107 (p. 106).

Chapter 4
Beyond Drag: Trans-Queer Embodiments and Repronormativity

In 1989, Leigh Bowery devised a performance for the opening of the exhibition *Success Is a Job in New York: The Early Art and Business of Andy Warhol* at the Serpentine Gallery in London. Accompanied by Nicola Bateman and Mr. Pearl, Bowery entered one of the gallery rooms and surrounded by an excited and curious group of visitors he quickly took off his flowy gown, elaborate helmet and boots. Almost naked with his genitals covered with a bushy blond merkin and his fleshy chest squashed inside a bra made of tape, with a shaved head and no bold make-up, he carried out a live ritual of physical transformation under a soundtrack of acid house. Mr. Pearl removed the bra with a pair of scissors while Bowery, with Bateman's help, put on a tight garment that looked like a cropped vest extending into a mask covering his entire head and most of his face. This strange mint green creation, with a bunch of feathers sticking out at the top of the head and a clownish red nose, gave Bowery an appearance similar to a *Muppet Show* character. As he posed momentarily to entertain the well-dressed spectators, Bateman took out of a bag a fuchsia corseted bodysuit and in no time the operation to get Bowery inside began.

For the next few minutes, the three of them struggled to get Bowery's corpulent body inside the garment and when they eventually succeeded a marathon of lacing commenced. The arms, torso, hips, legs – the whole back of the bodysuit from feet to nape – consisted of dense lacing, which Bateman and Mr. Pearl made sure was fastened firmly while Bowery's imposing figure stood still. When the legs and arms were laced up, Bateman, who was styled as a classy lady with a neat hairdo and smart attire, stripped naked and walked among the spectators. Mr. Pearl continued lacing up Bowery's back while Bateman danced ferociously in the next room with a beer in her hand and a dildo attached to her crotch. The performance ended several minutes later once the last lace was fastened in Bowery's nape. The transformation was complete in the midst of cheers and applause. Standing tall and awfully restricted, Bowery took a few poses and with robotic but graceful movements left with Mr. Pearl.[1] The bulky individual who had entered the room looking like a male in crisis turned into a monstrous gender-ambiguous creature of commanding stature and vigorous shape. What the audience had just witnessed was an act of subjectification, a queer becoming (Figure 4.1).

Bowery's ability to employ a highly queer visual language that upsets human experience and disrupts the traditional binary construction of gender beyond conventional notions of drag is a recurring theme in his performative costuming and one that is routinely celebrated by commentators on his work. His intricate art production can arguably be acknowledged as a visual articulation of Eve Kosofsky Sedgwick's seminal definition of 'queer' as 'an open mesh of possibilities', which interestingly emerged around the same time.[2] This is not necessarily relevant only in relation to his dissonant, sexually enigmatic embodiments but also due to the complex nature of his practice, which defies categorization and troubles canonical narratives of art and performance. To use Henry Rogers' words, Bowery is 'quintessentially queer'.[3]

From the perspective of Lacanian psychoanalysis, Alison Bancroft views Bowery as 'a paradigm of queer sexualities' and the embodiment of transgressive jouissance.[4] Specifically, she identifies two key visual aspects that persist in Bowery's costuming, rendering his self-presentation profoundly queer. The first is concerned with his fixation on faked female bodily traits, such as the convincing illusion of a full cleavage and the realistic impression of female pubic hair. His commitment to achieving an artificial but passable vision of femaleness required a great deal

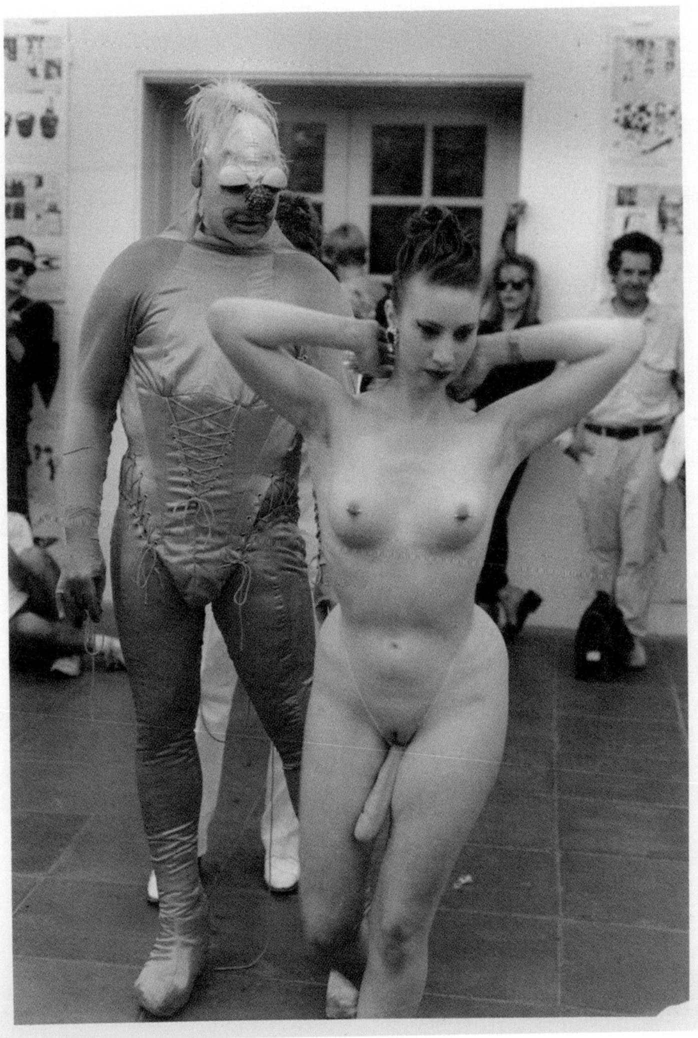

Figure 4.1: Leigh Bowery and Nicola Bateman performing at the Serpentine Gallery, London, 1989. Photograph by Gordon Rainsford. Courtesy of the Bishopsgate Institute, London.

of endurance and gaffer tape. The ample bosom underneath his elaborate bras and tops was the result of his chubby flesh being squeezed and secured into place with tape, while the triangular female hairy crotches, the merkins, were made from pieces of old wigs and glued onto his taped-back penis. The second visual aspect that Bancroft associates with Bowery's queer costuming is related to the ways he manipulates his head and especially the face, through which normatively gendered subjects become intelligible at first in the social world.

Tracing the ancient tradition of masquerade, Efrat Tseëlon touches on the liberating 'multiple metaphoric possibilities' of the masked face 'as a site of excess, ecstasy, intrigue and moral danger, harbouring erotic, riotous and mysterious associations'.[5] In terms of contemporary approaches to personhood, she asserts that masquerade challenges the modernist fiction of monolithic identity and the discourse of otherness it produces by representing not only the malleability of identity but also the embodiment of difference and the other. Whether transformed by layers of make-up that modified the features or stiflingly enveloped in fabric, Bowery's face is almost always concealed, making him a strange genderless being beyond human recognition. This disrupts normative narratives of essence and appearance, troubling, as a result, the inherent process of making sense of one's existence and gender. The floral ballgown he wore at the opening of Lucian Freud's retrospective at The Metropolitan Museum of Art in New York in 1993 is typical of this tendency. Covering almost every inch of bare skin, the long-sleeved dress that Bowery wore in front of Freud's monumental nude paintings of him had a fitted flat torso with a massive hoop skirt and a turtleneck that extended into a balaclava-like hood (Figure 4.2). Bowery's flagrant artifice contradicts the distinctively effortless aura of purity in Freud's paintings, which stemmed from the painter's antipathy, art critic Martin Gayford writes, for 'anything that obstructed his view of the natural, unadorned face and body'.[6]

Bowery's drastic transformation from an organic entity with rosy flesh in Freud's painting into a mysterious flashy creature with no face becomes a blaring statement of self-identification against essentialist-driven views on being and a playful repudiation perhaps of Freud's vision of Bowery's body. Their unlikely collaboration, which lasted over four years and arguably resulted

Figure 4.2: Leigh Bowery at the opening of Lucian Freud's exhibition at The Metropolitan Museum of Art, New York, 1993. Photograph by Don Pollard. © Don Pollard.

in some of Freud's greatest late works, evolved into a valuable experience for Bowery through which he learned to embrace his imperfections and be comfortable in his own skin. Their friendship would be a fruitful encounter for Freud too who proceeded to collaborate for paintings with Bowery's circle, most famously Sue Tilley, literally stripping them of their artificial freakishness and immortalizing their intimate unadorned side.[7]

Both the feminine signifiers and the masked face often coexist in Bowery's styling and, combined with his explosive demeanour, they disturb any sense of conventional aesthetic harmony and meaning. This constitutes a highly queer tactic because, as Tseëlon notes, the covered face allows awareness to shift to the body and, as a result, an array of different registers come into play.[8] A sense of Bowery's queer fusion is captured in John Maybury's experimental video *Read Only Memory* (1998), a 90-minute assemblage of archive footage, psychedelic effects and computer graphics supplemented by ambient experimental music. Scantily dressed in merkins, an assortment of tops and elaborate full-face headdresses, Bowery makes a few appearances throughout the video, dancing wildly in slow motion amidst trippy colours and embryonic digital manipulations. Although he is featured only briefly, his presence became emblematic of the work (Figure 4.3). In an article dedicated to Maybury's early experimental work, Gary Morris wonders rather bluntly whether Bowery's embodiment in *Read Only Memory* is that of 'a fat, naked woman' or 'a post-op tranny'.[9] Despite the demeaning language towards plus-size women and non-normatively gendered persons that testifies to society's conditioned intolerance when it comes to the disruption of norms, his questioning points to the queer effect of Bowery's mannerisms and performative costuming. His ponderous figure, which he seeks to accentuate rather than adjust to bodily ideals, and his alien looks construct a well-calculated grotesque spectacle that is distant from lucid representations of gender, conspicuously thwarting its normative expressions of femininity and masculinity.

Figure 4.3: John Maybury, *Read Only Memory*, 1998. Video stills. © John Maybury. Courtesy of the artist and Lux Moving Image, London.

Bowery's failure to embody a normatively gendered subjectivity through his costuming is, for Bancroft, 'a deliberate creative strategy' that calls attention to the fragility of gender expression and complicates assumptions about one's sex and gender based on dress.[10] Kristen Galvin similarly observes that through camp aesthetics of artifice, humorous appropriation and conflicting narratives, Bowery challenges not only the oppressive discourse of normativity but also cultural assumptions of drag practice. During the 1990s, drag increasingly infiltrated the mainstream most notably through Jenny Livingston's documentary *Paris Is Burning* (1990), which profiles the African American and Latinx drag ball subculture of New York; and RuPaul, the self-proclaimed 'supermodel of the world' who dominated dance charts and MTVat the time.[11]

Undeniably, Bowery's artistic vision appears much more complex than a successful mimesis of femininity or masculinity and it could be for this reason that he dismissed the label of 'drag artist' and generally avoided attending and performing in drag clubs. His bewildering presence aimed instead at disrupting normative bodies and gender as a monolithic identity, promoting a deeply personal fantasy of surrealist genderfuck. Detached from the clichéd polarized gender display of traditional drag, Bowery's spectacular self-presentation is described by Rogers as 'a life-work that may well be considered *trans-queer*' for it theatrically traverses the conceptual formulations of 'queer' and 'trans'.[12] Likewise, Michael Bracewell views Bowery as 'a hermaphrodite character' whose 'vulgar femininity' might reference drag parody, but is made distinctively trans through his performative costuming.[13]

Bowery might have distanced his performative costuming from drag, characterizing the latter as banal entertainment, but in the 1990s drag practice provided a significantly fertile theoretical ground for a deeper understanding of gender subjectivities and the elaboration of what became known as queer discourse. From the moment 'queer' was reclaimed from its pejorative use at the political margins of the (then) LGBT community in the 1980s it has stood as an umbrella term for the variety of sexual and gender minorities that dissent from heteronormative contexts. Heather Love claims that although 'transgender' (or simply 'trans') is mainly linked to non-normative gender embodiment and 'queer' is mostly associated with non-normative desire and sexual practices, establishing a clear distinction, both theoretically and practically, is a tricky task. Love writes,

> If *queer* can be understood as refusing the stabilizations of both gender and sexuality implied by the categories gay and lesbian and opening onto a wider spectrum of sexual nonnormativity, *transgender* emerged as a term to capture a range of gendered embodiments, practices, and community formations that cannot be accounted for by the traditional binary.[14]

Drag practice was afforded an important role in queer discourse when it was famously employed by Judith Butler as a vivid metaphor to illustrate their influential theory of gender performativity. Being a culturally constructed fiction, gender, according to Butler, has no ontological status but is constituted and maintained through 'the repeated stylization of the body' and the enactment of 'a set of repeated acts' that are already socially established, creating the effect of a natural and stable gender identity that serves an oppressive heteronormative institution.[15] In this respect, gender is always a process of becoming; it is performative. Therefore, schematically speaking, rather than being born women or men, individuals are conditioned to act as women or men, creating and upholding this binarism. Determined by the anatomy of two distinct sexes, gender binarism as a regulatory norm is the historical outcome of what Michel Foucault calls a 'biopolitical' regime of power, which rose to prominence during the nineteenth century in the West along with medical and scientific discourses and was centred around the control and standardization of life.[16] In favour of a normalizing society and as a means of accessing and regulating both the individual body and the population, the deployment of sexuality became the most significant biopolitical apparatus. This apparatus ultimately led to the pathologizing and criminalizing of non-normative gender expressions and deviant sexual identities, naturalizing heterosexuality mainly due to its reproductive capacity.

Traditional drag, which is for the most part based on mimesis and exaggeration of stereotypical normative gender traits and roles, can be viewed as a parody of the fabricated inner truth behind the existence of gender for '*[b]y imitating gender, drag implicitly reveals the imitative structure of gender itself – as well as its contingency*', Butler notes.[17] However, after much debate within feminist circles for employing a practice that is often deemed to be fundamentally demeaning to women, Butler underlines elsewhere that drag 'is a site of a certain ambivalence' and it does not necessarily translate to the subversion of gender norms.[18] Drag's theatricalization of the repeated bodily gestures, movements and styles that constitute gender norms can contribute to 'both [their] denaturalization and reidealization', depending on whether it exposes the hollow essence of gender or reveals an inner desire of identification with a representation of womanhood that is widely condemned by many feminists.[19] Drag performers that fall into the second category are those who anticipate the effect of realness, that is the craving and ability to create a convincing gendered subjectivity by embodying gender normativity as ideally as possible. To flesh out her argument, Butler discusses the drag balls documented in *Paris Is Burning* where contestants compete in drag in various categories, denoting certain social stereotypes, with 'realness' being a standard of how convincing their embodiments and performances are. Butler and a number of theorists are critical of this strategy of achieving an 'indistinguishable' performance of gender for it reinforces the reiteration of dominant social norms as well as the polarization of gender.

Typical of realness and an idealized representation of femininity are the embodiments of drag superstar RuPaul who broke into show business in the early 1990s and later brought greater visibility to the subculture of drag queens with his successful television series *RuPaul's Drag Race*. Blessed with a lean and long physique and an eye for detail, RuPaul's artificiality points to a perfected image of glamorized Black womanhood that leaves the reiteration of norms intact. Contrary to subversive drag practices of the same period that were not concerned with realness, such as that of the Divine David (aka David Hoyle) and Vaginal Davis for instance, RuPaul's canonical embodiments presented a less threatening image to the patriarchal dominant culture and the rest of power mechanisms that regulate gender. This being said, the gender-bending capacity of even the most 'harmless' drag practices can still be intriguing and may acquire political significance.

Bowery's closest contact with drag embodiment was for the needs of his role as Madame Garbo in the surreal comedy *The Homosexual: or, the Difficulty of Sexpressing Oneself* (1993). Written by Argentine playwright Copi in 1971 (original title *The Homosexual: or, the Difficulty of Expressing Oneself*), the play was directed by Stewart Laing and Gerrard McArthur and toured various theatre venues in the United Kingdom. This was not only an experiment with a genre of performance that is seemingly very different from his usual impromptu practice but also provided a rare depiction of Bowery in a more conventional drag masquerade. Dressed in a conservative skirt suit, a fur hat and wearing drag make-up, Bowery's character is a married woman who had a penis transplant in Casablanca against her will and claims, paradoxically, to be the father of the child of a promiscuous male-to-female pregnant girl whose mother also happens to be a trans woman. Although the play involved all the leading male actors in drag, it can hardly be classified as a traditional drag performance, which is usually about short acts or lip-syncing and emphasis is often given on mimesis of perceptions of womanhood. Its surreal and complicated plot opens a space for rethinking the relationship between gender, biology and societal norms. In an essay discussing shamelessness and queer identity, Peta Tait remarks that Copi's play, which was banned in Argentina until 1984, paints an amusing picture of a highly camp trans world where gender fluidity and sex reversal are the norms and 'where being a social outcast is reclaimed as an adventurous life'.[20]

Bowery's broader practice, which is equally much more complex than traditional drag or conventional theatrical performance, involves a dynamic exchange between fashion, pop culture and parodic interpretation to critically expose their normative premises and diminish their dominating power. Discussing the work of Vaginal Davis, José Esteban Muñoz makes similar comparisons to commercial drag to concretely illustrate the former's 'terrorist' practice in the ways it foregrounds the interrelation of issues around race, gender and sexuality. [21] Writing in the late 1990s, he argues that the sleek drag practice that had infiltrated the mainstream presented a charming but 'sanitized and desexualized queer subject' in line with assimilationist sensibilities of liberal pluralism.[22] Although increased social acceptance and tolerance of trans identities are desirable outcomes for many, this play-by-the-rules representation fails to foment a fruitful dialogue about difference and its political dimensions. In contrast, Muñoz writes, artists like Davis – and, I maintain, Bowery – represent 'a queerer modality of drag that is performed by queer-identified [...] artists in spaces of queer consumption'.[23] Such queer practices, which often make use of humour and parody, are not self-absorbed or concerned with realness but rather engaged in productive cultural critique. They stand for what Chuck Kleinhans describes as 'low camp': the intentional celebration of what is considered 'bad taste' and offends bourgeois values for the purpose of 'mak[ing] a statement'.[24] The pioneering performances of The Cockettes and the Gay Girls Riding Club are earlier examples of this tendency.

Camp and dominant culture share a tense relationship. Kleinhans elaborates on this reciprocal tension by looking at the different ways camp, as a celebration of superficial aesthetic hyperbole, is registered in commercial film production and underground cinema, discussing among others John Waters' films, which Bowery cherished for their insurgent spirit. Fundamentally queer in its conception, camp constantly draws inspiration from and challenges the kitsch sensationalism of mass culture through parody as a subcultural mode of resistance. A sound example of this kind of parodic camp mentality, which is arguably absent from the propriety of traditional drag, is Andrew Logan's spectacular Alternative Miss World events that have taken place intermittently in various London venues since 1972, with Bowery taking part with a friend known as Gill in 1986.

Based on the unwittingly tacky – and to many offensive – concept of beauty pageants, Logan's competition involves contestants regardless of their gender identity, age, body size and ability who parade in creative costumes and are judged on poise, personality and originality. Registered as 'Miss Fuck It', the duo in one of their chaotic appearances involved an excessively dressed Bowery dashing on stage and dragging vehemently a small bicycle with a naked Fat Gill on it barely balancing and trying not to crash. The now-legendary art event both appropriates and twists beauty stereotypes by distorting the same mechanism that promulgates them in mass culture. Unlike normative drag pageants, which Logan admits to finding unimaginative, Alternative Miss World has provided a space for limitless possibilities of being as embodied by established art dealer James Birch who paraded as a box of chocolates or Bruce Lacey's 'Miss R.O.S.A.B.O.S.O.M.' entry that involved a radio operated robot the artist built to win the title in 1985. Essentially, the event generously offers an opportunity for what Muñoz calls 'counterpublic terrorism', that is the effect of humour and parody in the public domain as strategies of disidentification from dominant culture.[25] Bowery's public personas unquestionably exercise their own version of counterpublic terrorism, if not typically against gender directly then through the reworking of the cultural apparatus that sustains the normative properties of gender.

Camp Parody against Heteronormative Mass Culture

Whilst Bowery's work could not be easily absorbed into the mainstream, he deeply desired fame and his practice often balanced between dominant taste and subcultural modes of expression, projecting his disidentificatory mindset. The concept of disidentification is thoroughly elaborated in the work of Muñoz and particularly in his theorizing of the intricate ways in which queers of colour often identify with demeaning representations of their ethnicity or queerness as an emancipating response to dominant exclusionary representations. Although not always effective, disidentification is broadly defined as 'the survival strategies the minority subject practices in order to negotiate a phobic majoritarian public sphere that continuously elides or punishes the existence of subjects who do not conform to the phantasm of normative citizenship'.[26] Operating in the middle ground between identification and counteridentification, to disidentify translates as the transformation of exclusionary texts to shift their meaning for one's own cultural purposes and, as Muñoz emphasizes, this transformation essentially 'works within and outside the dominant public sphere simultaneously'.[27]

A photoshoot published in the satirical fashion magazine *BLOW* in 1994 parodying the most scandalous advertising campaign of that year exemplifies the tension between pop culture and camp subculture in Bowery's disidentificatory practice, which in his case concerns white heteronormative cultural stereotypes. The photo is a re-creation of the famous 'Hello Boys' billboard advertisement in which a not-yet-famous Eva Herzigova poses in lace lingerie for the promotional purposes of Wonderbra, a supposedly miraculous push-up bra. The supermodel, who is depicted in a sepia tone, looks enthusiastically down at her enhanced cleavage alongside the product's logo and bold text that reads in capital letters 'Hello Boys'. The eye-catching campaign, which skyrocketed Herzigova's modelling career, won two prestigious creative advertisement awards in 1994 and in a poll conducted by the British Outdoor Media Centre in 2011 was voted the most iconic advertisement of all time, leaving in second place the provocative 'Labour Isn't Working' by Saatchi & Saatchi for Margaret Thatcher's Conservative Party.

Contrary to the typical feminist outrage that imagery of semi-naked women has often evoked since the 1960s for sexually objectifying them, the strategically designed 'Hello Boys' campaign (created by Nigel Rose and shot by Ellen von Unwerth), viewed from a postfeminist perspective, was deemed celebratory of the modern financially independent woman who is body-confident and in charge of her sexuality.[28] Bowery posed for photographer Fiona Freund in the same pose as Herzigova for a black-and-white image that reproduced precisely the layout and text of the original campaign. Wearing only a black lingerie set and a shoddy wig that resembles the model's tousled hairstyle, he also looks downwards at his man breasts astounded. With sloppy make-up, skin blemishes and a flabby body, he looks nothing like the flawless young woman in the original campaign. It becomes apparent that Bowery is not interested in the slightest in resembling Herzigova's 'ideal' body or reproducing the same erotic effect. On the contrary, his cheeky camp appropriation expresses his deep-rooted disidentification with the once-desired fashion industry and its regularizing impact on culture and society. His performed disidentification, as a process of what Muñoz terms 'recycling and rethinking encoded meaning', is fleshed out with him looking by all means splendidly terrible (Figure 4.4).[29]

Although the 'Hello Boys' appropriation is not typical of Bowery's resourceful practice and experimental approach to self-fashioning, which set him apart from what is commonly perceived as drag, it does provide a useful opportunity to elaborate on his distorted camp visual language as a strategy of survival and disidentification in a way that departs from a fetish for excessive

Figure 4.4: 'Hello Boys', *BLOW*, September 1994. Photograph by Fiona Freund. Courtesy of James Pretlove.

styling. Susan Sontag's seminal definition of camp as merely 'love of the unnatural: of artifice and exaggeration' has become a superficial leitmotif among reviewers of Bowery's work.[30] The kind of disidentificatory approach to mass culture and its heterosexist sensibilities that Bowery performs is inextricably linked to the essence of camp as a queer strategy of self-defence and visibility, for disidentification manifests through camp tactics of reforming identity. Camp emerges as a result of the queer person's deep disenchantment with the dominant order and the preclusion of having one's desires represented in a discourse that is conditioned by the tenets of compulsory reproductive heterosexuality. Camp, therefore, is first and foremost queer and profoundly political, an aspect that is brushed aside in Sontag's otherwise important essay on camp and restored by subsequent scholars, such as Richard Dyer and Jack Babuscio.[31] Similarly, Bowery's work has been loosely theorized as camp by some commentators and scholars due to its characteristic visual hyperbole, neglecting the critical complexities and radical potential underneath the glittery surface.

What has been substantially overlooked is the fact that his camp appropriation of popular culture, which frequently permeates his distinctively postmodernist practice, is symptomatic of his disidentificatory impulse and allows for re-contextualization and valuable critique.

Beyond its critique of normative aesthetics, Bowery's parodic representation of the 'Hello Boys' campaign challenges a problematic aspect of the lingerie advertisement, which can be traced in the way heteronormativity is legitimized as a reciprocal discourse through the public dissemination of imagery and slogans that position men at the epicentre of female sexual pleasure. Suspicious of the postfeminist appeal certain advertisements (like the one under study) count on, Dee Amy-Chinn argues that the Advertising Standards Authority (ASA) in the United Kingdom, which regulates non-broadcast advertising, encourages the circulation of images that are, nevertheless, suggestive of women as sexual objects exclusively for heterosexual male consumers.[37] Through close examination of several case studies she demonstrates how adverts that portray women as active sexual subjects – especially as subjects whose desires transcend the heteronormative matrix – can very often be found to be offensive by part of the public and are consequently withdrawn by ASA from public consumption.

The ASA's strict control safeguards the reiteration of norms and is symptomatic, Amy-Chinn maintains, of the enduring dominance of heteronormative patriarchal discourses even in a seemingly progressive hyper-sexual culture. Although no man is pictured with Herzigova, the bold phrase 'Hello Boys' next to her sexualized depiction leaves no doubt that the campaign is calling for male attention or, more accurately, it seeks to appeal to women consumers who desire to attract male attention through imagery that satisfies heterosexual male fantasies and adds, perhaps, some extra anxiety to those women who feel excluded or intimidated by Herzigova's slender body. Another reading could be that the model is addressing her breasts, anthropomorphizing and objectifying them as they pop up from the phenomenal bra. The diminutive 'boys' in the slogan creates a strangely maternal effect on the model's part in an otherwise highly sexualized content, which communicates a repronormative feeling on the verge of the repropornographic.

Bowery's humorous queer appropriation wrecks the campaign's heteronormative framework and aesthetic for he brazenly claims the position of the female subject who attracts male attention. His ambiguous low camp embodiment creates an opportunity for criticizing the ways heteronormativity and imposed normative ideals dominate commercial popular culture by excluding a whole spectrum of diverse sexual expressions, gendered subjectivities and body types and hints at alternative pathways for desires and identifications remaining on the margins. Even the slogan 'Hello Boys' turns into an ironic mockery next to his ambiguous 'disturbing' femininity, sealing the queer overtones of the image whether he's calling out to men or addressing his breasts in an anti-repropornographic gesture. He effectively puts to the test Dyer's thesis on camp, which he views as a product of gay oppression capable of 'demystify[ing] the images and world-view of art and the media'.[33]

Camp is for Dyer a reminder of the manufactured narrow view on lifestyle and modes of being that the media in their majority foster but, most importantly, a reminder of the countless true possibilities one can take hold of. Accordingly, Bowery's less-than-perfect image touches on the fabricated stereotype of sleek beauty and heteronormativity that broadcast media portray as ideals of an ultimate and unattainable reality and promotes queer social visibility unapologetically. His multi-layered interpretation of 'Hello Boys' corroborates the close-knit relationship between disidentification and camp as valuable tools for voicing repressed desires and facilitating nonconformist gendered subjectivities. Yet, Bowery's innovative, transgressive vision becomes more apparent through his eccentric performances and highly stylized appearances in bizarre garments, strange make-up and unusual body modifications; all of which allow him to take the qualities of camp and disidentification to a new level, aligning his practice with the tenets and body politics of progressive trans discourse. His avant-garde approach to embodiment goes to such lengths that as a matter of fact it queers not just gender and sexuality but human existence itself.

Transgressing Gender: Hybrid Realities and Cyborg Dreams

Delving into Bowery's work one soon determines that, unlike drag, it goes beyond ordinary concerns surrounding gender expression and its representation. Galvin situates Bowery's performative costuming in opposition to the mainstream arrival of drag in the 1990s mostly for resisting the 'commercial or consumerist interest in the body beautiful'.[34] However, it is also his investment in an unexpected genderqueer aesthetic that messes up the gender binary and fundamentally differentiates his practice from conventional drag, consequently delimiting the possibility of wider acceptance.

By distorting gender to the degree Bowery usually does, his costumed personas ultimately strain against the limits of the category of the human, considering that persons, according to Butler, can only become intelligible in the social sphere through embodying gender 'in conformity with recognizable standards of gender intelligibility'.[35] By 'intelligible' genders Butler refers to the clear-cut gender binary that follows a heteronormative and repronormative continuum among biological sex, culturally constructed gender, desire and sexual practice. When this linear sequence of intelligibility is disrupted by the cultural emergence of beings who fail (or refuse) to conform to gender norms, as Bowery's embodiments do, the notion of the person itself is called into question. Visibly trans bodies and other kinds of gender identities that do not fulfil these norms of cultural intelligibility appear as developmental failures and are suppressed by power structures, resulting in social stigmatization, discrimination, restricted fundamental civil rights and often violence. Their visibility and proliferation, Butler argues, are crucial for constructive criticism of the oppressive and normalizing mechanism in the name of intelligibility. In this regard, Bowery's unprecedented trans-queer embodiment turns into a politically charged cultural vehicle for anti-assimilation and for calling attention to the intertextual possibilities of trans identities, intersex and other gender-variant bodies.

The binary gender system in the West is most painfully imposed upon intersex and trans bodies that strive to pass in their gender role and successfully fulfil a standard image shaped by culture. Hovering between two oppositional genders – neither of which can be fully attained – they have been targeted both by the medical apparatus that seeks to pathologize them and adjust them accordingly to accepted standards of gendering and by certain hostile formations within academia and feminism. As such, trans men are often regarded by so-called trans-exclusionary radical feminists (TERFs) as gender traitors who align with patriarchy or simply as butch lesbians who comply with essentialism. Similarly, many trans women have received harsh criticism for reinforcing stereotypical views of femininity and have in many cases been attacked by TERFs who feel uneasy with and violated by their presence in 'women-only' spaces.

In what became perhaps the most discussed anti-trans polemic, *The Transsexual Empire: The Making of the She-Male* (1994), Janice Raymond elaborates a frenzied conspiracy theory about how trans women are artefacts manipulated by a male-dominated medical discourse in order to possess 'real' women by appropriating their bodies. In response to her transphobic panic, Sandy Stone in her seminal posttranssexual manifesto proposes that trans individuals give up on the struggle for 'passing', the continuous process that is to blend seamlessly with members of their gender and be rewarded in return with society's acceptance.[36] Although passing is occasionally easier and more successful for some trans, it does always require that parts of their identities are subdued or left behind in favour of a new stable subjectivity, which is compliant with the traditional gender binary system and reinforces it. By resisting this, trans individuals, Stone maintains, will reshape their identities 'not as a series of erasures in the service of a species of feminism conceived from within a traditional frame, but as a political action begun by reappropriating difference and reclaiming the power of the refigured and reinscribed body'.[37] The unashamed exploration of a multitude of physicalities and expressions will allow them to speak from a position outside the constraints of normative gender; for Stone, it is only through their ambiguity being openly read that they will access the 'post' era and become posttranssexuals.

If power begets resistance, as Foucault insists, Bowery's trans-queer manifestations are subversive for they theatrically represent resistance to discipline, normativity and essentialism by projecting a posttranssexual mentality and physicality.[38] Such bodies, as posttranssexual becomings, defy normativity in their appearance, practice or stylization and fail to be situated easily in dominant categories and roles. Even though Bowery identified and passed as male outside his performative costuming, his aesthetic is utterly trans for it does not only reach across gender but goes beyond the notion of the human itself.

The instability of gender identity and its multiple manifestations are most notably celebrated in the visual arts in the work of genderqueer photographer Del LaGrace Volcano. The gender-fluid temperament that Bowery's performative costuming elicits is explicitly divulged in Volcano's fierce representations: butch masculinities, lesbian BDSM desires, trans men, intersex bodies and self-portraits of a frequently transfigured subjectivity feature heavily in the work. Assigned female at birth, Volcano has assumed a variety of gendered and sexed subjectivities throughout the years. More recently the artist identifies as a 'herm', a neology that describes Volcano's personal path as 'a lovable gender queer with a colorful *herm*story' that also serves as a preferred pronoun.[39] Volcano embraces the ambiguity produced by herm's body and seeks to create work that speaks for those individuals like hermself who refuse to correspond to a gender binary narrative, promoting the playful spirit of gender fluidity and uninhibited sexuality.

Being a self-proclaimed 'intentional mutation' and 'intersex by design' rather than by diagnosis, Volcano denies the pathologizing of non-binary individuals and rejects culturally established ideals of beauty.[40] Herm's persistence in the representation of trans bodies and devotion to raising awareness are translated by Dominic Johnson as likely '*incontrovertible* feminisms', for such bodies are often disputed in feminist discourse and their representations are overlooked in histories of art.[41] Often photographed in subcultural settings, Volcano and herm's subjects perform their gendered subjectivities and sexual desires or display their culturally abject bodies to trouble dominant heteronormative manifestations of coupling and hegemonic concepts of the beautiful body. The documentary quality of Volcano's work and the identification of the artist with herm's subjects complicate their relationship and convey a sense of community, permitting an intimate and productive exchange to take place. As Volcano writes, herm is 'committed to making images *with* (speaking) subjects rather than taking images *from* passive and silenced objects'.[42]

In *Not a NeoNazi* (1997), Volcano photographed the Berlin-based performer Bridge Markland as a masculine shirtless skinhead in an empty derelict room. The image can be found in one of herm's published portfolios documenting the relatively recent subcultural phenomenon of drag kings. According to Jack Halberstam's definition, the drag king – much like his counterpart the drag queen – is usually a female who dresses up in distinctly male attire and performs masculinity theatrically.[43] Contrary to the plausible performance of maleness in the theatrical genre of male impersonation, the drag king attempts, often through parody, to expose the performativity of male masculine behaviour.

A virtuoso of roleplay and transformation who specializes in gender-bending performances, Markland is depicted in generic skinhead attire consisting of a belted high-waisted pair of denim jeans and braces. She gazes fiercely into the camera and poses effortlessly with a cigarette in her mouth, adopting a body language that signals trouble. Her trademark shaved head and her strikingly rigid face are immediately perceived as hyper-masculine but as the eyes move downwards the viewer is confronted with her bare breasts, which remain deliberately visible with no evident anxiety to conceal them. The tape covering the nipples, apart from being a BDSM signifier or a witty attempt at self-censorship, draws attention to this feminine part of the body, queering the subject and the broadly heteromasculine overtones of skinhead toughness. There is nothing else in this image suggesting that the subject might be female. The black-and-white film and the dark empty room supplement the minimal aesthetic and reinforce the assertive masculinity of the subject (Figure 4.5).

Volcano admits finding this image 'intensely disturbing', considering that Markland is a Jewish bisexual woman appropriating the visual signifiers of a militaristic look that became widely associated with oppressive far-right politics.[44] Indeed, as Murray Healy observes, by 1982 the skinhead had evolved from a youth-subcultural expression of the working class into a Neo-Nazi emblem in popular consciousness.[45] The conservative masculinity that skinheads in the 1960s had aspired to as a means of embodying an authentic fixed subjectivity and retaining boundaries was ultimately adopted by supporters of far-right ideologies who claimed the identity and developed its dress codes. Although not all skinheads during the 1980s shared fascist sentiments, the revival became for the most part associated with hooliganism, racist attacks and queer-bashing. On another

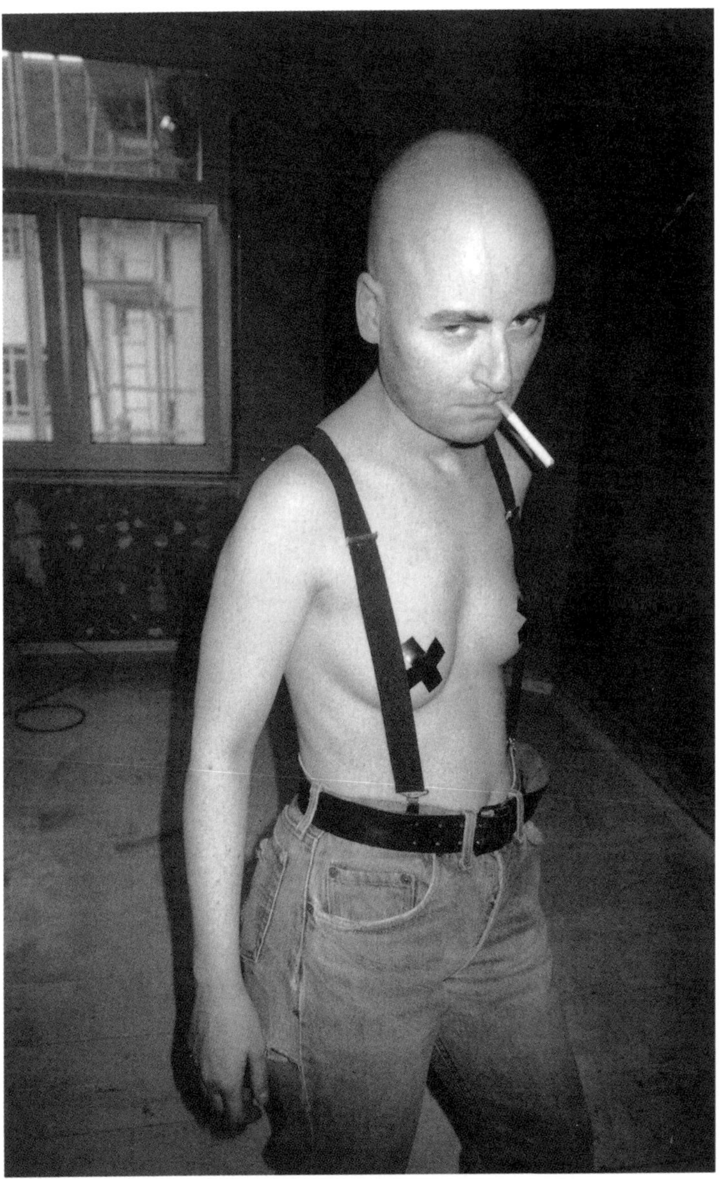

Figure 4.5: Del LaGrace Volcano, *Bridge Markland, Not a NeoNazi*, 1997. © Del LaGrace Volcano.

note, the figure of the macho and violent skinhead provoked a sort of sexual attraction and titillated BDSM fantasies particularly among some gay men who also appropriated the appearance, complicating further the already precarious notion of authentic heteronormative masculinity.[46] By embodying an irritable (nominally homophobic) skinhead and queering him, Markland speaks back to the uncompromising ideal of toxic masculinity that members of the subculture and some gay men so desperately sought to achieve.

If dominant male masculinities tend to appear in the domain of the real, refraining from the performative and the artificial, as Halberstam asserts, Markland effectively uncovers the skinhead's masculine artificiality by appropriating its signifiers. This is a common strategy among drag kings where emphasis is given to the 'tricks and gadgets of the sexism on which male masculinity depends'.[47] As a genderqueer woman easily passing as a male had her breasts not been exposed, Markland wrecks the gender dichotomy and troubles the heteronormative principle of masculinity as an exclusively male privilege. As Jewish, she mocks and disintegrates the symbolic meaning behind the skinhead who came to be viewed mainly as a homophobic and xenophobic admirer of Hitler. Perhaps Markland's drag is just a playful appropriation of the fetishized bad-boy toughness the skinhead look brought about in certain BDSM gay scenes; after all, as the title suggests, the subject is not a Neo-Nazi. Unlike Bowery's problematic appropriation of the swastika in his 'Nazi Dominatrix' look, Markland interestingly retains some of the interpretative ambiguity of her embodiment by avoiding such explicit references.

Not a NeoNazi is exemplary of what Jay Prosser calls the '(trans)-mutation between the aesthetic and the documentary' in Volcano's work, which stresses the fact that herm's work is closer to the real over the pictorial without compromising its artistic value.[48] Through herm's documentation of a purposely 'failed' drag – failed in the sense that Markland is not keen on covering up the anatomical signs of her femaleness – the prospect of an anti-normative embodiment of gender envisioned by posttranssexual enthusiasts becomes visible. Despite the fact that Bowery's costuming is not drag in any conventional sense and his work is premised on aesthetic criteria transcending the frontier of the real and the documentary, it can equally invoke readings of a highly trans-queer multi-gendered hybridity.

A picture of Bowery taken in 1994 by Josef Astor contrasts Volcano's unpolished photographic approach and eludes ventures of rational interpretation. Judging from the simple setting and gradient background, Bowery was most likely photographed in a studio and is depicted in black-and-white as a gender-ambiguous humanoid. His costumed body seduces and confuses. The strange creature in the picture is hairless with a shaved head and no brows and looks like a deranged puppet. It has big bold eyes that look like they are bleeding as they stare upwards with astonishment and two metallic wires (probably safety pins) pass through its pierced cheeks and into the corners of the mouth as if they are forcing its aghast expression. The neck is elongated by a tight corseted garment and the arms are enclosed in unusually high gloves that cover the shoulders. A sturdy belt just below the creature's exposed pushed-up chest disproportions the silhouette by lengthening the lower part of the body, which appears with no genitals and is peculiarly shaped with uneven wide hips and asymmetrical lower limbs. One leg is bulky and oddly formed like a pillar while the other resembles that of a human, with a patterned thigh-high stocking and a platform heel. Even the posture looks unnatural and overly dramatic as the arms elegantly stretch slightly out to the sides as though the creature is struck by an apocalyptic catastrophe. The abstract background situates the figure in a non-tangible environment, intensifying its alien embodiment, which on the whole is beyond social experience and the human (Figure 4.6).

Unlike Markland's queer drag in *Not a NeoNazi*, Bowery's performative costuming constructs a highly imaginative and artificial narrative that makes gender futile and obsolete by rendering him a profoundly genderless creature in line with Donna Haraway's vision of a cyborg 'in a post-gender world'.[49] Although Bowery's representation passes as non-human and thus does not explicitly engage with malleable gendered subjectivities and complexities of identification, his is an equally disturbing image to that of Markland that can be seen to encapsulate 'the utopian dream of the hope for a monstrous world without gender'.[50] Writing in the early 1980s, Haraway argues that socialist and feminist debates based on traditional dichotomies and seeking a universal theory are no longer adequate under advanced

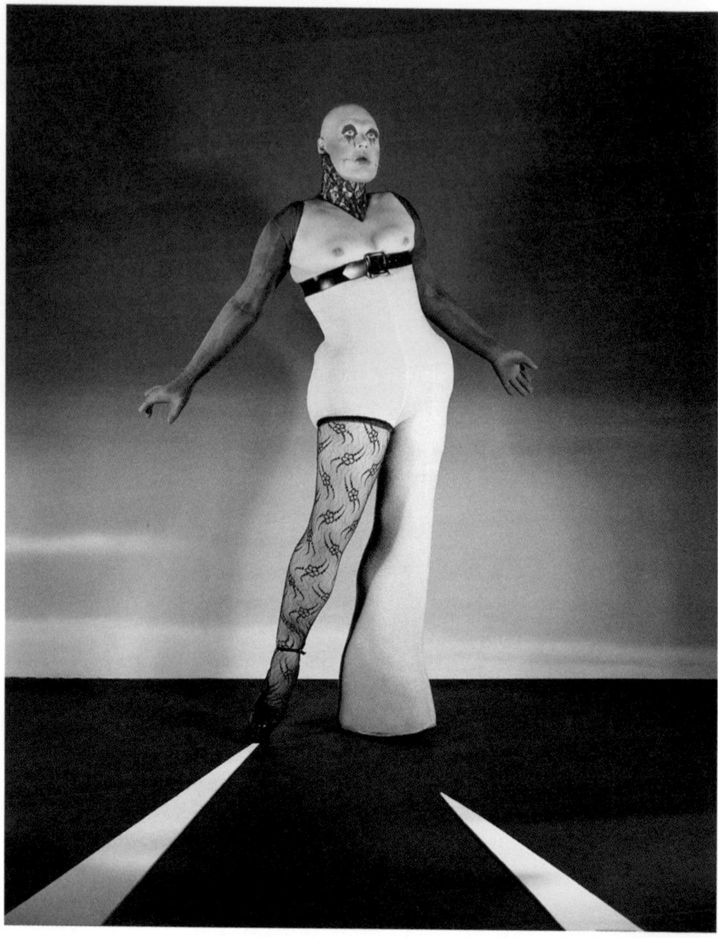

Figure 4.6: Josef Astor, *Leigh Bowery*, 1994. © Josef Astor.

capitalism and the rapidly evolving social relations shaped by science and technology.

In doing away with essentialism and other Western traditions that produce dualisms like gender, inevitably forming relations of domination, and refusing to demonize technology for the new challenges it brought to struggle against power, Haraway engages the cyborg from science fiction narratives metaphorically as a postmodern symbol of 'resistance and recoupling'; its hybrid nature, she maintains, represents 'transgressed boundaries, potent fusions, and dangerous possibilities' of a potentially radical political significance.[51] Moving beyond the limitations of traditional gender (and other binary structures) and calling for the reconstruction of hybrid identities determined by affinity and personal choice, Haraway anticipates in a broad way the post-transsexual embodiment subsequently fleshed out by Stone.

However, not all representations of cyborg bodies carry subversive interpretations, Anne Balsamo writes.[52] As a symbol of transgression and 'unfamiliar "otherness"' that complicates human identity and its interlocking aspects of experience, the cyborg came to signify a promising postmodernist paradigm of contesting the naturalness of the body by undoing the damaging binary constructions that produce difference and by underlining the constructedness of all identities.[53] Haraway's socialist feminist cyborg utopia overlooks the fact that dominant representations of cyborg bodies in popular science fiction perpetuate cultural gender stereotypes and reassert conventional notions of human and machine: the eponymous robot officer in the movie series *RoboCop* (1987) or the replicant Rachel from *Blade Runner* (1982) are two of the examples Balsamo examines to maintain that both male and female cyborgs are stereotypically associated with masculine and feminine characteristics, respectively. Bowery's genderless cyborg embodiment seems to tackle this problematic schema in mainstream cyborg fantasies that meticulously sustain the polarization of gender by reflecting the general unrest surrounding gender debates at the time.

According to Jennifer González, representations of cyborgs in contemporary visual culture emerge as a result of the failure of traditional bodies, as 'ontological model[s] of human beings', to stand up to new challenges of lived experience in times of radical sociocultural change.[54] For instance, a photomontage by Hannah Höch titled *The Beautiful Girl* (1920), which depicts an assemblage of female body parts and automobile accessories in line with the Dadaist aesthetic, is suggestive of the ambiguous social role of women in the post-First World War era of modernization. Bowery's more recent cyborg embodiment anticipates and encompasses the anxieties around the disavowal of identity-based categories and the debates surrounding trans embodiment that gained momentum in visual culture and feminist discourse throughout the 1990s, from influential art exhibitions, such as *Oh Girl, It's a Boy* (1994) at the Kunstverein München; *In a Different Light* (1995) at the Berkeley Art Museum; and *Rrose Is a Rrose Is a Rrose: Gender Performance in Photography* (1997) at the Solomon R. Guggenheim Museum in New York, to the triumphant outset of queer theory with its mantra of creative subversion by way of gender performativity. In pop culture, a similar aesthetic, symptomatic of the cyborgian zeitgeist, is found on the cover of Marylin Manson's industrial glam metal album *Mechanical Animals* (1998) in which the lead singer appears as a white androgynous extra-terrestrial being. At a time of deep crisis in identity and corporeality, Bowery's cyborg becoming anticipates as well as glorifies the dissolution of all boundaries and inscriptions that inhibit the human body and determine the notion of the human.

Bowery's cyborg feminist undertones are most distinctly manifest in his fixation with overemphasizing the belly in some of his costumes to clearly suggest a pregnant silhouette as well as his most emblematic performance during which he explicitly emulates a birth scene. In 'Globe' or 'Pregnant Tutu Head', Bowery references directly the pregnant body but remains true to his devotion to the bizarre. He appears immersed in a sculptural creation in earthy colours that distorts the human figure to such extremes that any attempt at reading the subject as normatively gendered or human is doomed. Inspired by Transformers, the toy robots that change shapes, the look consists of several pieces that cover every inch of bare skin. His whole head is enclosed in a big pompom that sticks out from a high wide-neck top with three-quarter length sleeves and a big round lump that protrudes at the front where the abdomen is, while the feet are enclosed in huge cup-shaped constructions (Figure 4.7).

Bowery's cyborg representation of pregnancy disturbs its cultural links to womanhood and cisgender bodies (bodies whose gender identity corresponds to the sex assigned at birth) and deregisters the typically heteronormative conditions that regulate reproduction as a solid pretext of the gender binary. In the same way, cases of trans and intersex pregnancies made possible

Figure 4.7: Tom Pilston, *Leigh Bowery (Outside His Home at Farrell House in East London)*, 1991. © Tom Pilston/Panos Pictures.

mostly (but not exclusively) through artificial insemination call into question the constitution of what Nadyne Stritzke and Elisa Scaramuzza call 'repronormativity', which they define as:

> [T]he complex reciprocity of social institutions, thought structures, modes of perception, practices, and manners of life that govern and give preference to binary gendered heterosexual procreation. It is based on the unconsciously internalized assumption that mankind is binary gendered and may only reproduce itself through heterosexual procreative intercourse.[55]

Bowery's queer pregnant embodiment gloriously ruins this linear repronormative narrative not only by steering clear of the normative representation of bodily gender traits that are commonly perceived as female (apart from his pronounced belly) but also by utterly thwarting any recognized notion of humankind, suggesting the difficulty of bodies (however monstrous or alien) to often represent themselves as wholly without gender. In Bowery's surrealistic sphere, pregnancy hardly becomes intelligible as a symbol of female fertility but is rather registered as a supernatural wonder of an anthropomorphic being without a coherent gender.

This unprecedented grotesque pregnancy is obviously at odds with ordinary romanticized pregnant bodies of females that populate visual culture and often represent maternity as the sacred feminine force behind the continuation of the species and the heteronormative nuclear family. A relatively recent exhibition at The Foundling Museum in London, titled *Portraying Pregnancy: From Holbein to Social Media* (2020), illustrates the ongoing canonical association of pregnancy with the female heterosexual body. Spanning a period of more than 500 years, the exhibits included a selection of drawings, paintings, photographs and other artefacts of mainly British art that deal with the representation of pregnancy. From depictions of the pregnant Virgin Mary and embellished portraits of noble ladies during the Tudor period to contemporary paintings by male artists depicting their wives (such as Duncan Grant and Lucian Freud) as well as sensual photographs of celebrities showing off their bumps (most notably Demi Moore by Annie Leibovitz for *Vanity Fair* and, more recently, Beyoncé by Awol Erizku), the exhibition presented a rather narrow view on the allegedly inseparable relationship between gestating bodies and womanhood, propagating a stereotypically repronormative outlook that excludes the representation of procreation among the broad spectrum of queer subjectivities. This is particularly striking given that in recent years sensational images of 'pregnant men' in the press have frequently 'scandalized' the public since trans man Thomas Beatie first made headlines with his pregnancy in 2008.

Stefan Horlacher remarks that, as a significant source of knowledge, art can acquire a radical potential for its ability to create spaces for cultural resistance where 'ludic, creative, and experimental thinking becomes possible' and 'humankind can transcend itself and create new ways of living and alternative concepts of understanding, also of one's own gender and sexual identity'.[56] Indeed, in a series of self-portraits titled *Inter*me*, Volcano upsets the widespread fantasy of explicitly gendered ideals and the sociocultural expectations they create – heteronormative pregnancy being one of them. Having as a reference David Beckham's body image of immaculate masculinity, a prevailing ideal that herm admits finding fascinating but problematic, Volcano produced for *Inter*me* three photographic triptychs of herm's nude intersex body that portray a more realistic, yet inevitably puzzling, masculine embodiment. What complicates further this narrative of ambivalent masculinity is a close-up photograph of a heavily pregnant belly that appears in the middle of the first triptych and belongs to Volcano's long-term partner Matt Wurm, who at the time was pregnant with their first child. By interrupting the pictorial pattern of queer subjectivity, 'The Pregnant Punctum', as Volcano calls this image, essentially interrupts repronormative assumptions and through its intimate autobiographical mood carves out a space for queer kinship and all the possibilities and formations of gender dismissed as non-normative.[57]

Bowery's monstrous pregnancy can be seen to anticipate, allegorically at least, the urgency for increased visibility of those forms of procreation that diverge from repronormative binarism and become stigmatized as unnatural or are forcibly restrained through various complex medical and legal protocols or are sometimes even prohibited. His work avoids Volcano's brutally honest confrontational quality, afforded by herm's intimate documentary and autobiographical imagery, but the voluntary enfreakment Bowery endures by means of his performative costuming, body modification and eccentric make-up produces a queer subjectivity that equally communicates an uneasy feeling of otherness. His fascination with the big round belly, which displaces any masculine residue in his alien embodiment, ultimately culminated in a series of whimsical performances in which he famously 'gave birth' to an actual human being, taking childbirth to a whole new queer dimension.

From *Female Trouble* to Wigstock: A 'Birth' of Disidentification

The biggest crowd Bowery ever performed in front of was at Wigstock in 1993, an annual one-day drag festival in Tompkins Square Park in downtown New York. Referencing Woodstock, a massive three-day countercultural music event of peace and love in 1969, Wigstock begun in 1985 as a small-scale local celebration aspiring to bring to light the subculture of drag queens, which had until then been confined to nightclubs such as the nearby Pyramid Club.[58] By 1993 the festival had grown into a colourful spectacle of various drag acts and dance music performances that attracted thousands of people. Bowery was invited by the hostess and main organizer, the renowned drag queen Lady Bunny, after she witnessed Bowery's performance at The Fridge in London, in which he notoriously sprayed the audience with an enema. Once again, Bowery's brief but remarkable appearance managed to become the highlight of the evening.

Following a rich line-up of glittery drag queens, who mainly lip-synced in sequin-garnished gowns and performed their well-rehearsed dance routines (including RuPaul who promoted his newly released track 'House of Love'), Bowery took the stage. When the music started he appeared in a modest,waisted buttoned-up jacket and a knee-length skirt in a matching tacky pattern, low-heeled granny shoes and a turban-like headpiece. Every part of his bloated feminine figure was completely covered, including the head, which was enclosed in a tight white mask with only three small openings for the eyes and the mouth and bold make-up painted on. The absence of visible skin and the disfiguring mask that gave him extremely pronounced cheekbones and unnatural features transformed him into a horror lady. Walking clumsily around the stage he started singing live the classic hippy song 'All You Need Is Love' (1967) by the Beatles without any apparent effort to stay in tune. After a few minutes of terrible singing and sloppy movements the performance became even more awkward as he reclined on a table and started groaning and shaking his legs up in the air while something inside him tore the white tights up and debouched from between his legs. Much to the spectators' astonishment, it was a huge naked 'baby' played by Bateman who had been hidden underneath Bowery's costume throughout the performance supported upside-down by a harness. With no hair and smeared with red jelly to simulate the blood-covered state of a newborn, Bateman sat quietly on the table looking puzzled while Bowery shouted with excitement: 'Oh my God! Wigstock's first baby!', a pun, according to Francesca Granata, on the two confirmed births during Woodstock.[59] Then, 'mother' Bowery cut the umbilical cord (in fact a string of sausages) with his teeth, embraced and kissed his child and both left the stage happily amid warm applause.[60]

The 'Birth', as it is often called, is Bowery's most discussed performance, which he enacted numerous times after it was first presented at Gerlinde and Michael Costiff's Kinky Gerlinky club night in London in 1992. It is also Bowery's performance that has attracted the most scholarly attention mainly due to its multiple possibilities for feminist critique and the several entry points it offers to relevant discourses of gender embodiment and queerness. It is routinely theorized as camp, which in opposition to mainstream drag culture acquires significant political

Figure 4.8: Leigh Bowery and Nicola Bateman performing the 'Birth' at RoXY, Amsterdam, 1994. Photograph by René Habermacher. © René Habermacher.

value for eschewing the boundaries of the gendered body and for touching on the sensitive subject of queer reproduction (Figure 4.8). Much like with his enema act, Bancroft aligns Bowery's 'Birth' with an aesthetic turn witnessed in queer performances at the time of AIDS, which tended to explore corporeal taboos that were deemed more challenging than 'the cliché of gay performance as a melodramatic man in a dress miming ballads badly'.[61] Furthermore, by enacting a birth scene, Bowery explicitly illustrates what his trans-queer costuming is largely suggestive of: that the embodiment of femininity is not tied to anatomical or biological factors and that gestation and childbirth specifically are not the exclusive prerogative of women. His emulates a sort of perverse birth in which Bateman, with her mature slimy body, tears his clothes and seemingly bursts out of his flesh like a horrific organism, as in Ridley Scott's science fiction film *Alien* (1979).

Viewed from a more traditional feminist angle, the 'Birth' for Granata evokes comical acts in the carnival tradition that involved corpulent men giving birth and exposes the disturbing and gynophobic Western assumptions that see the female body as grotesque and monstrous.[62] Although parodies of women's bodies and experiences are fairly common in drag, one hardly expects to encounter a birth scene – especially such a sophisticated one – as a representation of womanhood in a popular drag festival. Bowery's highly camp tactics, she argues, denounce stereotypical understandings of womanhood and dispute the usually idealized femininity of drag, which she describes as 'masquerade'.[63] Similar to Bancroft, Granata pays attention to the dismantling of the alignment of women with maternity in Bowery's 'Birth' and notes his high queerness, underscored by seemingly 'giving birth' to an adult woman. More recently, Galvin refers to the 'Birth' as Bowery's 'most direct, radical, and elaborate play on biology, gender and sexuality', arguing that through its distorted camp expression in the midst of the AIDS epidemic Bowery challenges the homophobic tenet of what Lee Edelman calls 'reproductive futurism': the premise that the child is a symbol of possibility of the future that contrast the narcissistic hopelessness of the non-reproductive queer.[64] Apart from the existing queer feminist readings it instigates, Bowery's 'Birth' performance, as a camp strategy of survival, negotiates a massively heterosexualized culture by empowering those identities that are excluded from repronormative discourses.

Bowery's 'Birth' performance was largely inspired by a scene from Waters' cult film *Female Trouble* (1974) in which Dawn Davenport, a delinquent high-school student incarnated by Waters's muse Divine (aka Harris Glenn Milstead), gives birth to her daughter alone on the couch of her home and cuts the umbilical cord with her teeth. The first time it was performed at Kinky Gerlinky, a legendary monthly club night held at The Empire in Leicester Square, Bowery paid tribute to Waters' film by re-enacting the controversial scene. With the jazzy funk song sung by Divine in the movie's opening credits playing in the background, he walked heavily on stage looking huge. Chewing gum and dressed in an outfit that resembled that of Davenport he approached the edge of the stage where a corded telephone was placed on a big table and pretended to dial a number and have an intense conversation. Minutes before going into labour in the movie, Davenport calls the father of her child (also played by Divine in male attire) from a public telephone booth to inform him about her state and ask for money. It was probably his infuriated response that hastened her water to break when he replied pompously 'You never gettin' any money from me, cow!' and hung up. Channelling Davenport, Bowery grabbed his huge belly devastated, laid on the table if in pain and 'gave birth' to Bateman in front of an ecstatic audience.[65]

Galvin describes Bowery's inventive appropriation of Davenport as 'meta-drag': a camping of an existing highly camped representation of 'white trash prowess and anti-beauty politics' that is recontextualized from the terrain of underground cinema to the subcultural queer club.[66] Bowery's tribute to *Female Trouble* and straightforward impersonation of Davenport reveals his identificatory impulse towards Divine, whose drag ethos, drenched in Waters' wild trash aesthetic and flagrantly displayed through his terroristic demeanour and perverted mind, most likely inspired Bowery (Figure 4.9). The versatile creative paths they both followed were informed by common experiences of disenchantment towards normative ideals of mainstream culture and traditional drag. Reluctant to assimilate, Bowery found a platform for expressing his camp individuality in London's subcultural nightclub scene just like Milstead had found his alter ego Divine years earlier through Waters' twisted gang of society's

Figure 4.9: Divine as Babs Johnson in *Pink Flamingos*, 1972. Directed by John Waters. Trailer still. New Line Cinema at Wikimedia Commons.

outcasts and the films they produced together. The enactment of birth, which became emblematic in their practices, constitutes a provocative theme for it is culturally linked to an unglamorous side of womanhood that ruins typical fantasies of sexual objectification.

As fascinating and wondrous as giving birth might be, it remains a taboo subject tied to Julia Kristeva's view of the abject body that evokes horror, fear and disgust with its wastes and fluids as it defies the desire for cleanliness and propriety and brings into the open the person's prospective physical decay and ultimate death.[67] It is perhaps for this reason that vulvas – no matter how glorified nude bodies can be – are historically deemed grotesque in Western visual culture. Mary Russo takes on the Italian origin of 'grotesque', literally meaning 'of a cave', and argues that the term serves as a metaphor for the 'cavernous anatomical female body', which, as a 'cave of abjection', generates misogyny in the form of the 'blood, tears, vomit and excrement' associated with pregnancy.[68] Even though since the mid-twentieth century the body has arguably undergone massive transformations in performance art by testing and transgressing its boundaries constantly and mapping out new trajectories for embodied experiences, the aesthetics of pregnancy and childbirth persist as a controversial topic with limited manifestations.[69]

In visual culture more broadly representations of pregnancy also remain rare in the public domain and evoke a sort of 'cultural anxiety' that motivated Sandra Matthews and Laura Wexler to compile and critically engage with a collection of images of pregnant women in the twentieth century. In *Pregnant Pictures* they argue that the difficulty in representing pregnancy stems in part from the fact that Western cultures have traditionally attempted to keep the maternal aspect distinct from the sexual in women's roles and to denaturalize the sexual associations of pregnancy, which ordinarily invokes orthodox heterosexual intercourse regardless of whether this is the case.[70] In their account of over 200 images of representations of pregnancy, published in 2000, the focus is – not surprisingly – solely on cisgender women and childbearing is treated throughout via a heteronormative lens and as 'an aspect of female sexuality' that is 'different from the male norm'.[71]

This is not to suggest that the authors, willingly or not, made an omission by neglecting trans men's pregnancies but rather to highlight the fact that those pregnancies deviating from the repronormative binarism have been largely denied representation in the cultural and social realm regardless of the progressive nature of the representational project.[72] The long invisibility of trans procreation has been orchestrated by medical and public discourses that kept them for many years in the margins but, most importantly, also by widespread legislation that denied reproductive rights to trans persons who desired to change their civil status, considering that gender affirmation surgery, which may render one sterile, was for many years a prerequisite for a trans individual to enjoy legal recognition of their preferred gender.[73] Thus, any trans pregnancies were officially recorded as repronormative – as the trans person was deemed either to have not transitioned or else successfully de-transitioned (even if provisionally) – failing, as a result, to reach out and register the instability of gender in culture's consciousness.

Before the highly publicized case of Beatie's pregnancy initiated a greater public dialogue and took trans procreation out of the closet, male birth had remained for the majority an inconceivable scenario that could only be encountered as a cinematic fantasy. The Hollywood romantic comedy *Junior* (1994), for example, narrates the story of a male cisgender scientist whose devotion to fertility lab research and the lack of funding to test a new drug led him to experiment with his own body and become pregnant with scientific intervention. The storyline, JaneMaree Maher writes, is symptomatic of the then relatively new scientific developments in reproductive technology (such as the use of in vitro fertilization and ultrasound), which provided much hope and ease, displacing the focus on women's reproductive ability by opening the way for exciting new prospects in procreation.[74]

Male pregnancy as a new prospect is what *Junior* seeks to humorously portray, albeit with evident anxiety that the delicate lines of heteronormative binarism are not crossed. The role of the pregnant scientist is taken by hard-bodied Arnold Schwarzenegger whose acting career is built around the image of the hyper-masculine action hero, which is now demystified for the purpose of comedy by his mundane portrayal as a vulnerable and highly sensitive expecting man in hormonal meltdown. Yet, the plot rehabilitates any suspicions of emasculation caused by his pregnancy when he proceeds to conveniently fall in love (and have sex while still pregnant) with a female colleague whose frozen egg, unbeknown to both, had been used for fertilization. A baby girl (a boy would potentially be deemed too 'homo awkward') is eventually delivered neatly and almost effortlessly via a caesarean section. The final scenes of the film are even more cringeworthy, with the couple enjoying happy family moments with their child at the beach and the female colleague/girlfriend now heavily pregnant with their second child. Normativity restored.

Since reproduction persists as a cultural territory that is still defined by distinctively heteronormative discursive conditions and representations of birth scenes are largely confined to medical textbooks, Bowery's enactment acquires a double symbolism. It does not only exonerate a bodily function that is restricted to the terrain of private experiences but also denaturalizes its correlation to strictly female embodiment and its subsequent repronormative cultural associations by performing it in his usual trans-queer costuming and in a space of queer consumption. His 'Birth' performance hints at trans and non-binary procreation as a marginal minoritarian conduct, making it relevant during a time marked by optimistic scientific progress in assisted reproductive methods, which have benefited non-normative pregnancies greatly, but mainstream culture and power structures have sought to relieve of any trace of queerness.

That Bowery is queer is an understatement given the subtle complexities in his diverse body of work that imply a performative, non-fixed engagement with identity. While gender-bending performance has arguably lost much of its edge now due to its increased visibility perhaps, Bowery's embodied fluidity for the sake of an unimaginable, unfamiliar and awe-provoking whole of shifting signifiers appears more relevant than ever and renders conventional drag an obsolete repetition. His trans ethos, eminent in his numerous hybrid embodiments, gives Haraway's cyborg fantasy flesh and bone as it reminds us of the malleability of bodies and the multiple potentialities inhibited by the tyranny of gender. By means of his distinctive visual vocabulary and abject performative tactics, Bowery constantly upsets and disidentifies with normative expressions of gender, which Kate Bornstein so compellingly calls a 'social disease'.[75] Messing with all sorts of coherent cultural narratives, Bowery is the apotheosis of queerness for, as Muñoz writes, 'to perform queerness is [...] to constantly find oneself thriving on sites where meaning does not properly "line up"'.[76]

Notes

1. Dick Jewell, *Leigh Bowery, Serpentine Gallery* (London, 1989) [VHS]. Jewell's personal archive.
2. Eve Kosofsky Sedgwick, 'Queer and Now', in *Tendencies* (London: Routledge, 1994), pp. 1–19 (p. 7).
3. Henry Rogers, 'Leigh Bowery: Life-Works', in *The Art of Queering in Art*, ed. by Henry Rogers (Birmingham: Article Press, 2007), pp. 21–32 (p. 22).
4. Alison Bancroft, 'Leigh Bowery: Queer in Fashion, Queer in Art', *Sexualities*, 15.1 (2012), 68–79 (p. 69).
5. Efrat Tseëlon, 'Reflections on Mask and Carnival', in *Masquerade and Identities: Essays on Gender, Sexuality and Marginality*, ed. by Efrat Tseëlon (London: Routledge, 2001), pp. 18–37 (p. 29).
6. Martin Gayford, 'Ein riesiger unbekümmerter Narrenprinz: Lucian Freuds Bilder von Leigh Bowery', in *Leigh Bowery: Verwandlungskünstler*, ed. by Angela Stief (Vienna: Piet Meyer Verlag, 2015), pp. 261–81 (p. 267). A script in English was provided by the author.
7. Freud's painting of Tilley, *Benefits Supervisor Sleeping* (1995), became known as the most expensive painting sold by a living artist at the time of its sale in 2008.
8. See Tseëlon.
9. Gary Morris, 'Lysergic Landscapes: John Maybury's *Read Only Memory*', *Bright Lights Film Journal*, 31 January 2009, <https://brightlightsfilm.com/lysergic-landscapes-john-mayburys-read-only-memory/> [accessed 27 February 2025].
10. Bancroft, p. 70.
11. See Kristen Galvin, 'Anatomy's a Drag: Queer Fashion and Camp Performance in Leigh Bowery's Birth Scenes', *Critical Studies in Men's Fashion*, 4.2 (2017), 185–202.
12. Rogers, p. 29. Emphasis in original.
13. Michael Bracewell, 'Leigh Bowery's Immaculate Conception', in *The Space Between: Collected Writings*, ed. by Doro Globus (London: Ridinghouse, 2011), pp. 126–33 (p. 131).
14. Heather Love, 'Queer', *TSQ: Transgender Studies Quarterly*, 1.1–2 (2014), 172–76 (pp. 172–73). Emphasis in original.
15. Judith Butler, *Gender Trouble: Feminism and the Subversion of Identity* (New York: Routledge, 1990), p. 45.
16. See Michel Foucault, *The History of Sexuality, Volume 1: An Introduction* (New York: Pantheon Books, 1978).

17. Butler, p. 187. Emphasis in original.
18. Judith Butler, *Bodies That Matter: On the Discursive Limits of "Sex"* (New York: Routledge, 1993), p. 85.
19. Butler, *Bodies That Matter*, p. 85.
20. Peta Tait, 'Performing Shamelessness: Leigh Bowery, Copi and Queer Body Physicality', in *What a Man's Gotta Do?: Masculinities in Performance*, ed. by Adrian Kiernander, Jonathan Bollen and Bruce Parr (Armidale: CALLTS, 2006), pp. 208–21 (p. 211).
21. See José Esteban Muñoz, *Disidentifications: Queers of Color and the Performance of Politics* (Minneapolis: University of Minnesota Press, 1999).
22. Muñoz, p. 99.
23. Muñoz, p. 99.
24. Chuck Kleinhans, 'Taking Out the Trash: Camp and the Politics of Parody', in *The Politics and Poetics of Camp*, ed. by Moe Meyer (London: Routledge, 1994), pp. 157–73 (p. 163).
25. Muñoz, p. 100.
26. Muñoz, p. 4.
27. Muñoz, p. 5.
28. See Janice Winship, 'Women Outdoors: Advertising, Controversy and Disputing Feminism in the 1990s', *International Journal of Cultural Studies*, 3.1 (2000), 27–55.
29. Muñoz, p. 31.
30. Susan Sontag, 'Notes on "Camp"', *Partisan Review*, 31.4 (1964), 515–30 (p. 515).
31. See Richard Dyer, 'It's Being So Camp as Keeps Us Going', in *Camp: Queer Aesthetics and the Performing Subject: A Reader*, ed. by Fabio Cleto (Edinburgh: Edinburgh University Press, 1999), pp. 110–16; and Jack Babuscio, 'The Cinema of Camp (aka Camp and the Gay Sensibility)', in *Camp: Queer Aesthetics and the Performing Subject: A Reader*, ed. by Fabio Cleto (Edinburgh: Edinburgh University Press, 1999), pp. 117–35.
32. See Dee Amy-Chinn, 'This Is Just for Me(n): How the Regulation of Post-Feminist Lingerie Advertising Perpetuates Woman as Object', *Journal of Consumer Culture*, 6.2 (2006), 155–75.
33. Dyer, p. 115.
34. Galvin, p. 200.
35. Butler, *Gender Trouble*, p. 22.
36. See Sandy Stone, 'The Empire Strikes Back: A Posttranssexual Manifesto', in *The Transgender Studies Reader*, ed. by Susan

Stryker and Stephen Whittle (New York: Routledge, 2006), pp. 150–76.

37. Stone, p. 231.
38. See Foucault.
39. Del LaGrace Volcano, 'Hermstory', in *The Feminism and Visual Culture Reader*, ed. by Amelia Jones (London: Routledge, 2010), pp. 27–30 (p. 29). Emphasis in original.
40. Del LaGrace Volcano, *Sublime Mutations* (Tübingen: Konkursbuch Verlag, 2000), p. 5.
41. Dominic Johnson, 'Transition Pieces: The Photography of Del LaGrace Volcano', in *Otherwise: Imagining Queer Feminist Art Histories*, ed. by Amelia Jones and Erin Silver (Manchester: Manchester University Press, 2016), pp. 340–55 (p. 345). Emphasis in original.
42. Del LaGrace Volcano and Ulrika Dahl, *Femmes of Power: Exploding Queer Femininities* (London: Serpent's Tail, 2008), p. 14. Emphasis in original.
43. See Jack (formerly Judith) Halberstam, *Female Masculinity* (Durham, NC: Duke University Press, 1998).
44. Del LaGrace Volcano and Jack Halberstam, *The Drag King Book* (London: Serpent's Tail, 1999), p. 22.
45. See Murray Healy, 'Real Men, Phallicism and Fascism', in *The Subcultures Reader*, ed. by Ken Gelder (London: Routledge, 1997), pp. 367–83.
46. Although the skinhead subculture appears to be widely heterosexist, it was by no means homogeneous. Not only there were some openly gay skinheads (see, for example, the Gay Skinhead Group organization), but some gay skinheads were, hypocritically and paradoxically, Neo-Nazis and supporters of the homophobic far-right National Front and the British National Party, perplexing the modern understanding of 'gay' as a left-wing phenomenon. Nicky Crane, the organizer of the fascist British Movement organization in Kent during the 1980s and the most feared troublemaker at the time, came out publicly as gay years later denouncing his political past.
47. Halberstam, p. 266.
48. Volcano, *Sublime Mutations*, p. 9.
49. Donna J. Haraway, *Simians, Cyborgs, and Women: The Reinvention of Nature* (New York: Routledge, 1991), p. 150.
50. Haraway, p. 181.
51. Haraway, p. 154.

52. See Anne Balsamo, 'Reading Cyborgs Writing Feminism', in *The Gendered Cyborg: A Reader*, ed. by Gill Kirkup, Linda Janes, Kathryn Woodward and Fiona Hovenden (London: Routledge, 2013), pp. 148–58.
53. Balsamo, p. 151.
54. Jennifer González, 'Envisioning Cyborg Bodies: Notes from Current Research', in *The Gendered Cyborg: A Reader*, ed. by Gill Kirkup, Linda Janes, Kathryn Woodward and Fiona Hovenden (London: Routledge, 2013), pp. 58–73 (p. 61).
55. Nadyne Stritzke and Elisa Scaramuzza, 'Trans*, Intersex, and the Question of Pregnancy: Beyond Repronormative Reproduction', in *Transgender and Intersex: Theoretical, Practical, and Artistic Perspectives*, ed. by Stefan Horlacher (New York: Palgrave Macmillan, 2016), pp. 141–63 (p. 146).
56. Stefan Horlacher, 'Transgender and Intersex: Theoretical, Practical, and Artistic Perspectives', in *Transgender and Intersex: Theoretical, Practical, and Artistic Perspectives*, ed. by Stefan Horlacher (New York: Palgrave Macmillan, 2016), pp. 2–27 (p. 14).
57. See Del LaGrace Volcano, Jay Prosser and Eliza Steinbock, 'INTER *me: An Inter-Locution on the Body in Photography', in *Transgender and Intersex: Theoretical, Practical, and Artistic Perspectives*, ed. by Stefan Horlacher (New York: Palgrave Macmillan, 2016), pp. 189–224.
58. Wigstock ran annually from 1985 to 2001, marking the end of the summer. Originally held in Tompkins Square Park, the festival later moved temporarily to Union Square before eventually taking place at the Hudson River piers. In 2018, Lady Bunny and Neil Patrick Harris revived the festival.
59. Francesca Granata, *Experimental Fashion: Performance Art, Carnival and the Grotesque Body* (London: I.B. Tauris, 2017), p. 63.
60. See *Wigstock: The Movie*, dir. by Barry Shils (New York: Samuel Goldwyn, 2003) [DVD]. Author's transcription.
61. Bancroft, p. 75.
62. See Granata.
63. Granata, p. 68.
64. Galvin, p. 187.
65. See Dick Jewell, *Kinky Gerlinky* (2004) [DVD].
66. Galvin, p. 192.
67. See Julia Kristeva, *Powers of Horror: An Essay on Abjection* (New York: Columbia University Press, 1982).

68. Mary Russo, *The Female Grotesque: Risk, Excess, and Modernity* (New York: Routledge, 1994), p. 2.
69. Pregnancy as an aesthetic experience and creative process has been explored in performances by Cathy von Eck, Sandy Huckleberry and, most notably, Marni Kotak who gave birth to her son Ajax in front of a restricted audience at the Microscope Gallery in New York in 2011. See EL Putnam, 'Performing Pregnant: An Aesthetic Investigation of Pregnancy', in *New Feminist Perspectives on Embodiment*, ed. by Clara Fischer and Luna Dolezal (Cham: Palgrave Macmillan, 2018), pp. 203–20.
70. See Sandra Matthews and Laura Wexler, *Pregnant Pictures* (New York: Routledge, 2000).
71. Matthews and Wexler, p. 13.
72. In an article negotiating photographs of pregnancy as sites of cultural struggle, published eleven years after *Pregnant Pictures*, Wexler discusses among others the well-publicized images of Beatie's pregnancy that granted visibility to trans childbearing. See Laura Wexler, 'More Pregnant Pictures', *Photography and Culture*, 4.3 (2011), 309–20.
73. See Lara Karaian, 'Pregnant Men: Repronormativity, Critical Trans Theory and the Re(conceive)ing of Sex and Pregnancy', in *Law, Social and Legal Studies*, 22.2 (2013), pp. 211–30.
74. See JaneMaree Maher, 'A Pregnant Man in the Movies: The Visual Politics of Reproduction', in *Continuum: Journal of Media and Cultural Studies*, 22.2 (2008), 279–88.
75. Kate Bornstein, *Gender Outlaw: On Men, Women, and the Rest of Us* (New York: Vintage Books, 1995), p. 78.
76. Muñoz, p. 78.

Epilogue: Bowery Futures

The end of 2019 marked 25 years since Leigh Bowery's death. To commemorate the anniversary of his passing and celebrate the re-release of their only album *Open Wide* (1997), the remaining core members of Minty – Matthew Glamorre, Richard Torry and Nicola Bateman – reunited for a unique show (with the addition of Bishi Bhattacharya) that took place on 21 December that year at State51, an industrial studio space in Shoreditch, London. Hidden in a dark backstreet off Brick Lane and remote from the trendy bars, the venue was filled with a mixed crowd of mostly old friends and club freaks from the 1980s – many of them retaining a flamboyant attitude in dress and make-up – waiting in anticipation and hanging around a makeshift bar by the entrance with a cup of mulled wine. One of the highlights of the evening was the premiere of *Like a Dream* (2019), a short film directed by Glamorre and Luke Losey to honour Bowery's memory that was projected in between sets on a big screen at the background of the stage.

The finely produced film opens with eerie sounds and a nearly naked and densely inked Ron Athey standing in a dark, atmospheric setting with a young woman hanging curled and upside down in front of his body. Anyone familiar with Bowery's work would recognize that the woman is supported in this position by a special harness devised by Bowery to facilitate his infamous 'Birth' performances. Athey carefully places her on an altar of sorts where she lays motionless in a flesh-tone bodysuit and an elaborate sparkling headpiece, with her long auburn hair sliding down. In the following shot he is seen above her speaking in tongues ecstatically and making a whirring sound, gesturing dramatically with his arms and rolling his eyes as if he is possessed by a superior power through which he enacts some mystic ritual. The young woman rises. She is ethereally beautiful like a nymph in a Pre-Raphaelite fantasy and dances gracefully with a shimmering veil around Athey who stands imperiously with hands on hips until he descends towards the ground. Dreamy ambient sounds and blurry sparkles replace the darkness as a glamorous creature, draped in a sequinned gown and a white, balaclava-like facemask, emerges in Athey's place. It is Bowery, or a vision of him beamed from another dimension to convey a message: 'This is like a dream. This seems so unreal. I can't believe this is true. [...] It's incredible. This is so beautiful', he repeats slowly in Bowery's actual voice gazing into the camera as Glamorre, Bateman and Torry gradually gather around him flamboyantly attired and greet him with a bow. 'There's so much we can do. Total pleasure. This is like a dream', Bowery repeats a few more times – bringing to mind his words in *The Laugh of No. 12* – before floating and fading into a galaxy haze to become a bright star (Figure E.1).[1]

The film, which came about after a forgotten vocal recording of Bowery was rediscovered, is packed with rich symbolism, biblical references and occult mystery. It is both a memorializing tribute to a lost friend and band member as well as a symbolic enactment of Bowery coming back for a moment to give his blessing for the resurrection of Minty. Its premiere on the

Figure E.1: Minty, *Like a Dream*, 2019. Film stills. © Candy Records. Courtesy of Matthew Glamorre.

winter solstice is not coincidental. In ancient pagan cultures the darkest day of the year represents the death and rebirth of the sun and holds a sacred powerful energy and spiritual significance manifest through various ceremonies. Being more like a real ritual, a sort of séance for communicating with Bowery's spirit rather than just a theatrical piece for the camera, the performance triggered a powerful emotional response to those involved who had been close to him, Glamorre tells me.[2]

The opening scene of Athey and the young woman in the harness is a direct reference to Bowery 'gestating' Bateman; only this time it is Athey, a 'magus' able to get into a trance and cross the veil between the worlds, who carries Amber Binnie, Bateman's daughter, as a virgin sacrifice and a conduit to Bowery's spirit. Her movement around Athey following the ritual of possession is reminiscent of Salome's seductive *Dance of the Seven Veils*, performed before King Herod Antipas, but also represents the ceremonial mystical dance of shamanic witches around fire, leading to Athey's collapse to re-emerge as Bowery's spirit. Athey's involvement is not only key in the narrative due to his personal experiences with spiritualism and his extreme performances dealing with altered states of consciousness but also invested in emotional load as both artists shared a mutual respect for each other and a similar sense of humour. 'They could've almost been brothers', Glamorre adds after a short pause for reflection. Athey's physique allows him to fit comfortably in Bowery's original outfits, which only a handful of people would have permission from Bowery's close friends to wear anyway.[3]

On the occasion of the 25th anniversary of Bowery's death a series of tribute articles sprung up online in style and fashion magazines, mainly celebrating his most iconic looks as groundbreaking and influential and ruminating on his wild clubbing days at Taboo. The main emphasis on fashion across these memorial articles is not surprising, considering that Bowery's brief but colourful practice only lasted for a decade and more or less gradually faded into relative obscurity until Fergus Greer's eye-catching collection of photographs was published at the turn of the millennium. Greer's photographs brought Bowery's performative looks to a wider, fashion-conscious audience and built his cult legacy as a mysterious nightclub creature whose exceptional outfits influenced some of the most innovative contemporary fashion designers.

His significant input to fashion aside, Bowery's influence is still powerfully present in nightlife: in the plethora of club nights that seek to sustain a modality of performance and eventful happenings and in the growing number of performers who employ performative costuming or those partygoers and flamboyant creatures of the night who experiment with alien embodiments and extreme dissonant subjectivities. Given his devotion to nightclubs as his main creative outlet and the status of subcultural icon afforded by his looks, this seems only reasonable. Bowery's widespread legacy can be traced to a vibrant period in New York's club culture history in the early 1990s, the Tranimal drag movement that flourished in Los Angeles at the end of the 2000s and an annual Bowery event, Bowerytopia, that was formed in Brisbane in 2016 and aims at bonding the local queer community by celebrating the empowering possibilities of performative costuming. These three instances highlight not only the powerful impact Bowery's practice still holds on visual and club cultures but also its increased significance to contemporary political matters surrounding identity and the queer body.

Club Kids

Even from the early post-Taboo days, Bowery's reputation managed to outgrow London, reaching the other side of the Atlantic and exerting influence on a vivid period in the cultural history of New York marked by a delirious nightclub scene run by a bunch of nightlife entrepreneurs and committed partygoers known as Club Kids. After Andy Warhol's death in 1987 the historically thriving nightlife of New York seemed to have reached a turning point. Surrounded by a clique of 'superstars', Warhol had been a fixture in the city's premium nightclubs and underground venues for the previous two decades and his sudden passing was thus translated by cultural journalist Michael Musto in *The Village Voice* as 'the death of downtown'.[4] About a year later, *New York Magazine* dedicated a cover story to a newly formed tight-knit group of teenagers dubbed the 'Club Kids' who had just begun to get noticed for their parties in venues, such as The Tunnel and The World, where attendees were required to dress up to gain entry.

Drag culture and an expanding ballroom scene that encouraged sartorial experimentation had already been very prominent in New York's subcultural nightlife, but these early Club Kids moved away from commonplace drag embodiments, creating strange gender-bending clownish looks. The initial Pop-Art-infused fashions made of product packages gave space to the typical Club Kid look that often referenced early childhood with pastel pyjamas and onesies, vintage metal lunch boxes, bright make-up and platform shoes that constructed a distorted image of innocence. Gradually, an anything-goes mentality that encompassed a variety of styles and looks took over as long as they were ridiculously excessive or alien. Bowery is regularly mentioned as a sort of patron saint for the Club Kids who assimilated his aesthetic and followed his lead on nightclub extravagance, prompting a sensational cultural phenomenon that induced moral panic in conservative Americans. Club promoter and one of the instigators of the scene, Michael Alig, a dropout of the Fashion Institute of Technology in New York, had incorporated in his outfits many elements evidently inspired by Bowery's looks: from large, coloured spots covering his face to patterned jumpsuits with low-cut necklines and an exposed bottom. Without denying the resemblance he described the Club Kids' styling as an 'aesthetic sampling' of 'bits and pieces' from Bowery and Warhol, the crowd at Pyramid Club and the East Village punks.[5]

Bowery visited New York for the first time in 1983 after being invited by now renown event producer Susanne Bartsch to present his work as an emerging fashion designer. He subsequently returned many times to perform and socialize with the subcultural *haut monde*, turning into a sort of celebrity in the club scene. An ex-Londoner who introduced several ideas to New York nightlife through her famous events during the 1980s, Bartsch was behind club nights at Savage (which were inspired by Taboo), Bentley's and Copacabana – all of which Bowery attended when he was in town, making a name for himself and even appearing in *PAPER* magazine, New York's independent style bible at the time. In his memoir and historical account of the Club Kids, Walt Cassidy, a prominent member of Alig's crowd also known as Waltpaper, notes that Bowery made an appearance at a significant downtown ballroom event at The World in 1988. Dressed in a yellow ensemble and the head harness fitted with lightbulbs, Bowery came second in the category 'Beat Face and Haute Coiffure' after duo Kurt and Bart, who were very fond of him, surprisingly managed to steal the show in matching Kabuki-style looks, sowing the seeds of theatrical excess. 'Their visionary commitment to silliness and irreverence created a bridge from the Bowery-infused London scene and set the tone for what would quickly become the hallmark of New York City's blossoming Club Kid contingent', writes Cassidy.[6]

Although little has been published about Bowery's activities and performances in New York's nightclubs, such as Jackie 60, the Red Zone and The Limelight, it looks like he hardly missed a chance to be part of exciting events in the city and go to parties. Housed in an impressive Gothic Revival building with ornate stained-glass windows, originally used as an Episcopalian church, The Limelight in Chelsea was one of the most remarkable mega clubs in town, with its opening party in 1983 hosted by none other than Warhol. Sue Tilley recalls that the original concept for Bowery's performance at The Limelight involved jumping up and down on a trampoline that would be slashed at some point with a jigsaw, causing him to fall through the stage. However, his club performances often deviated from the plan and this one was no exception.[7] His uncomfortable costume, which featured a toilet seat worn around his neck and platform shoes, combined with a significant alcohol consumption made the trampoline act impossible and Bowery kept falling off. To make things worse (or better) the club management only provided an electric drill and thus Bowery had to improvise by running around the stage randomly making holes in the floorboards. Despite the unexpected issues one can only imagine that he still did not fail to deliver spectacular weirdness. On the contrary, his brief performance at the Red Zone did go as planned. After he went on stage fully attired, Charles Atlas and Mr. Pearl appeared dressed as beauticians and threw eggs at him.

What perhaps best documents Bowery's arrival in New York's subcultural scene is his appearances in Nelson Sullivan's prolific video collection that chronicles the city's underground queer communities during the 1980s. An amateur videographer immersed in partying and nightlife, Sullivan with his portable VHS camcorder was a regular sight in downtown New York.

For more than a decade he walked around recording himself and his surroundings, constantly documenting events and the lives of his scenester friends that included artists and club personalities; RuPaul, Lady Bunny, Quentin Crisp, Keith Haring, Joey Arias, Andy Warhol, band Deee-Lite and some of the Club Kids are featured in his videos among many others. Existing footage from his collection shows Bowery on various occasions: mingling with the disco-dancing crowd at Bentley's; being one of the MCs at Love Ball, Bartsch's AIDS benefit at the Roseland Ballroom; and having fun at a joint birthday party organized for him, video artist Tom Rubnitz and Atlas.[8] Whenever Bowery was in town he rushed from club to club drawing attention with his peculiar looks, soon becoming known as an eccentric club personality from London and disseminating the myth that surrounded Taboo. The underground embraced him and the younger generation of Club Kids, some of whom Bowery also socialized with, looked up to him and aspired to their own post-Warholian empire of freaks, which they actually achieved (Figures E.2 and E.3).

The Club Kids' breakthrough came in 1990 when after several club nights in various venues Alig hosted his wild Disco 2000 weekly party at The Limelight, turning it into a legendary hotspot of outrageousness and debauchery. Memorable events until its demise in 1996 include 'hot body' contests, pee-drinking incidents, blood-feast-themed parties and a champagne enema performance in Bowery style. Thousands of people flocked to the renovated Limelight with its spacious dancefloor, sophisticated laser lighting, smoke machines and go-go cages hanging from the ceiling. Behind these parties a community of Club Kids in a variety of elaborate costumes, along with their dancing mascot Clara the Carefree Chicken, epitomized a rapidly spreading enthusiasm for freedom and self-expression set to the beat of electronic dance music.

The success of the Club Kids would probably have not been so prominent without a well-sustained promotional strategy that included so-called 'outlaw parties' in public spaces that attracted hundreds, a luring television commercial for the party created by Atlas and *Project X* (1988–96), a magazine reporting on the latest club developments in the city that occasionally favouring snapshots and news of Bowery regarding his whereabouts. The unprecedented visibility of this particular club scene is arguably mostly indebted to its major exposure in widely broadcast daytime tabloid talk

Figure E.2: 'Looks to Look for', *Project X*, April–May 1992. Photographs by Michael Fazakerley. Courtesy of Ernie Glam.

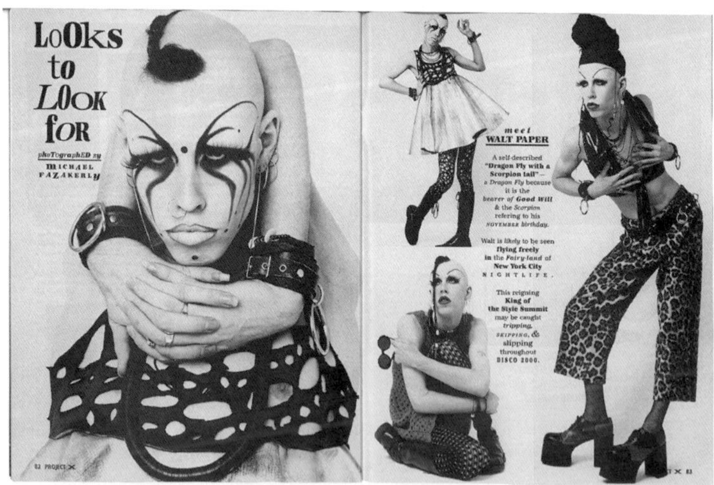

Figure E.3: 'Looks to Look for', *Project X*, date unknown. Photographs by Michael Fazakerley. Courtesy of Ernie Glam.

shows that Alig and his most devoted Club Kids gladly attended as 'celebutant' guests in their most scandalous looks, becoming national sensations by upsetting the conservative values of moralists and arousing the repressed desires of restless youth around the country. In an episode of *The Joan Rivers Show*, Bowery charmingly paraded through the studio with Club Kids Alig, James St. James, Ernie Glam and Amanda Lepore. Dressed in one of his costumes with a huge pompom covering his head, he briefly spoke in defence of self-expression, individuality and the desire to shock people, with Joan Rivers being impressed by and joking about his realistic boobs.

In an endeavour to extend their reach beyond the boundaries of the nightclub, the Club Kids in association with *Project X* organized a multimedia exhibition at the Willow Gallery in Soho, in which some of them, outrageously attired, were displayed as living installations, echoing Bowery's *tableaux vivant* at Anthony d'Offay's gallery. Cassidy writes that Bowery's presence at the show sent a wave of excitement among the performers, especially Alig who was very 'keen to impress' him with the progress they had made.[9] He also recalls the interactive installation he and his friend Desi created where they were placed close to each other connected by a tube as if Cassidy, scantily clad, had either aborted or given birth to a blood-covered Desi. Bowery in his 'Mrs. Peanut' look seemed very amused with their performance and kept directing visitors towards them, recalls Cassidy, wondering whether they had slightly inspired his famous 'Birth' extravaganza.

Bowery's strong presence in New York's subcultural landscape and the legend of Taboo might have motivated the emergence and refinement of the Club Kids by influencing their aesthetics and shaping their ethos; however, their scene evolved along the way more into a business-oriented endeavour in which their dissonant identities served as commodities and as the necessary lubricant to keep the machinery of the nightclub enterprise running smoothly. From the early days most of Alig's outlaw parties were funded as publicity stunts by the nightclub owners who happened to host his nights and in the credits of most *Project X* issues they appear as publishers. Although not necessarily orchestrated by club owners themselves, the frequent televised appearances of the Club Kids as brand ambassadors – in which a strong sense of performance radiates not only from the hosts' moral preaching but also their own apathetic stance and 'provocative' demeanour – were nothing but beneficial for the business.

There was indeed a mutual financial understanding between clubs and these flamboyant nightclub celebrities that went beyond the typical agreements usually pertaining to party organizers reaping just the profit from the entrance fee after a fun night with like-minded people. The Club Kids at The Limelight were essentially employed by its owner Peter Gatien and, even though they undoubtedly constituted a creative group of people that sought to be different, their motives – unlike Bowery's – were largely driven by commercial success and their difference was projected as a viable career strategy. The nationwide media exposure allowed them to frequently travel around the country and abroad to attend clubs as a sort of freak show, living out their celebrity fantasies and easily capitalizing on their looks. Annual style summits were also organized to promote the movement. This proved a great strategy for growing the Club Kids network by inspiring young creatives and misfits to move to New York and become part of Gatien's expanding crew of club freaks that collaborated closely with PR teams and photographers and worked across a number of mega venues he acquired after the huge success of The Limelight, namely Palladium, The Tunnel and Club USA.

Whether employed in administrative roles or as dancers, promoters, art team assistants and door managers, the Club Kids turned into a wide corporate brand flirting with the mainstream rather than just an underground obscure scene. As arrogant and delusional as they might have seemed during their many television appearances, they openly bragged about the good money they were making out of their hedonistic lifestyle and extreme looks, putting idealisms of self-identification and expression in second place. Apart from the dissident embodiments there is indeed little connection between the Club Kids and those earlier subcultural club scenes that bonded over exclusion, between the clubbing experience in an avaricious mega-club and the strong sense of community in an intimate underground venue. One might even conclude that the fame-hungry Club Kids were partly a youth movement but, more emphatically, an entrepreneurial corporation, that they were being exploited for the huge financial gain of club owners like Gatien and that themselves were more than happy to play this game and less concerned with identity politics or resistance against mass culture. Yet, it would be fair to speculate that the New Romantic scene especially would in all likelihood have met the same fate had it been given the chance.

The Club Kids and Gatien's clubbing empire clumsily came to a halt after a series of dramatic events unfolded during Mayor Rudolph Giuliani's term of office in the mid-1990s. By 1996, Giuliani's 'Quality of Life' campaign had gathered steam by targeting New York's nightclubs as wholly sinister venues promoting rampant antisocial behaviour and, consequently, Gatien was the first to come under scrutiny. Suspected of facilitating drug trafficking, his clubs were constantly infiltrated by undercover police officers and faced numerous raids and closures. To complicate matters, Alig, who had been struggling with drug addiction, was charged with and later pleaded guilty to murdering and dismembering former Limelight Club Kid and reputed drug dealer Andre 'Angel' Melendez during a drug-induced rage, the remains of whom he brutally dumped in the Hudson River. After no concrete evidence was found to support the drug conspiracy charges, Gatien – financially and mentally exhausted from his continuous trouble with the city, state and Federal Court – pleaded guilty to tax evasion in 1999 before eventually being deported to his native Canada by the Immigration and Naturalization Service. Shortly after The Limelight ceased to operate as a nightclub it turned into a gleaming three-storey shopping centre worthy of its newly gentrified surroundings, while the sensationalized story of Alig and the Club Kids provided a compelling plot for the American indie film *Party Monster* (2003).

In New York's rich subcultural history during the twentieth century – from the jazz clubs in Harlem to CBGB's punk in East Village and the New York Dolls (whom Malcolm McLaren briefly managed before returning to England to 'invent' punk with the Sex Pistols); the birth of hip hop in The Bronx and the No Wave scene in the Lower East Side; Warhol's Factory parties; the explosion of disco and Studio 54; the Black and Latinx queer voguers in uptown drag balls or Klaus Nomi with his cyborg looks and operatic voice – an Australian performer imported from London turned out to be a pivotal force in shaping the freak aesthetics of the city's club culture in the late 1980s.

Tranimal

On the West Coast, meanwhile, a group of party-goers and drag queens in San Francisco begun experimenting with theatrical embodiments, challenging prevailing ideas of beauty, identity and gender expression. This experimentation gave rise to a monstrous drag movement, which performer and musician Jer Ber Jones dubbed 'Tranimal' (a portmanteau of 'tranny' and 'animal') to emphasize its animalistic raw quality in contrast to the polished aesthetic of conventional drag queens.[10]

It has become an exhausting repetition, but Bowery, with his highly trans-queer performative costuming, is also in the case of Tranimal usually the first person cited as inspirational alongside other icons, such as Boy George, Grace Jones, Cindy Sherman and John Waters. Tranimal gained wider visibility and became established as the imaginative manifestation of creative, animalistic interpretations of drag after acclaimed photographer and visual artist Austin Young – who photographed Bowery and various drag scenes early in his career – came up with the idea of organizing Tranimal-conversion participatory art projects in collaboration with artists and drag personalities Squeaky Blonde and Fade-Dra Phey. Since the first event of this kind at the Machine Project in 2009, a not-for-profit arts organization based in Los Angeles, several followed in bigger venues, such as the Hammer Museum (2010), the Berkeley Art Museum (2011) and more recently the Los Angeles Music Center (2018).

These so-called 'Tranimal workshops' involve members of the public willing to submit themselves to the hands and vision of various guest local drag artists and stylists in order to undergo a spontaneous Tranimal makeover. A team of invited experts (including former Club Kid and RuPaul's long-time make-up artist Mathu Andersen) equipped with hairpieces and wigs, hideous hand-made creations, crafted masks, rugs, plastic body parts, lots of make-up and all kinds of unexpected found objects commit to transforming eager participants into ephemeral art. After the makeover, revamped as they are, they revel in a professional photoshoot by Young as atrocious supermodels. His Tranimal portfolio is replete with colourful portraits of otherworldly beings; most of them beyond categorization. The face is almost always fully covered and the body often appears disfigured and gender-ambiguous. A typical Tranimal strategy for re-shaping the human head is covering it with pantyhose that can be stuffed into any form imagined, manipulated and decorated, painted over and ripped, turning the wearer into a creepy soft sculpture. Bowery also experimented with a pantyhose-wrapped head, which allowed him to paint over facial features anew, giving him an eerie appearance. Yet, the Tranimal look takes this prompt much further by using padding and layering underneath to create a messy mass, with swollen lips covering half of the face or horrendous tumours sprouting chunks of hair, resembling glammed-up versions of the Elephant Man, the notorious Victorian-era 'freak' John Merrick who suffered from a rare congenital disorder (Figure E.4).

With gender rendered often unreadable within the post-anthropocentric framework of the movement, Tranimals distance themselves from the realistic or comical conventions of drag and play with gender stereotypes in a way that is clearly reminiscent of Bowery's earlier trans-queer embodiments. Their attempt to ignore gender and work outside its social structures not only challenges dominant perspectives on drag practice and the viewer's understanding of the performance of gender but also creates a fresh dialectical space in drag and gender studies. The distorted genderfuck Tranimal embodiments, scholar Nick Cherryman argues, complicate and at the same time comply with Judith Butler's celebrated thesis on drag being subversive only by exposing the performativity of gender.[11] Indeed, any indication of the participants' sex or gender is most often blotted out significantly in their aggressive transformation into a gender-unspecific Tranimal – and if gender is theoretically removed from drag, Butler's argument appears to be obsolete if not utterly pointless. Yet, gender performativity is so firmly embedded in social structures that it gets unavoidably in the way no matter the vigorous effort to overcome it. It is present in the anxiety to escape it, the very act of viewing the Tranimal and trying to make sense of it through one's automatic interpretation of its mannerisms and traits. Whether successfully read or not, Tranimal drag too serves as a subversive exposure and reminder of the unconsciously deep-seated performativity of gender. Although unattainable in its explicit attempts to eliminate the constructs of gender, Tranimal,

Figure E.4: Austin Young, untitled Tranimal, 2011. © Austin Young.

Cherryman concludes, opens the way for experimentation and exciting new types of drag.

The first Tranimal workshop at the Machine Project came about in conjunction with the Ultra Fabulous, Beyond Drag film festival (2009) at the Downtown Independent theatre and after a year it was repeated at the Hammer Museum as part of TRANSylvania Mania!, a queer Halloween event supported by the museum's public programme. What had started as a smaller-scale affair steadily evolved into a wider social experience and a participatory performative artwork beyond the confines of queer culture. The next Tranimal workshop at the Berkeley Art Museum took place in the context of Confuse-a-tron, an interdisciplinary event curated by artist, educator and director of Machine Project, Mark Allen, in which four – clearly very different in subject – drop-in sessions transpired simultaneously, aiming at disseminating knowledge and bringing diverse communities together. Taking an interest in creating social experiences where different subjectivities can mingle, Allen set up a participatory art project combining workshops on succulent cloning, making Korean kimchi, producing electronic sounds with cacti and melons, and transforming into a Tranimal model. Deriving from what Nicolas Bourriaud theorizes as 'relational aesthetics'– a set of artistic practices introduced during the 1990s where human relations and their social context are prioritized over passive consumption of art – Allen filled the museum space with children arranging planters, cooking enthusiasts chopping cabbages, technology geeks sticking cables into fruit and distorted gender-queer creatures posing in high heels and abused stockings on their heads.[12]

Following a similar interdisciplinary ethos, a subsequent experimental Tranimal master class at the Machine Project incorporated performance, photography and interactive sound design. After four participants were transformed into striking Tranimals and before Young captured their looks, Allen attached to their costumes light-sensitive circuit boards that reacted to movement and light by adjusting the sound frequencies while opera singer and performance artist Juliana Snapper guided them to explore the vocal expression of their new identities, resulting in an eyesore cyborg noise chorus. Almost a decade since the first workshop, Tranimals returned in 2018 for Sleepless: The Music Center after Hours, a recurring art night at the Dorothy Chandler Pavilion located within the Los Angeles Music Center. This event was organized in partnership with Fulcrum Arts, a charitable organization interested in the intersection of art and science, and hosted a rich line-up of performances, large-scale projections, virtual reality environments, Tranimal transformations and DJ sets. The inclusion of Tranimal workshops in the programmes and events of some of the most reputable art institutions is nothing but a glaring testament to the once-neglected art of performative costuming, which has now infiltrated and – to some extent – been embraced by the art establishment. While this reflects an increasingly open-minded curatorial approach witnessed in recent years, much of the credit for this shift undeniably goes to Bowery's enduring influence and the heightened visibility of his practice.

Bowerytopia

The potential of radical dressing in sustaining a queer community with a shared vision for diversity and self-expression against heteronormative ideals (which manifests sumptuously in Bowery's practice) has inspired a series of events curated by The Stitchery Collective in Brisbane. These events function as a homage to Bowery's important legacy to Australia's queer community and as significant sites for fostering creativity, blurring gender and bonding over the celebration of queerness.[13]

Prioritizing the social and cultural aspects of fashion and promoting inclusivity, accessibility and participation, the design collective came up in 2016 with Bowery Bowl, a costume competition celebrating Bowery's practice that was held in the East Brisbane Bowls Club in collaboration with the non-profit organization Backbone Youth Arts. The event, which strongly encouraged experimentation in costuming by using accessible materials, attracted a crowd of approximately a hundred people in a specially designed space with play installations and dance areas. A costume parade in front of a panel of judges who voted for the categories 'Best Bowery Look', 'Best Club Kid Look' and 'Queen of the Bowl' was the highlight of the evening. The two events that followed this first endeavour were larger in scale and more ambitious, albeit retaining the emphasis on Bowery's performative costuming as an empowering creative strategy for community building and diversity.

In 2018, The Stitchery Collective produced Bowery Haus as the closing party of Melt, an annual queer arts festival held at the Brisbane Powerhouse. Besides the impressive glittering set design, DJs and awards for the most flamboyant participants, special costuming and a glitter station were available to lure the unprepared latecomers or passers-by. Bowery Haus was repeated the following year at Melt festival with the addition of photographer Georgia Wallace who – similarly to Young's Tranimal workshops – was commissioned to take studio portraits of the participants to reward their effort in apparent homage to Greer's collaboration with Bowery. Some of them experimented with broader ideas of masquerade, while most reinterpreted the signature aesthetic aspects of Bowery's freakishness and copied his posing: a black shiny BDSM bodysuit, a blue face, clownish make-up and pigment dropping from the top of the head, elaborate headdresses, masks and shape-shifting garments. Enveloped head to toe in a tight floral bodysuit with a long skirt and sporting a big round belly, one participant channelled both the characteristic floral pattern of the 'Metropolitan' gown and 'Globe'. During their performance a matching simulated foetus attached to an umbilical cord came out of the belly by manipulating the costume, paying tribute to Bowery's 'Birth' performance. In recent years The Stitchery Collective presented Bowerytopia as part of the Brisbane Festival at The Tivoli, their biggest and most ambitious celebration of Bowery that attracts hundreds of costumed attendees for a vibrant party with performances, exhibitions, costume competitions, interactive photosets and a lot of posing (Figure E.5).

Utilizing Bowery's practice of performative costuming, The Stitchery Collective aims to create and promote a safe environment where the creative exploration of identity can be celebrated through participation and the blurring of boundaries between performer and audience. Drawing on the work of Angela Jones, they describe these Bowery events as instances of 'queer heterotopias' where '"othered" individuals can freely perform their identities and transgress dominant heteronormative ideals', turning into empowering 'political spaces' of resistance against normalization.[14] Bringing to the fore enduring queer cultures of costume, the events embrace inclusivity, diversity and playful experimentation with performance. By naming their queer parties after Bowery, The Stitchery Collective – more than any other cultural movement or trend that owes its formation to his practice – explicitly honour and value his

Figure E.5: Participants in Bowerytopia at The Tivoli, Brisbane, 2022. Photograph by James Caswell. © James Caswell.

performative costuming for its powerful disruptive potential that continues to speak to the desires and battles of flamboyant queer communities.

Thirty years after Bowery's death his legacy is more discernible and relevant than ever, extending beyond the confines of fashion design or art to the social sphere and becoming a paradigm of queer visibility and club culture extravagance. In fashion Bowery's influence continues to be significant, evident, for example, in Alexander McQueen's pale faces with sex-doll lips; Gareth Pugh's latex-wrapped models; Richard Quinn's floral gowns and balaclavas; Maison Margiela's head pompoms and merkins; and Rick Owens' Spring/Summer 2016 runway show where models paraded with gymnasts harnessed to their bodies upside-down. Here and elsewhere, Bowery's freakishness has resonated with the increasing urgency of identity exploration, self-expression and representation pertaining to queer politics and lives through the cultural histories of the Club Kids, Tranimal and the Bowery parties as well as through the numerous club nights with a similar ethos that continue to pop up.

Bowery's performative life project was an ongoing pursuit of refusing to adapt to certain ideals and asserting difference. His glorification of artificiality, his dedication and persistence in costuming the body and drastically altering his appearance speak to one's fundamental right to self-identification and representation beyond essentialist notions of naturalness. His determination to constantly re-design the self and his constant state of flux counter to the idea of an authentic identity tied to the biological or unadorned body is what particularly resonates with queer modes of being. Inextricably linked to nightclubs, his practice has – not unexpectedly – also left a distinctive mark on club cultures, which are, nevertheless, customarily associated with queerness. LOVERBOY (2015) at VFD; Deep Trash (2014–20) at Bethnal Green Working Men's Club; Sink the Pink (2008–) and INFERNO (2015–) at various venues are some recent notable examples of queer club nights in London where live art and clubbing coalesce and dressing up is strongly encouraged as an act of asserting difference.

Taboo was a melting pot of ideas. It's notoriety still holds an enduring fascination as well as Bowery's wildness as social commentary on sexuality does. His legacy is palpable in the enthusiasm for body experimentation in younger generations of clubbers and drag performers who explore alternative ideas of gendered subjectivities. Their investment in body modification and costuming resonates deeply with and endorses a greater attempt witnessed in mainstream culture in recent years to get rid of oppressive stereotypes, promote body positivity and non-conformity and celebrate gender fluidity and difference. Under this spirit of increased acceptance even the high fashion magazine *Vogue* commissioned a series of short videos in 2019, titled *Extreme Beauty*, in which thirteen creatives transform into their unique monstrous alter egos while talking about their backgrounds and life experiences; Bowery is often cited as an inspiration. It seems that the world he sought to shock with his investment in extremity and quirkiness to confront negative societal norms has in many ways eventually caught up with him.

Back in 2002, Boy George stated prophetically: 'In twenty years' time there will be these Leigh Bowery gangs. There will be this cult of Leigh Bowery [...] in the same way as [Stanley Kubrick's] *Clockwork Orange*.'[15] Hopefully, this new Bowery breed does not incite terror, as Alex's group of outlaw 'droogs' do in Kubrick's iconic film, but instead poetically fosters wider visibility and acceptance of difference. They are Bowery's legacy, representing the best outcome of a transformative practice of performative costuming that continues to merge art and life.

Notes

1. *Like a Dream*, dir. by Matthew Glamorre and Luke Losey (London: Candy Records, 2019). Glamorre's personal archive. Author's transcription.
2. Matthew Glamorre, unpublished interview with the author, London, May 2020.
3. Glamorre.
4. See Michael Musto, 'The Death of Downtown', *Village Voice*, 28 April 1987, pp. 15–20.
5. Christopher Bollen, 'Michael Alig', *Interview*, March 2010, <https://www.interviewmagazine.com/culture/michael-alig> [accessed 27 February 2025].
6. Walt Cassidy, *New York: Club Kids* (Bologna: Damiani, 2019), p. 60.
7. See Sue Tilley, *Leigh Bowery: The Life and Times of an Icon* (London: Hodder & Stoughton, 1997).
8. See 5NinthAvenueProject, YouTube, <https://www.youtube.com/5ninthavenueproject> [accessed 27 February 2025]. Sullivan's ambition to share his vast collection of footage through his own cable television show was tragically interrupted by his sudden death in 1989. His archive is now preserved at The Fales Library and Special Collections at New York University.
9. Cassidy, p. 198.
10. Although the term 'tranny' – like 'queer' and 'freak' – has been used sometimes in an attempt to reclaim it from its negative association, its flippant use by drag performers remained problematic for trans people.
11. See Nick Cherryman, 'The Tranimal: Throwing Gender Out of Drag?', in *Contemporary Drag Practices and Performers: Drag in a Changing Scene, Volume 1*, ed. by Mark Edward and Stephen Farrier (London: Methuen, 2020), pp. 132–42.
12. See Nicolas Bourriaud, *Relational Aesthetics* (Dijon: Les Presses du Réel, 2002).

13. See Madeline Taylor, Anna Germaine Hickey and Remi Roehrs, 'Celebrating Bowery: Radical Costume Parties as Queer Heterotopia in Brisbane', *Studies in Costume and Performance*, 5.1 (2020), 85–100.
14. Taylor, Hickey and Roehrs, p. 91.
15. Boy George in *The Legend of Leigh Bowery*, dir. by Charles Atlas (London: BBC4, 2008).

Bibliography

5NinthAvenueProject, YouTube, <https://www.youtube.com/5ninthavenueproject> [accessed 27 February 2025].

Adamson, Glenn, and Jane Pavitt, 'Postmodernism: Style and Subversion', in *Postmodernism: Style and Subversion, 1970–1990*, ed. by Glenn Adamson and Jane Pavitt (London: V&A Publishing, 2011), pp. 12–97.

Als, Hilton, 'Cruel Story of Youth', in *Leigh Bowery*, ed. by Robert Violette (London: Robert Violette, 1998), pp. 10–25.

Amy-Chinn, Dee, 'This Is Just for Me(n)': How the Regulation of Post-Feminist Lingerie Advertising Perpetuates Woman as Object', *Journal of Consumer Culture*, 6.2 (2006), 155–75.

Anthony d'Offay Gallery, *Leigh Bowery* (press release) (1988). 261830-1001, Ephemera, Tate Library, Tate Museum.

Atlas, Charles, '1990–2010: Video Shorts; Video Collages; Video Featurettes', in *Charles Atlas*, ed. by Lauren Wittels (Munich: Prestel, 2015), pp. 144–79.

Auslander, Philip, *Performing Glam Rock: Gender and Theatricality in Popular Music* (Ann Arbor: University of Michigan Press, 2006).

Babuscio, Jack, 'The Cinema of Camp (aka Camp and the Gay Sensibility)', in *Camp: Queer Aesthetics and the Performing Subject: A Reader*, ed. by Fabio Cleto (Edinburgh: Edinburgh University Press, 1999), pp. 117–35.

Balsamo, Anne, 'Reading Cyborgs Writing Feminism', in *The Gendered Cyborg: A Reader*, ed. by Gill Kirkup, Linda Janes,

Kathryn Woodward and Fiona Hovenden (London: Routledge, 2013), pp. 148–58.

Bancroft, Alison, 'Leigh Bowery: Queer in Fashion, Queer in Art', *Sexualities*, 15.1 (2012), 68–79.

Berghaus, Günter, *Theatre, Performance, and the Historical Avant-Garde* (New York: Palgrave Macmillan, 2005).

Blyn, Robin, *The Freak-Garde: Extraordinary Bodies and Revolutionary Art in America* (Minneapolis: University of Minnesota Press, 2013).

Bogdan, Robert, *Freak Show: Presenting Human Oddities for Amusement and Profit* (Chicago: The University of Chicago Press, 1988).

Bollen, Christopher, 'Michael Alig', *Interview*, 24 March 2010, <https://www.interviewmagazine.com/culture/michael-alig> [accessed 27 February 2025].

Bordowitz, Gregg, 'The AIDS Crisis Is Ridiculous', in *The AIDS Crisis Is Ridiculous and Other Writings, 1986–2003*, ed. by James Meyer (Cambridge: The MIT Press, 2006), pp. 43–67.

Bornstein, Kate, *Gender Outlaw: On Men, Women, and the Rest of Us* (New York: Vintage Books, 1995).

Bourriaud, Nicolas, *Relational Aesthetics* (Dijon: Les Presses du Réel, 2002).

Bracewell, Michael, *England Is Mine: Pop Life in Albion from Wilde to Goldie* (London: Flamingo, 1998).

Bracewell, Michael, 'Leigh Bowery's Immaculate Conception', in *The Space Between: Selected Writings on Art*, ed. by Doro Globus (London: Ridinghouse, 2012), pp. 126–33.

Bürger, Peter, *Theory of the Avant-Garde* (Minneapolis: University of Minnesota Press, 1984).

Butler, Judith, *Bodies That Matter: On the Discursive Limits of 'Sex'* (New York: Routledge, 1993).

Butler, Judith, *Gender Trouble: Feminism and the Subversion of Identity* (New York: Routledge, 1990).

Califia, Patrick, *Speaking Sex to Power: The Politics of Queer Sex* (San Francisco: Cleis Press, 2002).

Cameron, Deborah, *Feminism and Linguistic Theory*, 2nd edn (New York: Palgrave Macmillan, 1992).

Carlson, Marla, *Performing Bodies in Pain: Medieval and Post-Modern Martyrs, Mystics, and Artists* (New York: Palgrave Macmillan, 2010).

Carr, C., 'The Pain Artist', in *On Edge: Performance at the End of the Twentieth Century* (Middletown: Wesleyan University Press, 2008), pp. 321–24.

Cassidy, Walt, *New York: Club Kids* (Bologna: Damiani, 2019).

Cherryman, Nick, 'The Tranimal: Throwing Gender Out of Drag?', in *Contemporary Drag Practices and Performers: Drag in a Changing Scene, Volume 1*, ed. by Mark Edward and Stephen Farrier (London: Methuen, 2020), pp. 132–42.

Chicago, Judy, *Through the Flower: My Struggle as a Woman Artist* (New York: Authors Choice Press, 1975).

Clarke, John, 'Style', in *Resistance through Rituals: Youth Subcultures in Post-War Britain*, ed. by Stuart Hall and Tony Jefferson (Abingdon: Routledge, 2002), pp. 175–91.

The Clothes Show, BBC One, 17 November 1986.

Craik, Jennifer, *Fashion: The Key Concepts* (Oxford: Berg, 2009).

Crimp, Douglas, 'On the Museum's Ruins', in *The Anti-Aesthetic: Essays on Postmodern Culture*, ed. by Hal Foster (New York: The New Press, 1998), pp. 49–63.

Crimp, Douglas, 'Portraits of People with Aids', in *Melancholia and Moralism: Essays on AIDS and Queer Politics* (Cambridge: The MIT Press, 2002), pp. 83–107.

The DAG: Bite the Hand that Feeds (London: Live Art Development Agency, 2012) [DVD].

Davis, Lennard J., 'Crips Strike Back: The Rise of Disability Studies', *American Literary History*, 11.3 (1999), 500–12.

Doyle, Jennifer, 'Blood Work & "Art Criminals"', *Art21 Magazine*, 10 December 2008, <http://magazine.art21.org/2008/12/10/blood-work-art-criminals> [accessed 27 February 2025].

Doyle, Jennifer, *Hold It against Me: Difficulty and Emotion in Contemporary Art* (Durham, NC: Duke University Press, 2013).

Dworkin, Andrea, *Intercourse* (New York: Basic Books, 2006).

Dyer, Richard, 'It's Being So Camp as Keeps Us Going', in *Camp: Queer Aesthetics and the Performing Subject: A Reader*, ed. by Fabio Cleto (Edinburgh: Edinburgh University Press, 1999), pp. 110–16.

Engler, Martin, 'The Multiple Bodies of Leigh Bowery', in *Leigh Bowery: Beautified Provocation*, ed. by René Zechlin (Heidelberg: Kehrer Verlag, 2008), pp. 55–60.

English, Bonnie, *A Cultural History of Fashion in the 20th and 21st Centuries: From Catwalk to Sidewalk* (London: Bloomsbury, 2013).

Fiedler, Leslie, *Freaks: Myths and Images of the Secret Self* (New York: Simon & Schuster, 1978).

Flanagan, Bob, *The Pain Journal* (Los Angeles: Semiotext(e), 2000).

Foss, Daniel, *Freak Culture: Life-Style and Politics* (New York: E. P. Dutton, 1972).

Foster, Hal, *The Return of the Real: The Avant-Garde at the End of the Century* (Cambridge: The MIT Press, 1996).

Foucault, Michel, *The History of Sexuality, Volume 1: An Introduction* (New York: Pantheon Books, 1978).

Fraser, Mat, *Devolving the Mutant, Mat Fraser's Live Art 1999–2011: From Societal Oppression to Personal Succession* (London: Live Art Development Agency, 2011) [DVD].

Freud, Sigmund, 'Humour', in *The Standard Edition of the Complete Psychological Works of Sigmund Freud, Volume XXI (1927–1931): The Future of an Illusion, Civilization and Its Discontents and Other Works*, ed. by James Strachey (London: Vintage, 2001), pp. 159–66.

Fried, Michael, 'Art and Objecthood', in *Art and Objecthood: Essays and Reviews* (Chicago: The University of Chicago Press, 1998), pp. 148–72.

Frost, Laura, *Sex Drives: Fantasies of Fascism in Literary Modernism* (Ithaca: Cornell University Press, 2002).

Galvin, Kristen, 'Anatomy's a Drag: Queer Fashion and Camp Performance in Leigh Bowery's Birth Scenes', *Critical Studies in Men's Fashion*, 4.2 (2017), 185–202.

Gammel, Irene, *Baroness Elsa: Gender, Dada, and Everyday Modernity* (Cambridge: The MIT Press, 2003).

Garland Thomson, Rosemarie, *Extraordinary Bodies: Figuring Physical Disability in American Culture and Literature* (New York: Columbia University Press, 1997).

Garland Thomson, Rosemarie, 'Staring Back: Self-Representations of Disabled Performance Artists', *American Quarterly*, 52.2 (2000), 334–38.

Garland Thomson, Rosemarie, *Staring: How We Look* (Oxford: Oxford University Press, 2009).

Gayford, Martin, 'Ein riesiger unbekümmerter Narrenprinz: Lucian Freuds Bilder von Leigh Bowery', in *Leigh Bowery: Verwandlungskünstler*, ed. by Angela Stief (Vienna: Piet Meyer Verlag, 2015), pp. 261–81.

Glamorre, Matthew, unpublished interview with the author, London, May 2020.

Goldberg, RoseLee, *Performance Art: From Futurism to the Present* (London: Thames & Hudson, 2011).

Gombrich, Ernst H., *The Story of Art* (Oxford: Phaidon, 1978).

González, Jennifer, 'Envisioning Cyborg Bodies: Notes from Current Research', in *The Gendered Cyborg: A Reader*, ed. by Gill Kirkup, Linda Janes, Kathryn Woodward and Fiona Hovenden (London: Routledge, 2013), pp. 58–73.

Gonzalez Rice, Karen, *Long Suffering: American Endurance Art as Prophetic Witness* (Ann Arbor: University of Michigan Press, 2016).

Granata, Francesca, *Experimental Fashion: Performance Art, Carnival and the Grotesque Body* (London: I.B. Tauris, 2017).

Greenberg, Clement, 'Avant-Garde and Kitsch', in *Art and Culture: Critical Essays* (Boston: Beacon Press, 1961), pp. 3–21.

Greenberg, Clement, 'Post Painterly Abstraction', in *The Collected Essays and Criticism: Modernism with a Vengeance, 1957–1969*, ed. by John O'Brian (Chicago: The University of Chicago Press, 1993), pp. 192–96.

Grosz, Elizabeth, 'Intolerable Ambiguity: Freaks as/at the Limit', in *Freakery: Cultural Spectacles of the Extraordinary Body*, ed. by Rosemarie Garland Thomson (New York: New York University Press, 1996), pp. 55–66.

Halberstam, Jack (formerly Judith), *Female Masculinity* (Durham, NC: Duke University Press, 1998).

Hann, Rachel, 'Debating Critical Costume: Negotiating Ideologies of Appearance, Performance and Disciplinarity', *Studies in Theatre and Performance*, 39.1 (2019), 21–37.

Haraway, Donna J., *Simians, Cyborgs, and Women: The Reinvention of Nature* (New York: Routledge, 1991).

Hart, Lynda, *Between the Body and the Flesh: Performing Sadomasochism* (New York: Columbia University Press, 1998).

Haslam, Dave, *Life after Dark: A History of British Nightclubs and Music Venues* (London: Simon & Schuster, 2015).

Hawkins, Matthew, 'Member of the Thinking', in *Michael Clark*, ed. by Suzanne Cotter and Robert Violette (London: Violette Editions, 2011), pp. 298–307.

Healy, Murray, 'Real Men, Phallicism and Fascism', in *The Subcultures Reader*, ed. by Ken Gelder (London: Routledge, 1997), pp. 367–83.

Hebdige, Dick, *Subculture: The Meaning of Style* (London: Routledge, 1988).

Heiser, Jörg, 'What Is Appropriate: The Role of Art in Responding to the Holocaust', *Frieze*, April 2010, 92–97.

Heller, Steven, *The Swastika: Symbol beyond Redemption?* (New York: Allworth Press, 2000).

Henkes, Andrew J., 'A Party for the "Freaks": Performance, Deviance and Communitas at *Club Fuck!*, 1989–1993', *The Journal of American Culture*, 36.4 (2013), 284–95.

Hevey, David, *The Creatures Time Forgot: Photography and Disability Imagery* (London: Routledge, 1992).

Horlacher, Stefan, 'Transgender and Intersex: Theoretical, Practical, and Artistic Perspectives', in *Transgender and Intersex: Theoretical, Practical, and Artistic Perspectives*, ed. by Stefan Horlacher (New York: Palgrave Macmillan, 2016), pp. 1–27.

Hughes, Robert, 'The Decline and Fall of the Avant-Garde', *Time*, 18 December 1972.

Hunwick, Paul, 'Leigh Bowery – Obituary', *i-D: The New Faces Issue*, February 1995. PP.22.J, Periodicals, National Art Library, Victoria and Albert Museum.

Hutcheon, Linda, *The Politics of Postmodernism* (London: Routledge, 2002).

i-D: The Money Issue, September 1984. PP.22.J, Periodicals, National Art Library, Victoria and Albert Museum.

Jaeger, Jack, 'Interview with Leigh Bowery', in *Take a Bowery: The Art and (Larger than) Life of Leigh Bowery* (Sydney: Museum of Contemporary Art, 2004), pp. 152–53.

Jameson, Fredric, *Postmodernism, or, the Cultural Logic of Late Capitalism* (London: Verso Books, 1991).

Jewell, Dick, *Kinky Gerlinky* (London, 2004) [DVD].

Jewell, Dick, *Leigh Bowery, Serpentine Gallery* (London, 1989) [VHS]. Jewell's personal archive.

Johnson, Dominic, *Glorious Catastrophe: Jack Smith, Performance and Visual Culture* (Manchester: Manchester University Press, 2012).

Johnson, Dominic, 'Intimacy and Risk in Live Art', in *Histories and Practices of Live Art*, ed. by Deirdre Heddon and Jennie Klein (Basingstoke: Palgrave Macmillan, 2012), pp. 121–47.

Johnson, Dominic, 'Marginalia: Towards a Historiography of Live Art', in *Critical Live Art: Contemporary Histories of Performance in the UK*, ed. by Dominic Johnson (Oxford: Routledge, 2013), pp. 13–30.

Johnson, Dominic, 'Perverse Martyrologies: An Interview with Ron Athey', in *The Art of Living: An Oral History of Performance Art* (London: Palgrave, 2015), pp. 195–218.

Johnson, Dominic, 'Transition Pieces: The Photography of Del LaGrace Volcano', in *Otherwise: Imagining Queer Feminist Art Histories*, ed. by Amelia Jones and Erin Silver (Manchester: Manchester University Press, 2016), pp. 340–55.

Johnson, Dominic, *Unlimited Action: The Performance of Extremity in the 1970s* (Manchester: Manchester University Press, 2019).

Jones, Amelia, *The Artist's Body*, ed. by Tracey Warr (London: Phaidon, 2000).

Jones, Amelia, *Body Art/Performing the Subject* (Minneapolis: University of Minnesota Press, 1998).

Jones, Amelia, 'How Ron Athey Makes Me Feel: The Political Potential of Upsetting Art', in *Pleading in the Blood: The Art and Performances of Ron Athey*, ed. by Dominic Johnson (London: Live Art Development Agency and Intellect, 2013), pp. 152–78.

Jones, Amelia, *Irrational Modernism: A Neurasthenic History of New York Dada* (Cambridge: The MIT Press, 2004).

Jones, Amelia, '"Presence in Absentia": Experiencing Performance as Documentation', *Art Journal*, 56.4 (1997), 11–18.

Juno, Andrea, and V. Vale, *Bob Flanagan: Supermasochist* (New York: Re/Search Publications, 1993).

Kaprow, Allan, 'The Legacy of Jackson Pollock', in *Essays on the Blurring of Art and Life*, ed. by Jeff Kelley (Berkeley: University of California Press, 2003), pp. 1–12.

Kaprow, Allan, 'The Real Experiment', in *Essays on the Blurring of Art and Life*, ed. by Jeff Kelley (Berkeley: University of California Press, 2003), pp. 201–18.

Karaian, Lara, 'Pregnant Men: Repronormativity, Critical Trans Theory and the Re(conceive)ing of Sex and Pregnancy in Law, *Social and Legal Studies*, 22.2 (2013), pp. 211–30.

Karantonis, Pamela, '"Punk's Dead, Michael": Artifice, Independence and Authenticity in Leigh Bowery's Self-Fashioned Post-Punk Performative', *Punk and Post-Punk*, 4.2–3 (2015), 205–22.

Kauffman, Linda S., 'Sadomedicine: Bob Flanagan's "Visiting Hours" and Last Rites', *Performance Research*, 3.3 (1998), 33–40.

Kleinhans, Chuck, 'Taking Out the Trash: Camp and the Politics of Parody', in *The Politics and Poetics of Camp*, ed. by Moe Meyer (London: Routledge, 1994), pp. 157–73.

Klem Osterud, Amelia, *The Tattooed Lady: A History* (Golden: Speck Press, 2009).

Klesse, Christian, '"Modern Primitivism": Non-Mainstream Body Modification and Racialized Representation', in *Body Modification*, ed. by Mike Featherstone (London: Sage Publications, 2000), pp. 15–38.

Klocker, Hubert, 'The Dramaturgy of the Organic', in *Viennese Aktionism*, ed. by Hubert Klocker (Klagenfurt: Ritter Verlag, 1989), pp. 41–55.

Klocker, Hubert, 'Viennese Actionism/Bodypolitics', in *Viennese Actionism: Günter Brus, Otto Muehl, Hermann Nitsch, Rudolf Schwarzkogler* (Seville: Ministry of Culture of Andalusia, 2008), pp. 21–30.

Kosofsky Sedgwick, Eve, 'Queer and Now', in *Tendencies* (London: Routledge, 1993), pp. 1–19.

Krauss, Rosalind, 'Sculpture in the Expanded Field', in *The Anti-Aesthetic: Essays on Postmodern Culture*, ed. by Hal Foster (New York: The New Press, 1998), pp. 35–47.

Kristeva, Julia, *Powers of Horror: An Essay on Abjection* (New York: Columbia University Press, 1982).

Kuppers, Petra, *Disability and Contemporary Performance: Bodies on Edge* (New York: Routledge, 2003).

The Legend of Leigh Bowery, dir. by Charles Atlas (London: BBC4, 2008) [DVD].

Lehnert, Gertrud, 'Die Kleider des Leigh Bowery', in *Leigh Bowery: Verwandlungskünstler*, ed. by Angela Stief (Vienna: Piet Meyer Verlag, 2015), pp. 73–94.

Like a Dream, dir. by Matthew Glamorre and Luke Losey (London: Candy Records, 2019). Glamorre's personal archive.

Love, Heather, 'Queer', *TSQ: Transgender Studies Quarterly*, 1.1–2 (2014), 172–76.

Lyotard, Jean-François, *The Postmodern Condition: A Report on Knowledge* (Minneapolis: University of Minnesota Press, 1984).

MacKinnon, Catharine, *Feminism Unmodified: Discourses on Life and Law* (Cambridge: Harvard University Press, 1987).

Maher, JaneMaree, 'A Pregnant Man in the Movies: The Visual Politics of Reproduction', *Continuum: Journal of Media and Cultural Studies*, 22.2 (2008), 279–88.

Malbert, Roger, 'Exaggeration and Degradation: Grotesque Humour in Contemporary Art', in *Carnivalesque* (London: Hayward Gallery Publishing, 2000), pp. 74–97.

Marcus, Greil, *Lipstick Traces: A Secret History of the Twentieth Century* (London: Faber & Faber, 2001).

Marsh, Anne, 'Einhorn unter Tauben', in *Leigh Bowery: Verwandlungskünstler*, ed. by Angela Stief (Vienna: Piet Meyer Verlag, 2015), pp. 161–82.

Matthews, Sandra, and Laura Wexler, *Pregnant Pictures* (New York: Routledge, 2000).

McConville, Brigid, and John Shearlaw, *The Slanguage of Sex: A Dictionary of Modern Sexual Terms* (London: Futura, 1985).

McEvilley, Thomas, *The Triumph of Anti-Art: Conceptual and Performance Art in the Formation of Post-Modernism* (Kingston: McPherson & Company, 2005).

McRuer, Robert, *Crip Theory: Cultural Signs of Queerness and Disability* (New York: New York University Press, 2006).

Mießgang, Thomas, 'Die Kunst des Ausgehens: Wie Leigh Bowery im Rausch des Londoner Nachtlebens seinen Körper lesbar machte und als Regisseur eines Theaters der Künstlichkeit in Erscheinung trat', in *Leigh Bowery: Verwandlungskünstler*, ed. by Angela Stief (Vienna: Piet Meyer Verlag, 2015), pp. 53–71.

Mills, Jane, *Womanwords: A Vocabulary of Culture and Patriarchal Society* (London: Virago, 1991).

Mitchell, David, and Sharon Snyder, 'Exploitations of Embodiment: *Born Freak* and the Academic Bally Plank', *Disability Studies Quarterly*, 25.3 (2005) <https://dsq-sds.org/article/view/575/752> [accessed 27 February 2025].

Mitchell, John, and Vincent Trasov, *The Rise and Fall of the Peanut Party: Journal: Twenty Days in November* (Vancouver: AIR, 1976).

Morris, Gary, 'Lysergic Landscapes: John Maybury's *Read Only Memory*', *Bright Lights Film Journal*, 31 January 2009, <https://brightlightsfilm.com/lysergic-landscapes-john-mayburys-read-only-memory/> [accessed 27 February 2025].

Muñoz, José Esteban, *Disidentifications: Queers of Color and the Performance of Politics* (Minneapolis: University of Minnesota Press, 1999).

Musto, Michael, 'The Death of Downtown', *Village Voice*, 28 April 1987, 15–20.

'Newsflash–', *i-D: The Spectator Issue*, November 1985, 22–23. PP.22.J, Periodicals, National Art Library, Victoria and Albert Museum.

Nickas, Bob, 'Talk of the Gown: Bob Nickas on Leigh Bowery', *Artforum*, February 2004, 52.

O'Brien, Martin, 'Lie Back and Take It: BDSM, Biomedicine and the Hospital Bed in the Work of Bob Flanagan and Sheree Rose', *Body, Space and Technology*, 15 (2016) <http://doi.org/10.16995/bst.18>.

O'Dell, Kathy, *Contract with the Skin: Masochism, Performance Art, and the 1970s* (Minneapolis: University of Minnesota Press, 1998).

Patel, Kantilal Alpesh, 'Leigh Bowery Cape', in *Queer Communion: Ron Athey*, ed. by Amelia Jones and Andy Campbell (Bristol: Intellect, 2020), pp. 323–26.

Phelan, Peggy, *Unmarked: The Politics of Performance* (Oxford: Routledge, 1993).

Pitts, Victoria, *In the Flesh: The Cultural Politics of Body Modification* (New York: Palgrave Macmillan, 2003).

Polhemus, Ted, 'The Performance of Pain', *Performance Research*, 3.3 (1998), 97–104.

Putnam, EL, 'Performing Pregnant: An Aesthetic Investigation of Pregnancy', in *New Feminist Perspectives on Embodiment*, ed. by Clara Fischer and Luna Dolezal (Cham: Palgrave Macmillan, 2018), pp. 203–20.

Reynolds, Simon, *Totally Wired: Post-Punk Interviews and Overviews* (London: Faber & Faber, 2009).

Richards, Mary, 'Ron Athey, A.I.D.S. and the Politics of Pain', *Body, Space and Technology*, 3.2 (2003) <http://doi.org/10.16995/bst.224>.

Richards, Mary, 'Specular Suffering: (Staging) the Bleeding Body', *PAJ: A Journal of Performance and Art*, 30.1 (2008), 108–19.

Rief, Silvia, *Club Cultures: Boundaries, Identities, and Otherness* (New York: Routledge, 2009).

Rimmer, Dave, *New Romantics: The Look* (London: Omnibus Press, 2013).

Rogers, Henry, 'Leigh Bowery: Life-Works', in *The Art of Queering in Art*, ed. by Henry Rogers (Birmingham: Article Press, 2007), pp. 21–32.

Rosenberg, Harold, 'The American Action Painters', *Art News*, 51.8 (1952), 22–50.

Rugoff, Ralph, 'Visiting Hours', *Grand Street*, 53, Summer 1995, 65–73.

Russo, Mary, *The Female Grotesque: Risk, Excess, and Modernity* (New York: Routledge, 1994).

Said, Edward W., *Orientalism: Western Conceptions of the Orient* (New York: Vintage Books, 1979).

Sandahl, Carrie, 'Bob Flanagan: Taking It Like a Man', *Journal of Dramatic Theory and Criticism*, 15.1 (2000), 97–106.

Sandler, Irving, *Art of the Postmodern Era: From the Late 1960s to the Early 1990s* (Colorado: Westview Press, 1998).

Sarkar, Bhaskar, 'Industrial Strength Queer: Club Fuck! and the Reorientation of Desire', *Media Fields Journal*, 7 (2013) <http://mediafieldsjournal.squarespace.com/industrial-strength-queer/> [accessed 27 February 2025].

Savage, Jon, *England's Dreaming: Anarchy, Sex Pistols, Punk Rock, and Beyond* (New York: St. Martin's Press, 1992).

Sayre, Henry M., *The Object of Performance: The American Avant-Garde since 1970* (Chicago: The University of Chicago Press, 1989).

Shalson, Lara, *Performing Endurance: Art and Politics since 1960* (Cambridge: Cambridge University Press, 2018).

Siebers, Tobin, 'Disability Aesthetics and the Body Beautiful: Signposts in the History of Art', *Alter*, 2.4 (2008), 329–36.

Sontag, Susan, 'Fascinating Fascism', in *Under the Sign of Saturn* (New York: Vintage Books, 1981), pp. 73–105.

Sontag, Susan, 'Notes on "Camp"', *Partisan Review*, 31.4 (1964), 515–30.

South of Watford, ITV, 25 April 1986.

Stewart, Susan, *On Longing: Narratives of the Miniature, the Gigantic, the Souvenir, the Collection* (Durham, NC: Duke University Press, 1993).

Stiles, Kristine, 'Readings: Performance and Its Objects', *Arts Magazine*, November 1990, 35–47.

Stone, Sandy, 'The Empire Strikes Back: A Posttranssexual Manifesto', in *The Transgender Studies Reader*, ed. by Susan Stryker and Stephen Whittle (New York: Routledge, 2006), pp. 150–76.

Strange, Steve, *Blitzed!: The Autobiography of Steve Strange* (London: Orion Books Ltd, 2002).

Stritzke, Nadyne, and Elisa Scaramuzza, 'Trans*, Intersex, and the Question of Pregnancy: Beyond Repronormative Reproduction', in *Transgender and Intersex: Theoretical, Practical, and Artistic Perspectives*, ed. by Stefan Horlacher (New York: Palgrave Macmillan, 2016), pp. 141–63.

Sykora, Katharina, 'Ego-Abenteuer zwischen Aktion und Bild', in *Leigh Bowery: Verwandlungskünstler*, ed. by Angela Stief (Vienna: Piet Meyer Verlag, 2015), pp. 209–32.

Taboo: The Boy George Musical (London: Blackhorse Entertainment, 2004) [DVD].

Tait, Peta, 'Performing Shamelessness: Leigh Bowery, Copi and Queer Body Physicality', in *What a Man's Gotta Do?:*

Masculinities in Performance, ed. by Adrian Kiernander, Jonathan Bollen, and Bruce Parr (Armidale: CALLTS, 2006), pp. 208–21.

Taylor, Madeline, Anna Germaine Hickey and Remi Roehrs, 'Celebrating Bowery: Radical Costume Parties as Queer Heterotopia in Brisbane', *Studies in Costume and Performance*, 5.1 (2020), 85–100.

Thornton, Sarah, *Club Cultures: Music, Media and Subcultural Capital* (Cambridge: Polity Press, 1995).

Tilley, Sue, *Leigh Bowery: The Life and Times of an Icon* (London: Hodder & Stoughton, 1997).

Tilley, Sue, and Cerith Wyn Evans, 'Conversation Between Sue Tilley and Cerith Wyn Evans', in *Take A Bowery: The Art and (Larger than) Life of Leigh Bowery* (Sydney: Museum of Contemporary Art, 2003), pp. 40–53.

Tilroe, Anna, 'The Laugh of No. 13', in *Take a Bowery: The Art and (Larger than) Life of Leigh Bowery* (Sydney: Museum of Contemporary Art, 2004), pp. 120–28.

Torry, Richard, 'What about Your Sex Life?', in *Leigh Bowery*, ed. by Robert Violette (London: Violette Editions, 1998), pp. 198–209.

Tseëlon, Efrat, 'Reflections on Mask and Carnival', in *Masquerade and Identities: Essays on Gender, Sexuality and Marginality*, ed. by Efrat Tseëlon (London: Routledge, 2001), pp. 18–37.

Ursprung, Philip, '"Catholic Tastes": Hurting and Healing the Body in Viennese Actionism in the 1960s', in *Performing the Body/Performing the Text*, ed. by Amelia Jones and Andrew Stephenson (London: Routledge, 1999), pp. 138–52.

Vale, V., and Andrea Juno, 'Fakir Musafar', in *Modern Primitives: An Investigation of Contemporary Adornment and Ritual*, ed. by V. Vale and Andrea Juno (San Francisco: Re/Search, 1989), pp. 6–36.

Volcano, Del LaGrace, 'Hermstory', in *The Feminism and Visual Culture Reader*, ed. by Amelia Jones (London: Routledge, 2010), pp. 27–30.

Volcano, Del LaGrace, *Sublime Mutations* (Tübingen: Konkursbuch Verlag, 2000).

Volcano, Del LaGrace, and Jack Halberstam, *The Drag King Book* (London: Serpent's Tail, 1999).

Volcano, Del LaGrace, and Ulrika Dahl, *Femmes of Power: Exploding Queer Femininities* (London: Serpent's Tail, 2008).

Volcano, Del LaGrace, Jay Prosser and Eliza Steinbock, '*INTER*me*: An Inter-Locution on the Body in Photography', in *Transgender and Intersex: Theoretical, Practical, and Artistic Perspectives*, ed. by Stefan Horlacher (New York: Palgrave Macmillan, 2016), pp. 189–224.

Wajnryb, Ruth, *Language Most Foul* (Crows Nest: Allen & Unwin, 2004).

Warren-Crow, Heather, 'Acquired Community: Leigh Bowery and *Hail the New Puritan's* Mise-en-Scène of AIDS', in *Different Bodies: Essays on Disability in Film and Television*, ed. by Marja Evelyn Mogk (Jefferson: McFarland & Company, 2013), pp. 39–54.

Watney, Simon, *Policing Desire: Pornography, AIDS and the Media* (Minneapolis: University of Minnesota Press, 1987).

Weinstein, Matthew, 'Trojan and Leigh', in *Leigh Bowery*, ed. by Robert Violette (London: Violette Editions, 1998), pp. 40–41.

Welchman, John C., *Art after Appropriation: Essays on Art in the 1990s* (New York: Routledge, 2001).

Werther, Janet, 'Discovering Stephen Varble', *PAJ: Performing Arts Journal*, 41.3 (2019), 17–27.

Wexler, Laura, 'More Pregnant Pictures', *Photography and Culture*, 4.3 (2011), 309–20.

'What Is Your Idea of Perfect Happiness?', in *Leigh Bowery*, ed. by Robert Violette (London: Violette Editions, 1998), pp. 8–9.

Wigstock: The Movie, dir. by Barry Shils (New York: Samuel Goldwyn, 2003) [DVD].

Winship, Janice, 'Women Outdoors: Advertising, Controversy and Disputing Feminism in the 1990s', *International Journal of Cultural Studies*, 3.1 (2000), 27–55.

Zapp Magazine #2 (Amsterdam: Zapp Productions, 1994) [VHS].

Zechlin, René, 'Introduction: The Human Body as an Artwork', in *Leigh Bowery: Beautified Provocation*, ed. by René Zechlin (Heidelberg: Kehrer Verlag, 2008), pp. 31–32.

Index

Page numbers in italics indicate illustrations.
'n.' after a page reference indicates the number of an endnote on that page.
Solo / collaborative works and collections by Leigh Bowery are listed alphabetically under the entry 'works'. His looks are listed alphabetically under the entry 'looks'.